Financial Accounting

An International Perspective

Second Edition

Arne Kinserdal

Professor of Business Economics,
Norwegian School of Economics
and Business Administration

FINANCIAL TIMES

PITMAN PUB

Motto   *'Tell me, I will forget.*
Show me, I may remember.
Involve me, I will understand.'

FINANCIAL TIMES
MANAGEMENT
LONDON · SAN FRANCISCO
KUALA LUMPUR · JOHANNESBURG

*Financial Times Management delivers the knowledge,
skills and understanding that enables students,
managers and organisations to achieve their ambitions,
whatever their needs, wherever they are.*

London Office:
128 Long Acre, London WC2E 9AN
Tel: +44 (0)171 447 2000
Fax: +44 (0)171 240 5771
Website: www.ftmanagement.com

A Division of Financial Times Professional Limited

First published in Great Britain 1995
Second edition 1998

© Financial Times Professional Limited 1998

The right of Arne Kinserdal to be identified as Author
of this Work has been asserted by him in accordance
with the Copyright, Designs and Patents Act 1988.

ISBN 0 273 63154 3

British Library Cataloguing in Publication Data
A CIP catalogue record for this book can be obtained from the British Library.

10 9 8 7 6 5 4 3 2 1

Typeset by Pantek Arts, Maidsto - ᵏ~~⁺
Printed and bound in Great Brit.

The Publishers' policy is to use p.

Contents

Preface

'Accounting is too important to be left to accountants.'

Accounting is often referred to as 'the language of business'. This is a good description because accounting plays an important role within business, and the annual accounts form the basis on which the performance of the firm is communicated and judged.

As with every language, accounting has its own terminology and its own rules. Without knowledge of these, it will be difficult to understand and use.

One important goal of this book is to give a basic understanding of accounting. An overview, understanding of the problems and reasoning required in accounting is the main theme. Accounting technique is not emphasized. Where technical understanding is necessary, it is basic reasoning that is given.

Accounting as 'the language of business' also has an international aspect which is growing in importance as the business world is becoming increasingly international. Much of this financial language is shared between countries, since basic assumptions and principles in financial accounting are the same, but we find many 'dialects', making this aspect even more complex than the national one.

This book gives a basic understanding of accounting from an international perspective. Whenever measurement and reporting problems are discussed, we also include an international aspect. References to the following six well-known international companies are given in a number of cases:

Marks & Spencer, Volkswagen, Danisco, Volvo, Bergesen Shipping, Coca-Cola.

In Chapter 12, the financial statements and accounting principles for these six companies are presented and commented upon.

In addition, the EU Fourth Directive is discussed in Chapter 10. This directive regulates the presentation and content of annual accounts and annual reports, the valuation methods and the information to be given. Since we will study what is prescribed and the framework laid down for choices among the alternatives, we will get an excellent overview both of the similarities and differences between countries.

The Glossary at the end of the book, 'Financial accounting from A to Z', consists of more than 400 words and expressions. This is more than a reference to subjects covered in the book, as it also explains relevant concepts usually found in annual reports.

The pedagogical dimension plays an important role in this book. Each chapter starts by stating the objectives of the chapter. At the end of each chapter there are summing-up questions and answers. Both the questions and answers are based on long experience in teaching accounting with a strong emphasis on the difficult and important points. At the end of most chapters there are test problems with suggested answers given at the end of the book.

Long teaching experience has convinced me that examples containing figures for illustration within the field of business economics clarify and give a better understanding of the problems. There are many such examples in this book.

The differences between English and American English have caused some problems. These have been solved by using both where necessary, with the English version first – for example, profit and loss account/income statement; stock/inventory.

I wish to thank my excellent secretary, Elisabeth Stiegler, for once more having done a fine job.

Arne Kinserdal
Bergen

Preface to the Second Edition

In this edition a new chapter has been added: Price change accounting ('Inflation accounting'). It has resulted from a demand by many users of the book, especially from the former Eastern European countries, to cover this aspect of financial accounting and reporting.

It might be asked why such a chapter is necessary, since inflation is now relatively low in most countries. There are two strong arguments in its favour: first, as the president of the German National Bank said recently, 'Inflation is never dead'; second, multinational companies will often face inflation in one or more of the countries in which they operate.

The new chapter has been added after the 'ordinary' chapters in the book, all of which are based on traditional historical cost accounting. Thus it represents a new dimension of financial accounting, much debated both in theory and in practice, and also confusing in many respects. The goal, therefore, has been to provide clarification and to show the direction to be taken when inflation returns.

All examples from practice have been updated in this edition, as have the six selected international case studies.

Arne Kinsderdal
Bergen

1 Basic assumptions in financial accounting

*'If you don't know the past,
you can't understand the present.'*

LEARNING OBJECTIVES

After studying this chapter you will:
- have considered what accounting is;
- know the difference between financial accounting and management accounting;
- have thought about who is interested in a financial report;
- have learnt four fundamentals of financial accounting;
- understand the six principles of financial accounting;
- be aware of the limitations of traditional financial accounting.

1.1 What is accounting?

Accounting is a system for measuring economic activity and communicating the result (of these measurements) to users.

This definition tells us that economic data must be recorded, measured and communicated. These three dimensions are key words for what accounting is. Let us look at them more closely.

Recording is the starting point for accounting data and also the documentation of data. The recording has to be done in a systematic way, that means according to a plan or a system, as economic events take place. This sets limitations. First, it must be possible to record the event, and second, the event must have a financial character. Many important events of value for the firm therefore fall outside the accounting system.

Measurement must be made according to specific rules. Some of them are quite clear and indisputable; others are open to alternatives. In many cases there are various possibilities for measurement. These must be clarified and written down as accounting policies.

Communication underlines that accounting is more than recording and producing measured figures. The final goal for accounting is to communicate the measured economic events to users.

From the above definition we see that the focus is on users. This seems reasonable. The great challenge is to present accounting figures so that the many different kinds of user understand the message. Later on in the chapter we will discuss this dimension.

Accounting is part of business economics. Historically, business economics started with accounting. Accounting still plays a central role within business economics, and the teaching field in accounting is the biggest within business economics. A key question is how accounting corresponds to economics. We will return to that question at the end of this chapter.

Accounting is not bookkeeping. The latter is a technique, although good and logical reasoning lies behind it. The basic understanding of this technique will be discussed in Chapter 5.

We conclude that accounting is a discipline requiring registration, measurement and communication.

1.2 The difference between financial accounting and management accounting

Traditionally, accounting is divided into two: accounting addressed to internal parties and accounting for use outside the firm. Internal and external accounting are good descriptions of the two, although the more common terminology is financial accounting and management accounting. These two fields of accounting have differences, but they also have close relationships. Since financial accounting gives information to external parties, this field is normally regulated by law. The strength of this regulation varies between countries. Much depends on the general standing of legal regulation in the specific country and that of the accounting profession. In every country, however, the profession will play an important role, both because it is not possible to regulate everything by law and also because legal regulation will always require just the minimum of accounting information.

Management accounting will generally have planning and control as its main objectives. This means that management accounting will vary between firms, because of differences in size and type. This will lead to different information needs. But despite this, there are also basic similarities between financial and management accounting. In small firms we often find that financial accounts are also used for management purposes. Much of the data used for management accounting is data recorded in the financial accounting system. The data have the same monetary values for both purposes, and are also a starting point for further analyses in order to direct and control the firm.

This book is about financial accounting, and from now on we will focus on problems in this area. Thus, when we refer to accounting, we will mean financial accounting.

1.3 The users of the annual report

We have underlined that the focus must be on the users when we discuss financial accounting. We will therefore start by listing the key user groups.

- *The owners.* The interest here will depend on the organizational form of the firm, its size and how close the owners are to the firm. Decisions on allocation of profit are based on accounting data.

- *The management.* For top management, the financial accounts will not normally be sufficient for management and control. However, these accounts do give a total view of the financial situation of the firm, decisions are taken on this basis, and the management is judged on profit, among other things.

- *The employees.* It seems obvious that the financial situation of the firm as measured in accounting is of interest to the employees. In negotiations about salaries, the economic situation of the firm will be used in the bargaining process. Accounting data are also directly used when employees have profit-sharing agreements.

- *Creditors.* Both loan creditors and trade creditors will be interested in the accounts both when meeting the firm for the first time and also in the continuing relationship.

- *Customers.* Even though the products and services of the firm are of most interest, customers will also want to evaluate the stability of the firm so as to ensure supplies.

- *Public authorities.* Here we will first have the tax authorities in mind. There will always be a connection between the financial accounts and the tax accounts. How close this connection is varies from country to country. We will discuss this in Chapter 7.

- *Competitors.* They are, of course, interested in the financial position of the firm. This also sets a limitation on what information the firm will publish.

- *Economic experts and financial analysts.* This group represents a broad range of people from economic consultants to financial analysts. They analyse the accounts and also ask critical questions.

- *Media.* This group includes financial periodicals, newspapers, television and radio. They analyse the economic situation of a firm and communicate their conclusions to a wide audience.

- *Trade unions.* In wage negotiations, accounting data will be one part of the data used.

- *Research and teaching.* Financial accounts from firms are used for economic analysis for a specific firm, for an industry or for the whole business world. This also gives possibilities for analysing the development in accounting reporting. In teaching, the use of financial reports both gives practical insight and sharpens the interest of students.

- *The local community and the nation.* In a local community, a firm can be extremely important for the total economy. In such a case the economy of the firm is of utmost interest. The economy of a nation is influenced by the result of firms' activities. Therefore, at this level, accounting information about the total economic picture will be important.

The listing of users and the analyses of the needs of the different users have shown that the economy of the firm is of wide interest and in fact influences us all. The communication problem when we have so many user groups is great. But one characteristic applies to all the groups, namely the ability to understand and to use accounting. Here we can classify in the following way: users with no or little accounting understanding, users with some understanding, and the experts. This is a classification well worth keeping in mind when accounting data are communicated. But the firm needs to be more user oriented and the user needs to be willing to spend more time in order to understand accounting. What is also clear is that if the experts have sufficient information and make critical analyses, all user groups will benefit.

1.4 Four fundamental concepts

It is important to know and to understand the basics underlying the measurements of financial accounts. We can summarize them using four fundamentals and six basic principles.

The four fundamental concepts are: the firm as a separate unit, the going concern, the accounting period and the monetary measurement.

1 *The separate entity concept* means that the firm is looked upon as a separate unit with a life of its own. This is like saying: we are employed at SAS, we work in Copenhagen, we study at NHH, etc. This means that financial accounts tell us about the economic resources of the firm and how management has performed. This concept will influence the models for reporting, the terminology and the measurements.

2 *The going-concern concept* means that the accounts are prepared and presented under the condition that the firm will continue. We know of course that not every firm will exist for ever, but generally the firm is expected to continue. This concept has direct consequences for measurements. Let us illustrate with two examples. When a retail store values stock at the end of the year, this is done under the condition that the goods will be sold in the ordinary course of business, not that the business is going to close down in the near future. If the firm does cease to exist, the stock would have to be valued in quite a different way. An industrial firm with work in progress at the end of a period will value these goods under the condition that they will be completed and sold in the ordinary course of business. If the firm were going to close down, the work in progress would perhaps have no value.

3 *The accounting period concept* is the result of the necessity to have economic information at certain intervals in order to know the result of any decisions made, to make certain decisions, for example concerning dividends, and to make necessary corrections over time. The period concept raises measurement problems. The correct measurement is obtained only when a firm is looked at from start to finish. For periods in between there will in most cases be uncertainty connected with the measurement at different points in time. There can be cases and circumstances where the best accounting information is given not as a period report, but as a finished activity report, for example with projects. But even for a given firm with this profile, accounting for a period will be necessary, except when an activity is established for a single project, lasting less than one year.

4 The monetary concept means that accounting information is expressed in monetary terms. That is done automatically when economic events are recorded. The monetary concept has strengths and weaknesses. The advantage is that a common measurement is established. The disadvantage is that the value of money changes over time. Traditional accounting does not take this last effect into consideration. Data recorded in 1970, 1980, 1990 and today are summarized and accounting data are presented as if the value of the money was the same at all these dates. In fact, this is like a situation where English pounds, German marks and Norwegian kroner are aggregated without taking the rate of exchange into consideration. This negative aspect of traditional accounting was much discussed in the 1970s and up to the middle of the 1980s, but less so in the late 1980s and 1990s.

The four fundamentals – separate unit, going concern, accounting period and monetary measurement – have long traditions in international accounting. They are based on rationality and practice with positive and logical backgrounds, but they also represent limitations. Both these features should be kept in mind when using accounting information.

1.5 Six basic principles

The six principles we discuss here are more concrete than the four fundamentals discussed in section 1.4. The six principles are: the transaction principle, the historical cost principle, the accrual principle, the matching principle, the prudence principle and the principle of consistency. Directly and indirectly these six principles influence all the measurements made within accounting.

1 The transaction principle
In the definition of accounting we included the recording function. Records are built upon the transactions that take place. At that time economic events can be measured. This means a restriction on the types of economic events that are taken into the accounts. It also means restriction on the timing for recording economic events. But at the time of transaction the data recorded are indisputable and represent facts. This is also the ideal situation for measurement analyses.

The transaction principle is used for all types of transactions, whether they are linked to revenues, expenses, investments or financing.

2 The historical cost principle
This principle is so central that traditional financial accounting is often referred to as historical cost accounting. Indirectly, this principle also follows from the transaction principle.

Historical cost means a restriction on what is measured within financial accounting. If a piece of land was bought in 1950, that value is shown in the accounts for all subsequent years. A building bought in 1980 will have a book value in later years based on the purchase price in 1980, reduced by annual depreciation on that amount. Thus the historical cost principle means that the accounts do not give today's value of the assets. This represents a great conflict between economic thinking and accounting. Much discussion has taken place in this area, but no model based on an assumption other than historical cost has yet been agreed upon, either in theory or in practice. There are two main reasons for this: historical cost represents the original investment that took place; and historical cost data represent facts, which means they are objective. But the conflict between relevance and objectivity will always exist.

3 The accrual principle

This principle is so fundamental that, in some countries, it is referred to as the accounting principle. This term is used in order to underline that the measurement is not based upon the cash principle. The accrual principle means that the profit for a period is measured by revenues and expenses, where expenses represent the cost in the period for a relevant item. If, for example, rent covering November and December has not yet been paid, the accrual principle means that the expense for the year in question must also include rent covering November and December.

4 The matching principle

It seems logical that when measuring the profit for a period, the revenues of that period have to be matched against those expenses necessary to generate the revenues. This philosophy lies behind the matching principle when measuring accounting profit. Let us illustrate the reasoning behind this principle by two examples both linked to the operations activity of a firm.

A firm has during the year recorded sales of 10 000. That amount represents the sales revenue for the year. If we assume that the firm bought goods for 8000 but still has goods for 1000 in stock (no stock at the beginning of the year), then the relevant expense for the year is 7000. The matching principle means that the sales for the year have to be matched against the cost of those goods. That means that the sales of 10 000 must be matched against the cost of goods sold at 7000.

The second example which illustrates the matching principle is linked to the collection of trade debts. If we assume a credit sale of 2000 and there is a probability that 500 will never be paid for, then this loss has to be taken in the current period. When we match the sales of the period with a loss potential, this loss has to be matched against the sales of the period.

5 The prudence principle (conservatism)

Measurement in accounting does not operate slavishly according to the historical cost principle. It is fundamental in accounting that assets and revenues should not be overvalued, and that liabilities and expenses should not be undervalued. This philosophy lies behind the prudence principle, and has a long tradition.

The prudence principle asserts that the amounts based on historical cost must be tested against the valuations of today. If, for example, stock at the end of a period has been bought for 5000 but now can be sold for just 4000, the prudence principle says that the company has to value and report the stock at 4000. Here the principle is applied to an asset, using the 'lower of cost or market value' valuation method. But the prudence principle is also applied to liabilities and to revenues and expenses.

We have to give a warning here: the prudence principle must not be regarded as implying that values should be minimized. This is not true. There must be realism behind the use of the principle, so that real alternatives are compared.

6 The principle of consistency

A key use of accounting data is to make comparisons. This is considered so important that in many countries the law requires that corresponding figures for the previous year shall be given together with the figures for the current year. In practice all companies present corresponding figures from the previous year. It is a condition, then, that the same accounting principles and measurement rules have been followed in both periods. This is what lies behind the principle of consistency. Without information to the contrary, a user of accounting data must take for granted that this principle has been observed.

It would, however, be a very static system if principles could never be changed. Therefore, accounting is open to changes in principle, but users have to be informed of these changes and the consequences for the accounting figures. Usually, this also means that corresponding figures from the previous period have to be presented according to the new principle, so that comparisons are valid.

The six basic principles – transaction, historical cost, accrual, matching, prudence and consistency – are found as principles in every country in the world.

1.6 Alternative models

As we have seen, historical cost is the base for measurement in financial accounting. Several alternative models have been proposed in accounting literature. These can broadly be classified into two alternatives: value-based models; or a model based on adjustment of historical cost data in order to reflect changes in the general price level.

The reason that historical cost is opposed by the proponents of value-based models is principally that it does not lead to useful financial statements. Thus the informational value of the historical cost model is challenged.

The case for market values can be illustrated in connection with assets, and is as follows: initially, assets are recorded at value, since cost at that time is identical with value. After acquisition, the accounting measurement should continue to express the values. This could be done by using current market prices. In many cases such market values are available, and then they could be used directly. In other cases market values would be approximations, for example by using specific indices. Within market values there are two different views: one asking what a similar asset will cost now, the other what the sales price for that asset would be ('as if sold').

This illustration had individual assets as the starting point. Theoretically, the value of the firm is a total view, measured as the net present value of expected future cash flows. In practice, such a system as an accounting system will be impossible to use, because of the uncertainty of the future cash flows, and also because some very valuable information contained in traditional accounting will be lost. But it is still important to keep the theoretical idea in mind. We will see examples of this logic in many circumstances later on. We will also underline that this ideal alternative exists in the financial markets for quoted companies. Here, the total value of the company's shares represents the expectations of future cash flows.

There is a difference of opinion among market value supporters concerning the way changes in values should be treated. Some argue that the changes should be directly included in equity, others that the changes should be part of income, at least the real part of the changes.

The general price-level model states historical cost data in a common monetary unit of equivalent purchasing power. This is not a valuation method, but an adjustment of nominal figures recorded in different periods into a common purchasing power equivalent. The figures in both the profit and loss account and the balance sheet are adjusted to the monetary unit of today.

We summarize the possible alternatives as shown in Fig. 1.1 (overleaf).

Comments:

One extreme is to look upon the value of the firm as a total, that is, to base the measurements on expected future cash flows. The other extreme is to report historical cash inflows and cash outflows. Between these two alternatives we

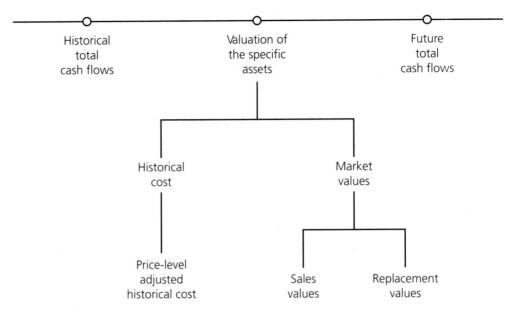

Figure 1.1 Valuation alternatives

find that accounting is dominant, i.e. that assets (and liabilities) are specified. The basis for the measurements in this case can be either historical cost or market values. The first one represents traditional financial accounting. Within the market value models we will find sales values and replacement values of the individual assets. We have also shown the alternative of adjusting historical data to the price level of today. Such an adjustment does not represent a valuation but means that all figures in the accounts are measured according to the same scale (monetary unit of today).

✔ Questions and answers

As mentioned in the Preface, the questions below are more than just a summing up. You will be able to prove whether you have understood what you have studied in this chapter. Suggested answers follow each question. But you should take time to give your own answer first.

1 **Why are registration, measurement and communication key words for understanding what accounting is?**

Answer:
When the objective of accounting is to give economic information, this information must be documented, that means data have to be recorded. Furthermore,

measurements must be made in order to give monetary values. Finally, accounting data will be used and this requires communication.

2 Why is accounting divided into financial accounting and management accounting?

Answer:

Because accounting has two clear and (usually) different objectives and needs, external and internal. In external accounting there will be a need for regulation, defined accounting models, valuation rules and a minimum of information requirement. This implies the data can be audited and can be used for comparison purposes. Internal accounting aims at giving the best information for planning, management and control. This means there has to be flexibility and a strong emphasis on the use in a specific firm. Details within the accounting system will generally have to be greater than in the area of financial accounting.

3 What conclusions can you draw when you study the many groups of users of accounting?

Answer:

First and foremost, if we include both present and potential users, there are very few in society who are not involved directly or indirectly. In addition, the ability to understand accounting varies tremendously. The grouping of users with no or little understanding, some understanding and the experts is important to keep in mind. It is also worth noting that the general user will gain from the critical appraisal of accounting data and information by the experts.

4 Why do you think the four fundamentals within accounting have come about? Analyse each of them separately.

Answer:

The firm as a *separate entity* seems natural when it has developed from something more than just one person's business or a single project. In modern times a firm has a management and in many circumstances is looked upon as something specific, independent of the ownership. It seems reasonable therefore that accounts give information on the economic activity of the firm, looked upon as a separate entity.

Going concern seems logical, because the normal situation is that the firm will continue. Therefore, it seems both unnecessary and a waste of time to look upon the firm as if this were the last year of its existence.

Accounting for a specific *period* rather than for the whole life of a firm seems both natural and necessary. If the alternative were applied, the time horizon would be too long and much accounting data would be lost. This would give an inefficient use of economic resources.

Accounting data are quantified data. Measurement in *money* is the most realistic concept to use, because records of transactions have been made in money and the accounts do the same.

5 **What consequences will the six accounting principles have for the contents of accounts? Analyse each of them separately.**

Answer:

The transaction principle means that a transaction of economic character must exist. Then it is possible to record and measure (in money).

The historical cost principle has as a consequence that accounting figures which do not give today's values but reflect the values at the time of registration. Traditional historical cost values typically differ substantially from current market values.

The accrual principle means that the profit for a period is based on revenues and expenses, not on cash flows. This principle gives more meaningful information.

The matching principle means that relevant revenues and expenses are matched against each other. This seems reasonable.

The prudence principle means that accounting data based on pure historical costs have to be compared with the situation existing today. A consequence is that accounting figures given in the balance sheet will not be overvalued.

The principle of consistency enables comparisons to be made between different time periods. This seems both logical and practical.

? Problems

1 Below, you will find a number of events. Not all of them are economic events. Neither will all economic events be recorded in the accounts. Which of the events will be recorded in the accounts?

   (a) The company pays 100 000 for goods received earlier.
   (b) The company buys office equipment. An invoice of 300 000 payable within two months follows the delivery.
   (c) The company negotiates a contract to sell goods for 400 000. The goods are to be delivered within three months.
   (d) The company is listed on the stock exchange. On this specific day the share price has fallen in value from 240p to 230p.
   (e) Wages to employees are paid from bank accounts, amounting to 180 000.
   (f) The government brings a new Budget into force, which means a significant reduction in corporate taxation.
   (g) Rent is paid for the first quarter next year, amounting to 200 000.
   (h) The new top manager starts work for the company.

(i) 6000 cash sales for a period are recorded.

(j) Sales on credit in the period are 20 000.

(k) The board of the company decides to increase the share capital from 30 000 to 40 000.

(l) The top manager gets travel expenses in advance of 20 000.

(m) An agreement is made with another company to do a common research and development project on 50/50 basis. The project is expected to have a total cost of 10 000.

2 Which of the six principles will be used in the examples below?

(a) At the end of the accounting period stock which had a purchase price of 50 000 now has a value of 40 000.

(b) A piece of land which was bought for 1000 many years ago now has a value of 5000.

(c) At the end of the year the company replaced old machinery with new at a cost of 10 000. The company depreciates the cost of such investment over five years with equal amounts each year. When the replacement took place, the old machinery was sold for 1000. It had been in use for five years.

(d) After serious consideration the company has decided that it will change the accounting policy as far as the lifetime of the machinery is concerned, from five years to eight years. This is more realistic, and also corresponds with the policies of competing companies.

2 Understanding the balance sheet

'There is something fine and logical with figures.
They know what they want and they do what they shall.'

Piet Hein

LEARNING OBJECTIVES

After studying this chapter you will:
- know what a balance sheet is;
- understand why the balance sheet is always in balance;
- have reflected on why and how the balance sheet is grouped;
- know the basic valuation rules of the items in the balance sheet;
- have studied James Super Market as a practical example.

2.1 What is the balance sheet?

We have said earlier that accounting communicates the economy of the firm. This is done first and foremost through two financial statements, the balance sheet and the profit and loss account/income statement.

The balance sheet shows the economic resources of the firm and how these resources are financed. The profit and loss account shows the result of the activities during a specific period. Thus the balance sheet gives the financial situation at a specific time, for example December 31, while the profit and loss account gives the profit for a period, for example one year.

We have said that the balance sheet will provide information about both the economic resources and how they are financed. The first one is given on the *asset* side of the balance sheet, the second on the *liability/equity* side. It is logical that there must always be a source of finance behind each resource in a firm. Either the firm has borrowed money in order to acquire an asset or the owners of the firm have financed it. The balance sheet must therefore always be in balance.

The asset side of the balance sheet will list the specific assets in the firm in a logical order: cash, bank accounts, debtors/accounts receivable, stocks/inventories, machinery, equipment and buildings. The order in this case is according to decreasing liquidity. We could also have started with buildings and ended with cash, according to increasing liquidity.

The liability/equity side of the balance sheet shows what financial resources were used to acquire the assets. Generally, the firm has only two possibilities, either to borrow money or to get the money from the owners. The liability/ equity side of the balance sheet will therefore show items such as creditors, liabilities to public authorities, bank loans, mortgage loans and equity. In this case the order is first liability and then equity. This order corresponds to the first alternative for compiling the asset side. Should the liability/equity side of the balance sheet correspond to the second alternative of the assets, equity must come first.

If we let A = Assets

E = Equity, and

L = Liabilities

we have now seen the fundamental relationship of the balance sheet:

A = L + E or A = E + L

The USA, Canada and the Scandinavian countries, among others, use the first alternative, while the UK and most continental countries use the second alternative. The EU model follows the second alternative. From now on we will use the second alternative. This means that the asset side follows increasing liquidity, and the liability/equity side starts with equity, followed by liabilities in order of date of maturity.

2.2 James Super Market

We shall illustrate the basic accounting statements with a practical example. It is taken from a small retail supermarket. The following information is given:

On January 2 this year, James Super Market (known as James Super) was ready for serving customers in a small community. James Super is established and owned by James Smith, a young man who had been working in the North Sea. He had saved money and now he wanted to open a supermarket in his home town. James had trade in his blood and, while he did his military service and was working in the North Sea, had taken courses in business economics, accounting and marketing. He invested 200 000 as capital in the supermarket, and he borrowed 400 000 from the local bank. There was no repayment on the loan for the first three years. He leased modern facilities, bought shop equipment for 500 000 and two women were employed. James had Local Bank Ltd as his bank connection and he opened an account there.

On January 2, we can compile this balance sheet for James Super:

Balance sheet, January 2, 19XX	(000s)
Assets	
Equipment	500
Bank account, Local Bank	100
	600
Equity and liabilities	
Equity (James Smith)	200
Loan, Local Bank	400
	600

We can see from the balance sheet which assets James Super has at the beginning and how these assets are financed.

James knew that the first year would be difficult, but he worked hard and business turned out better than he expected. At the end of the year James ascertains that his bank account is 70 000. At the same time, one of his big customers owes him 20 000. The stock is 380 000. This amount was found by counting the stock and valuing it according to purchase prices. He assumed that the equipment would last for ten years. James also found that he owed his trade creditors 260 000 for purchased goods and other creditors, which were the tax authorities, 40 000.

On this background we can prepare the following balance sheet at the end of the year:

Balance sheet, December 31, 19XX	(000s)	(000s)
	Dec. 31	Jan. 2
Assets		
Equipment	450	500
Stock	380	–
Trade debtors	20	–
Bank account, Local Bank	70	100
	920	600

	(000s)	(000s)
	Dec. 31	Jan. 2
Equity and liabilities		
Equity	220	200
Loan, Local Bank	400	400
Trade creditors	260	–
Other creditors	40	–
	920	600

Again, the balance sheet shows the assets in James Super and how they are financed. In this case the equity is found as a difference: when we know the total assets and the total liabilities, the difference must be equity, compare:

A = E + L or

E = A – L

We see that the equity at December 31 is 220 000. At January 2, equity was 200 000. The explanation of this difference must be the profit for the year. We will return to this fact in the next chapter.

We should recognize the following: the equipment has been reduced by 50 000. It has been used for one year now and, as we mentioned before, James assumed that it would last for ten years. It therefore seems reasonable to divide the cost of the equipment, 500 000, over ten years, providing the same amount (50 000) each year. We also see that James Super owes 40 000. This is a liability at December 31 and has to be included in the balance sheet in order to give a correct picture of the situation.

2.3 Grouping – sub-dividing the balance sheet

It was easy to get an overview of the balance sheet items in James Super. At January 2, there were only two assets, one liability and one equity item, that means four altogether. The items had increased to a total of eight at the end of the year, but still it was easy to get an overview.

In the balance sheet at December 31, we see the particular order of the items. The asset side starts with equipment, then stock, debtors and finally the bank account. On the equity/liability side of the balance sheet the liabilities start with the loan from Local Bank, then trade creditors and finally other creditors to be paid early next year. This order is not accidental: as we have said before, the asset side of the balance sheet is arranged according to increasing liquidity and the liabilities start with the long-term loan from Local Bank and ends with the liability to be paid very soon.

To standardize the balance sheet in a certain order is useful for interpreting accounting data. But there is also a need to group the items. The most common grouping of assets is *fixed assets* and *current assets*, and for liabilities *long-term liabilities* and *short-term liabilities*. Consequently:

$$A = FA + CA$$

where A = assets, FA = fixed assets and CA = current assets

and

$$L = LL + SL$$

where L = liabilities, LL = long-term liabilities and SL = short-term liabilities.

Fixed assets are assets acquired for permanent use in a business. They are the basis for business activities. Examples of such assets are buildings, machinery and equipment.

Current assets are assets not meant for permanent use in the business. On the contrary, they are acquired or developed to be sold and are connected with that function. Examples are debtors and stock.

Long-term liabilities are generally of a fixed, stable character. This does not mean that the same amount will be kept forever, but the amounts in this group will not have to be repaid shortly; normally the period is more than one year. Very often the long-term liabilities will be secured by mortgages. This also illustrates the link between long-term liabilities and fixed assets.

Short-term liabilities are liabilities falling due relatively soon, normally within one year. Examples are taxes and creditors.

The complete picture of a grouped balance sheet will be:

$$FA + CA = E + LL + SL$$

Let us look at the purpose of grouping in the balance sheet, and what we gain from such a grouping.

- The grouping itself will make the overview easier. There are fewer items on which to concentrate.

- For an outside user there will always be doubt about certain items as far as grouping is concerned. When the firm has made the grouping itself, grouping will be more consistent.

- The grouping itself is useful because it characterizes the firm, as the structure is different within different industries.

- Grouping is helpful when analysing a firm within a specific industry. This enables comparisons to be made with other firms in the same trade.

- The grouping of the balance sheet gives the possibility of analysing the relationship between assets and their financing.

- The valuation rules for the items within different groups can vary. We will return to this point later on.

Even though there were few items in the balance sheet of James Super, we will end this section with the illustration of the grouped balance sheet at December 31.

Balance sheet, December 31, 19XX	(000s)	(000s)
Assets		
Fixed assets		
Equipment		450
Current assets		
Stock	380	
Trade debtors	20	
Bank account, Local Bank	70	470
Total assets		920
Equity and liabilities		
Equity (James Smith)		220
Long-term liabilities		
Loan, Local Bank		400
Short-term liabilities		
Trade creditors	260	
Other creditors	40	300
Total equity and liabilities		920

2.4 Measurements

In Chapter 1 we outlined four fundamental concepts and six basic principles. Together they give the framework for valuation of the items in the balance sheet.

Let us reflect on this framework in our company, James Super. We restate the four fundamentals:

- the balance sheet shows the financial situation of James Super (separate accounting entity);
- the balance sheet is based on the going concern principle (James Super continues);
- the balance sheet shows the situation after one year (accounting period);
- the balance sheet is in monetary terms (money as a unit of measurement).

Not all the six basic principles are directly relevant in this case, but the two year-end accounting statements (the balance sheet and the profit and loss account/income statement) are linked, so directly and indirectly all six principles are used.

For James Super the principle of consistency is not relevant, since it is the first year of activity. The transaction principle, the accrual principle and the matching principle lie behind the figures in the balance sheet. We will return to these principles later on, in connection with the discussion of the profit and loss account. The two remaining principles, the historical cost principle and the principle of prudence, however, directly affect the balance sheet. We will therefore discuss the consequences of these two principles.

The historical cost principle means that the assets are linked to the time of acquisition and the cost situation at that time. That means that the stocks as at December 31 are priced according to when the goods were purchased. The equipment was bought at the beginning of the year for 500 000. According to the historical cost principle this is the basis for the valuation of that asset in the balance sheet. At December 31, this valuation is 500 000 less 50 000 as depreciation. The historical cost principle means that stocks/inventories and equipment do not show the value of these assets today but are based on the purchase cost.

The principle of prudence may be used for James Super. The balance sheet includes debtors of 20 000. If there is any doubt whether this will be paid the amount cannot be an asset in the balance sheet for the full amount of 20 000. Since the debtor in the balance sheet stands at 20 000, this means that James Super recognizes this claim as safe.

Regarding stock, this has, as mentioned before, been valued according to purchase prices. If the stock or part of it no longer has this value, it has to be written down. The test for this will be the expected sales price less sales and administrative costs (i.e. net realizable value). When the stock in the balance sheet of James Super is valued according to purchase prices, this means that writing down has not been necessary. The equipment has been reduced by depreciation. We must assume that ten years is a realistic time horizon when the purchase cost is divided into periods.

We have underlined that the items in the balance sheet are based on the historical cost principle and do not represent today's value. There could be differences between the two valuation alternatives. We have also underlined that the principle of prudence should always be adhered to, so that we can rely on the fact that there will be no overvaluation of assets.

Questions and answers

1   How do you define the balance sheet? Why must the balance sheet always be in balance?

Answer:
The balance sheet is an accounting statement at a certain point in time showing on the one hand the economic resources of the firm and on the other hand the equity and liabilities of the firm. Every asset recorded in the balance sheet must have been acquired once. Thus, it must have a source of finance either by liability at that time or by equity. It also follows from the transaction principle that an economic event always has two effects.

2   List, without any amount, the assets and liabilities you have today.

Answer:
Must of course be individual, but perhaps it will surprise you that you have so many.

3   Put amounts to the assets you listed in Question 2. The valuation criteria you may choose yourself, not limited to the traditional accounting principles.

Answer:
Must be individual, but you will learn that some of the assets are easy to measure without problems, for example cash, bank accounts; some will be more complicated, for example home, car, furniture, clothing. I suppose that when valuing the assets you have thought of either what the sale value will be today, or what you will have to pay for the same assets if you purchase them now.

4   Why do we group the balance sheet and what are the main groups?

Answer:
Easier overview; more consistent grouping when this is done by the firm; the balance sheet structure characterizes firms in different industries; gives possibility for

comparison between firms in the same industry; gives possibilities for analysis between assets and the way they are financed; and gives different valuation criteria for different groups.

Assets into FA and CA, liabilities into LL and SL.

5 Group the items below according to common principles of grouping. Within each group the items also should have a logical order:

Land, Creditors, Cash, Equity, Debenture, Overdraft, Unpaid telephone bills, Machinery, Value-added tax due, Stock/Inventory, Building, Quoted shares/investments, Loans to employees, Interest due, Amounts owed by customers, Advance payments to creditors.

Answer:

Assets	Equity and liabilities
Fixed assets	*Equity*
Land	*Long-term liabilities*
Building	Debenture
Machinery	*Short-term liabilities*
Loans to employees (supposed to be long-term)	Overdraft
Current assets	Creditors
Advance payments to creditors	Value-added tax due
Stock	Interest due
Amounts owed by customers	Unpaid telephone bills
Quoted shares (could be classified as fixed assets)	
Cash	

6 In Section 2.4 we claimed: 'The transactions principle, the accrual principle and the matching principle lie behind the figures in the balance sheet.' Which assets would that mean?

Answer:
The trade debtors, the trade creditors and other creditors illustrate the transaction principle and the accrual principle.

The matching principle requires that the stock/inventory at December 31 is carried forward as a balance item. It follows that the purchases during the year minus the stock/inventory at December 31 must be the cost of goods sold. When this cost is matched against the sales for the year we will have relevant amounts. The depreciation of equipment will also be a relevant matching against the revenue for the year.

7 In Questions 2 and 3 you listed your own assets and liabilities. What would the value be if you use the historical cost principle?

Answer:
Must be individual, but in many cases you will see great differences from the valuation you made in Question 3.

✔ Problems

1 The balance sheet items below should be grouped into assets, further grouped into fixed assets and current assets, equity and liabilities, further grouped into long-term liabilities and short-term liabilities (amounts in 1000s): Raw material 70, Tax from employees 30, Postal account 40, Debenture 1400, Quay 300, Work in progress 80, Bank overdraft 400, Finished goods 200, Building 900, Social Security contributions owed 120, Ship 200, Creditors 40, Machinery 1400, Office equipment 300, Bill payable 20, Advance payments from customers 30, Equity 1450, Debtors 200, Shares/Investment in Alfa (non-quoted) 200, Land 200, Bank loan 600.

2 The balance sheet below lacks amounts for six items. Given the following information you should be able to find these amounts.

Balance sheet, December 31, 19XX	(000s)
Assets	
Building	?
Machinery	?
Shares in Beta	?
Stocks	?
Debtors	?
Bank account	100
Total assets	___
Equity and liabilities	
Equity	?
Debenture	800
Local authorities	200
Other short-term liabilities	100
Total equity and liabilities	___

(a) The building was purchased for 800 ten years ago, and has 40 years' economic life.

(b) Machinery was acquired three years ago for 500; expected economic life five years.

(c) Shares/investment in Beta is a long-term investment. They were bought for 100 and estimated value today is 150.

(d) Stocks/inventories at purchase cost 300. Some of the goods are worth less than cost. Their purchase cost was 60 and realistic write downs will be 50 per cent.

(e) The list of debtors shows 200, but 20 is regarded as irrecoverable.

3 Understanding the profit and loss account/the income statement

'If figures had not existed, nothing would have been clear, neither isolated nor in connection with other things.'

Philolaus, about 500 BC

LEARNING OBJECTIVES

In this chapter you will:

- learn what the profit and loss account/the income statement is and what it shows;
- consider over the grouping in this statement;
- understand which valuations are made in the statement;
- examine an example of such a statement;
- study and understand the link between the balance sheet and the profit and loss account.

3.1 The profit and loss account – the most important statement

There are many reasons why the profit and loss account is the most important of the financial statements. As indicated by its name, the net result is shown here; in other words, from this statement you can see whether or not the firm made a profit during the period. To make profit is, in the long run, absolutely necessary for a profit-oriented firm. With a reasonable profit it will be easier to finance further investments, easier to maintain employment and easier to invest in research and development activities in order to secure the future of the firm.

The profit and loss account is also of interest because the underlying basis for profit can be analysed, namely the revenues and the expenses. In addition, the profit and loss account will be an important statement for planning and budgeting for future periods. It is often the case that the management of the firm is evaluated according to the results.

3.2 James Super Market

We can illustrate a profit and loss account by looking further into our case, James Super. We remember that this firm started on January 2, in the current year, and in Chapter 2 we looked at the balance sheet at the end of this year. The profit and loss account for the year is as follows:

Profit and loss account for 19XX	(000s)
Sales	5000
Interest from bank account	10
Total revenues	5010
Cost of goods sold	4000
Wages and social expenses	500
Rent	240
Operation of premises	90
Office expenses	60
Depreciation on equipment	50
Interest on loan	50
Total expenses	4990
Profit	20

We now have an explanation of the change in equity that we saw in the previous chapter. There, the balance sheet as at January 2 showed an equity of 200 000, while the balance sheet of December 31 showed 220 000. The increase in equity is explained by the profit for the year. So here we see the link between the profit and loss account and the balance sheet.

The profit and loss account shows the revenues and the expenses for the year. When these are matched, we can calculate the profit. We remind you that the principle for recording revenues is based on transactions, and that the expenses are measured according to the accrual principle.

Let us look closer into the recording of transactions in James Super.

The sale is recorded whether it has been for cash or on credit. What counts is that the sale has taken place during this year.

The cost of goods sold must be the expenses of the goods sold this year. At December 31, the stock at hand was 380 000. Since there was no stock at the beginning of the year, the cost of goods sold this year is found by deducting 380 000 from the purchases of the year.

Wages and social security expenses include wages to the employees. Also included is the social cost (national insurance, medical schemes, pensions) connected with having people employed. All expenses connected to this year are included.

Rent, operating premises and office expenses are all connected to this year, and thus relevant as expenses.

Depreciation on equipment was discussed earlier. Remember that the equipment was purchased for 500 000, and James estimated the lifetime of this equipment as ten years. With an equal yearly depreciation amount this means 50 000 as an expense for a year.

Interest on the loan from Local Bank is connected with this year (recorded on December 31) and is included in the expenses of the year. The loan amounts to 400 000 and with 12.5 per cent interest we see that the expenses are correctly calculated.

3.3 Grouping – sub-dividing the profit and loss account

The profit and loss account in James Super was relatively simple, and it was easy to get an accurate picture of the firm's performance. But it strikes us that certain revenues and certain expenses were of different types or groups. For example, there is a great difference between sales and interest from a bank account as revenue. There is also a big difference between expenses linked to the financing of the firm, the interest expenses, and the other operating expenses. For these reasons it seems reasonable and rational to group the items in the profit and loss account.

In practice, there will often be many items in the profit and loss account, and it is easier to read and to use the figures when they are grouped. Grouping of the profit and loss account will also clarify the items, as the firm is in a better position to group revenues and expenses accurately than are, say, individual investors.

The above arguments for grouping are witnessed both in practice and in legal regulations and recommendations covering financial disclosure.

Usually the grouping will be as follows:

- operating revenues and expenses;
- other revenues and expenses;
- extraordinary items;
- profit and loss allocations.

Revenues may be defined as the product of a firm. They are inflows from sales of goods, from rendering services, or other activities that constitute ongoing operations of the firm.

Expenses are costs incurred to generate revenues. They are outflows resulting from purchasing goods, incurring services, or from other activities that constitute ongoing operations of the firm.

Gains are distinguished from revenues and expenses by being more peripheral to the main activities of the firm.

Losses are, as gains, more peripheral to the main activities of the firm. A typical example of gains or losses is gain or loss on the sale of a fixed asset.

Operating revenues and expenses include all items linked to the operating activities of the firm. Here the word operating must be understood. It is used in various ways depending on the characteristics of the business. First of all operating activities are not the same for all types of business. They represent sales in retail firms and manufacturing firms, interest in finance firms, and services in the service trade. Revenues include positive influences from all activities in a firm. If for example a firm both produces goods for sale and also rents out premises, then both of them are revenues. They are, however, so different in nature that they should be shown separately.

Other revenues and expenses are connected with financial investments and other long-term investments, and also expenses connected with the financing of the firm. Thus, dividends received, interest received, interest expense and other expenses connected with loans are items we will find under this heading. There may also be other items here, for example expenses connected with discontinued operations.

Extraordinary items are events or transactions of unusual nature and infrequent occurrence. Unusual means that they do not happen very often, and the underlying event or transaction is exceptional and clearly in contrast to the ordinary and typical activities of the firm. Infrequency of occurrence means that the event is not expected to recur. Examples could be uninsured losses from floods, earthquakes, expropriations etc.

The classification of extraordinary items is usually very restrictive. This is an international tendency, and a story told at an international conference can illustrate this. An American researcher gave a speech and he strongly underlined how restrictive one should be when classifying items as extraordinary. He was asked whether it was possible to think of any extraordinary item at all. 'Well,' he said, 'expenses in connection with an earthquake.' Then another researcher replied: 'Yes, I agree, on the condition that this did not happen in California.'

Profit and profit allocation. The net result of operating revenues and expenses, of other revenues and expenses and of the extraordinary items will give the profit for the period. From this profit income taxes must be deducted. Then we have the *net profit*. This profit is either paid out as dividends or kept in the firm (retained earnings). The allocation of net profit may be shown in the profit and loss account.

Even though James Super is a small firm with, few items in the profit and loss account, we still need to group expenses and revenues:

Profit and loss account for 19XX	(000s)
Sales	**5000**
Cost of goods sold	4000
Wages and social expenses	500
Rent	240
Operation of premises	90
Office expenses	60
Depreciation on equipment	50
Operating expenses	**4940**
Operating profit	60
Interest income from bank account	10
Interest expenses	50
Net financial items	40
Net profit	20

Operating profit is, as we see, not influenced by financial items, nor by income from financial investments or financial expenses. As we shall see later, the operating profit figure gives an excellent opportunity to evaluate how effectively the resources of the firm have been managed. This figure will also be free of extraordinary items. Thus the operating profit gives a good starting point for comparison over time within the same firm and comparison between firms.

3.4 Measurements

It seems almost unnecessary to remind you that the four fundamental concepts lying behind accounting measurements also apply to the profit and loss account. The separate entity concept, the going concern concept, the accounting period concept and the monetary concept give the framework for reporting.

The six basic principles all directly affect the measurements in the profit and loss account. The transaction principle is used for the recording of revenues. The historical cost principle is the basis for measurement of the expenses. The accrual principle underlines that the measurement is not based upon the cash principle. The matching principle ensures that relevant expenses are matched against the revenues of the period. The prudence principle means that necessary write downs of assets are taken care of as expenses at the appropriate time. The principle of consistency enables comparisons to be made.

✔ Questions and answers

1   **Why is the profit and loss account the most important of the financial account statements?**

    Answer:
    Profits provide resources for activities such as research and development programmes and maintenance of operating capacity. The profit and loss account also gives information on operating performance, enables an examination of management performance, and provides figures for investors in evaluating the worth of the company.

2   **What is the difference between revenue and income?**

    Answer:
    Revenue is a gross figure, income is a net figure. For example, sales less operating expenses, both gross figures, give operating income, a net figure.

3   **The items below should be placed in the groups you think they belong to: interest income, wages and social expenses, gain on sales of machinery, depreciation on building, sales, operating expenses (trucks), cost of goods sold, depreciation on trucks, office and administration expenses, dividends received on shares owned, interest expenses, loss on trade debtors, rental income, loss on foreign currency.**

    Answer:
    As operating revenues and expenses: sales, rental income, gain on sales of machinery, cost of goods sold, wages and social expenses, operating expenses (trucks),

office and administration expenses, loss on trade debtors, depreciation on building, depreciation on trucks.

As financial items: interest income, dividends on shares, interest expenses, loss on foreign currency.

4 **Which of the following items should be found in the profit and loss account: sale of an old building, purchase of a new building, loss from sale of an old building, depreciation on a building.**

Answer:
Loss from sale of building, depreciation on a building.

? Problems

1 Below you will find revenues and expenses from the profit and loss account, all mixed up. Place them where they belong: interest on bank overdraft 100, wages and social security expenses 600, dividends on shares owned 50, sales 3800, loss on trade debtors 50, rent 300, interest on mortgage loan 200, cost of goods sold 2150, rental income 50, administration expenses 200.

2 What will be reported in the profit and loss account for the year ended December 31 in the following case? A firm invested 100 in a new factory. The factory was ready for use on July 1 this year. It was estimated to be worthless in 20 years. The old factory had been bought for 50 and the book value at December 31 last year was 5 after having been depreciated yearly by 1. The old factory was sold on June 30 for 8.

3 Below you will find figures from the profit and loss account as well as from the balance sheet, all mixed up. Show the two accounting statements, grouped: trade creditors 200, dividends on shares owned 10, bank account 50, wages and social security expenses 3600, stock 850, loss on trade debtors 50, equity 1200, shares/investment 100, rent expenses 300, machinery and equipment 900, sales 9090, depreciation on machinery and equipment 100, mortgage 800, cost of goods sold 4050, interest on mortgage loan 200, bank overdraft 300, administration expenses 800, trade debtors 600, tax liability 100, quay 200, other short-term liabilities 100, interest on bank overdraft 50.

4 Understanding the cash flow statement

'Cash is the lifeblood of every business firm.'

LEARNING OBJECTIVES

In this chapter you will learn:
- what the purpose of the cash flow statement is;
- why such a statement provides useful analytical information;
- how the best information is obtained by dividing the cash flows into operating activities, investing activities and financing activities;
- the difference between building up a statement of cash flow by using the direct method and by using the indirect method.

4.1 Why a cash flow statement is informative

In Chapter 2 we studied the balance sheet and in Chapter 3 the profit and loss account. As we know, the balance sheet shows the resources (assets) of a firm and how they are financed, either by equity or by liability. This picture is given at a certain point in time. The profit and loss account gives the profit for an accounting period and insight into how this profit was made. This is accomplished by reporting revenues and expenses for the period.

The profit and loss account and the balance sheet are the basic statements. However, many questions and explanations relating to changes in the liquidity of the firm are not so easy to answer from these two statements. Let us illustrate with an example. A firm has earned a high profit in the year, so why does it have liquidity problems? Such a question can be answered and explained by calculations from the basic statements, but it can be explained much more clearly and effectively by using a cash flow statement. Pedagogically, such a statement is extremely good if built up and presented in the right way. Historically, the cash flow statement is the youngest of the three statements, born in the US as a 'where–got, where–gone' statement, but in fact it is a cash accounting system in modern form.

4.2 Purposes of the cash flow statement

The main purpose of the cash flow statement is to focus on the cash outflows and the cash inflows during an accounting period. It is in fact a statement explaining the movements in the cash (liquidity) position of the firm.

The cash flow statement is essential both for internal and external users. The principles behind this statement are also an excellent tool in budgeting, where the liquidity budget is important.

As we will see, the cash flow statement is a bridge builder between the profit and loss account and the balance sheet, and concentrates on the changes in the balance sheet figures. This approach is rational and informative. Both investors and creditors will find that the information given in the cash flow statement is useful, because it explains the ability of the firm to generate cash, to manage cash flow, and to pay debts and dividends. In addition, as we have mentioned, the cash flow statement explains the difference between profit and cash generated from the operating activities.

In order to get the best possible information from a cash flow statement, the outflows and inflows of cash have to be analysed and presented in a systematic way. Let us see how this is done.

4.3 The model of the cash flow statement

The classification of cash flows is usually divided into *operating*, *investing* and *financing* activities.

Cash flows from operating activities are the cash effects of the activities linked to the profit for the year. In this category we find cash received from customers, cash paid to suppliers of raw materials and/or finished goods, cash payments of wages, and others.

Cash flows from investing activities show cash outflows and inflows connected with purchases and sales of fixed assets and long-term investments/loans.

Cash flows from financing activities give the cash inflows from new equity, for example the sale of shares, and new borrowing. The cash outflows will be payments to owners, for example dividends, and repayment of loans.

The total model of an informative cash flow statement will look like this:

Cash flow statement

	Current year	Previous year
Receipts from customers		
Interest and dividends received		
Payment for raw materials		
Other operating expenses		
Interest payments		
Income taxes paid		
Net cash from operating activities		
Purchase of fixed assets		
Purchase of investments		
Sale of fixed assets		
Net cash from investing activities		
Issue of shares		
Repayment of loans		
Dividends paid		
Net cash from financing activities		
Net increase (decrease) in cash		
Cash at the beginning of the year		
Cash at the end of the year		

In order to underline the connection between a revenue in the profit and loss account and the corresponding cash inflow and an expense in the profit and loss account and the corresponding cash outflow, we will illustrate this point with the following two examples.

Sales for a year were 100 according to the profit and loss account. In the balance sheet trade debtors were 30 at January 1 and 20 at December 31. This means that the cash inflow from trade debtors during the year was 110. Generally, we will have:

Cash from sales = Sales + decrease (– increase) in trade debtors

Cost of goods sold for a year was 80 according to the profit and loss account. The stock was 10 at January 1 and at 20 December 31. Trade creditors were 20 at January 1 and 25 at December 31.

This tells us that the purchase of goods in the year must have been 90 since the stock has increased by 10. Additionally, trade creditors have increased by 5. This means that the payment to trade creditors must have been 85. We see from the example that the cost of goods sold was 80, but the payment connected with purchase of goods was 85. The difference of 5 has two explanations: the change in stock and the change in trade creditors. Generally, we will have:

Cash for purchases = Cost of goods sold + increase (– decrease) in stock
– increase (+ decrease) in trade creditors

The last specific problem we want to raise and clarify is the expense depreciation in the profit and loss account. We have said that depreciation is, logically enough, an operating expense. But when reflecting further on this item, there is no cash linked to it. The cash was paid when a fixed asset was bought. Logically, it follows that the cash used for investment must be part of the cash flow statement, but it is reported in the cash flow in the investment activities section.

4.4 James Super Market

In order to gain a better understanding of the concept of cash flow statements, and also, at least indirectly, the procedural techniques of construction, we will look closer at our case, James Super.

As you will recall, James Super started on January 2 with an equity capital of 200 000, which represented the savings of the owner James Smith. If we prepare the balance sheet at this time it will look like this:

Assets	(000s)
Bank account	200
Equity	
Capital (James Smith)	200

James Smith borrowed 400 000 from Local Bank, and he invested 500 000 in equipment. Thus the balance sheet just after the investment was:

Assets	(000s)
Equipment	500
Bank account, Local Bank	100
	600
Equity and liabilities	
Equity (James Smith)	200
Loan, Local Bank	400
	600

At the end of the first year, the situation was as follows (see Chapter 2):

Balance sheet, December 31, 19XX	(000s)
Assets	
Equipment	450
Stock	380
Trade debtors	20
Bank account, Local Bank	70
	920
Equity and liabilities	
Equity	220
Loan, Local Bank	400
Trade creditors	260
Other creditors	40
	920

We also presented the profit and loss account for the first year, which was as follows (see Chapter 3):

Profit and loss account for 19XX	(000s)
Sales	5000
Cost of goods sold	4000
Wages and social expenses	500
Rent	240
Operation of premises	90
Office expenses	60
Depreciation on equipment	50
Operating expenses	4940
Operating profit	60
Interest from bank account	10
Interest on loan	50
Net financial expenses	40
Net profit	20

On this basis, we will have the following cash flow statement for James Super for the first year (we start with the position before the loan was raised and before the investment in equipment was made):

Cash from sales	4980	(5000 – 20)
Paid to suppliers of goods	–4120	(4000 + 380 – 260)
Paid operating expenses	–850	(890 – 40)
Interest from bank account	10	
Interest on loan	–50	
Net cash from operations	–30	
Investment in equipment	500	
Cash for investment	500	
Bank loan	400	
Cash from financing	400	
Net decrease in cash	130	
Cash at the beginning of the year	200	
Cash at the end of the year	70	

We see from the cash flow statement that we need all three activities (cash from operations, investment and financing) in order to explain the decrease in cash of 130 000.

Net cash from operating activities was negative in the first year. That explains part of the decrease in cash. We also see that the investment in the first year was higher than the loan from the bank, so this also helps explain the decrease.

If we look deeper into the cash changes connected with the operating activities, we see that, although the net profit was 20 in the first year, the cash effect was minus 30. This again can be explained by these facts: not all sales have been received in cash, the cash payment to suppliers of goods was higher than the cost of goods sold and not all operating expenses have been paid.

The model we have described above and applied in our case is constructed according to the direct method. That means gross amounts (flows) are shown in the section of cash flows from operating activities. The other alternative is the indirect method. In this case the starting point for the section of cash flow from operating activities will be net profit. This is the only difference between the two, as cash from investing activities and financing activities are the same.

Let us look at the statement of cash flow, the section of cash from operating activities, if we use the indirect method in our case:

Net profit	20
Adjustment to reconcile net profit to net cash:	
Depreciation	50
Increase in debtors	−20
Increase in stock	−380
Increase in creditors	300
Net cash from operations	−30

We see that the net cash flow from operating activities is the same in the two alternatives. Which one is best is an open question, although internationally the direct method has been preferred (for example in the US).

Questions and answers

1 **Why is it felt necessary to have a cash flow statement in addition to the balance sheet and the profit and loss account?**

Answer:
Because such a statement focuses on the movement of cash during a period, and gives an explanation of the changes in liquidity of a firm.

2 **Which sections do you usually find in a cash flow statement?**

Answer:
Cash from operating, investing and financing activities.

3 **How can you explain that a firm can have a high profit, but liquidity problems?**

Answer:
The profit is measured by matching revenues and related expenses. But the changes in liquidity depend on the cash outflows and the cash inflows. Both these cash flows can differ significantly from revenues and expenses. One good example is that the firm could have invested heavily during the year. That does not affect the expense for the year (except for the depreciation), but does affect cash.

4 **What is the difference between the direct and indirect method in presenting the cash flow statement?**

Answer:
The direct method shows the gross amounts, within the section, of cash flow from operating activities, while the indirect method starts with net profit and makes adjustments in order to reach the net effect on cash. It is only in this section of the cash flow statement (operating activities) that the two methods differ.

? Problem

1 Look at the following balance sheets for December 31 of the current year and previous year, the profit and loss account for this year, and a cash flow statement.

Examine the cash flow statement and provide explanations for the decrease of 15 in cash, despite a net profit of 10.

Then, check the figures in the cash flow statement on the basis of the balance sheets and the profit and loss account.

Balance sheet, December 31, 19XX

		Current year		Previous year
Fixed assets		105		50
Stock		45		30
Trade debtors		30		20
Cash		5		20
Total assets		185		120
Share capital		50		30
Capital reserve		10		–
Retained earnings		25		20
Total equity		85		50
Long-term liabilities		80		55
Trade creditors	10		15	
Other short-term liabilities	10		–	
Total short-term liabilities		20		15
Total equity and liabilities		185		120

Profit and loss account for 19XX

Sales	130
Cost of goods sold	100
Gross profit	30
Operating costs	15
Depreciation	5
	20
Net profit	10
Dividends	5
Retained earnings	5
Retained earnings brought forward	5
Retained earnings carried forward	10

Cash flow statement for 19XX

Payments from customers	120
Payments to suppliers	120
Payment of operating expenses	10*
Net cash from operating activities	−10
Investment in fixed asset	60
Net cash from investment activities	−60
New loan	25
New share capital	30
Net cash from financing activities	55
Net reduction in cash	15
Cash at December 31, last year	20
Cash at December 31, this year	5

*This figure can be explained in the following way:

Operating costs according to the profit and loss account are 15. Since the payment according to the cash flow statement is 10, an amount of 5 must be unpaid at December 31. This liability must be found in the item 'Other short-term liabilities' in the balance sheet. (We see that this item has increased by 10. The explanation for the other 5 must be the unpaid dividends.)

5 Basic understanding of bookkeeping

'Remember: Debit to the window side.'

Old, classical school story in the study of bookkeeping

LEARNING OBJECTIVES

The objective of this chapter is *not* to learn bookkeeping techniques, but to understand the basic reasoning behind them. This is necessary in order to understand accounting information, and also for using accounting data for financial analyses.

After studying this chapter you will:

- have seen the ingenious logic behind the double-entry bookkeeping system;
- understand the dual effect of a transaction;
- have obtained an overview on how the profit and loss account and the balance sheet are logically derived from the double-entry system.

5.1 Double-entry accounting

We have said that accounting is based on transactions, and we have also concluded that there are two effects of a transaction. For example, when a firm buys goods for cash, this affects both the cash (a decrease) and the stock (an increase). It is this double effect that lies behind the double-entry system.

The first book on double-entry accounting was published over 500 years ago (in 1494) by an Italian professor in mathematics and a friar, Luca Pacioli, although the system was known in practice some 200 years before that. It was the publication of this book that made the technique known throughout Europe. Before this, recordings were based on the single-entry accounting method. The invention of double-entry accounting was both rational and a positive development in the field of accounting. In the early days double-entry bookkeeping was considered an art, in fact it was defined as one of the fine arts. For example, a famous Norwegian orchestra established very early an academy for the fine arts: music, song, drawing and ... bookkeeping.

5.2 Accounts – debit and credit

Even though most firms now use business software to enable the books to be kept by computers, a basic understanding of the use of accounts and the logic behind debit and credit is valuable in the study of accounting.

An account is the place where all the information related to one type of asset, one type of liability, one type of equity, one type of revenue or one type of expense is to be found. The account consists of two sides and increases are recorded on one side, decreases on the other. Originally, bookkeeping was used and illustrated in the study of accounting by T-accounts, clearly separating the two sides of an account.

Using accounts in bookkeeping is more than just recording amounts related to the specific account. The accounts in a firm are grouped in a systematic way and linked together in a logical way through the plan of accounts. This plan specifies and classifies all the accounts to be used. The identification of the single account is usually done in a number system so that, for example, all assets start with number 1, all equity items with number 2, all liabilities with number 3, all revenues with number 4 and all expenses with number 5. Then, a second digit can be used for further grouping and a third digit for a specific account. For example, the number 132 could mean a specific type of stock.

As pointed out earlier, an account in double-entry bookkeeping has two sides, debit and credit. These words have their origin in early Italian accounting and were linked to the person. Thus a debit on a person's account means that the person must pay the firm a certain amount, and a credit means the opposite. In practice, and for educational purposes, we say that debit is on the left-hand side and credit is on the right-hand side.

5.3 Recording transactions

As mentioned in section 5.1, every transaction has a dual aspect and therefore needs to be recorded in two accounts. When, for example, a firm buys goods on credit, the stock account is debited and the trade creditor account is credited. When goods are sold on credit, the stock account is credited and the trade debtor's account is debited. This dual aspect also enables the firm to have a total overview at any point of time. Let us illustrate these dimensions in the case of James Super.

On January 2, James Super purchased frozen food from Meat Ltd. The invoice showed 10 000 to be paid on credit terms.

One way of treating this transaction could be to put the invoice aside (in the old days, nail it to the wall), and delay its recording until the invoice was paid. This alternative is very unsatisfactory, since the event itself is not duly recognized in a timely manner. We concluded earlier that, in accounting, the consequence of a transaction is basic. Therefore, the event of January 2 should be recorded in this way:

	Stock account		Trade creditors	
	Debit	Credit	Debit	Credit
January 2, Meat Ltd, invoice per Feb. 2	10 000			10 000

We have recorded that our stock has increased by 10 000, and we have also recorded that we owe Meat Ltd the same amount, payable on February 2. The double effect of this event is recorded when it took place, and the situation is up to date. In this case, an asset (stock) increased, and a liability (trade creditor) increased. If we start with the fundamental basic relationship in the balance sheet:

$$A = E + L$$

where

A = Assets

E = Equity, and

L = Liabilities

we see that generally, the above transaction is an example of an increase in one asset account and an increase in one liability account:

$$A (+) = E + L (+)$$

There was balance in the balance sheet before the transaction, and there is balance in the balance sheet after the transaction. We also understand that it is possible to make a balance sheet after every transaction. This, however, would not be very efficient. We will return to a rational way of doing it later on.

Let us continue our example:

On February 2, 10 000 is paid to Meat Ltd. The payment is made through the bank account. This should be recorded in the following way:

	Bank account		Trade creditors	
	Debit	Credit	Debit	Credit
February 2, Meat Ltd, invoice paid		10 000	10 000	

Again, the recording demonstrates that the transaction has two sides: the bank account has decreased and so has the liability. Generally, this is an example of a decrease in an asset and a decrease in a liability. Logically, there must still be balance in the balance sheet:

$$A (-) = E + L (-)$$

Let us look at the following event:

On January 15, wages are paid to the employees in an amount of 10 000.

The bookkeeping entries will be as follows:

	Cash account		Wages account	
	Debit	Credit	Debit	Credit
January 15, wages paid		10 000	10 000	

Again we will have a double effect of this transaction. The credit of cash is clear, but the debit to the wage account must be understood in a broader context: the wage account is an example of an expenditure necessary to do business. This expense represents a decrease in equity, but there will of course be revenues from having people employed in the shop. We have here an example of the following kind:

$$A (-) = E (-) + L$$

Let us now study the revenue side of the accounting system.

Sales by James Super for the month of January: 300 000. All sales have been on a cash basis. The following entry is made to record the sales:

	Cash account		Sales account	
	Debit	Credit	Debit	Credit
January 31, total sales	300 000			300 000

Generally, this is an example of:

$$A\ (+) = E\ (+) + L$$

Finally, we will have examples where a liability item results in a change in equity. Therefore, we will also have:

$$A = E\ (+) + L\ (-)\ \text{or}$$

$$A = E\ (-) + L\ (+)$$

It seems obvious that changes can also take place within two assets' accounts or within two liabilities' accounts. Let us look at one such example.

> On January 5, James Super draws 15 000 in cash from the bank account. The recording entries will be as follows:

	Cash account		Bank account	
	Debit	Credit	Debit	Credit
January 15, cash from bank	15 000			15 000

The consequence of this transaction is also a double one: the cash has increased, and the bank account has decreased. Again, the basic balance is sustained:

$$A\ (+)\ (-) = E + L$$

Similarly, for a transaction within the liability group we will have:

$$A = E + L\ (+)\ (-)$$

Also, for a transaction within the equity group we will have:

$$A = E\ (+)\ (-) + L$$

We can now end this section by underlining that every transaction has two aspects and always will have two effects on the balance sheet. This can either take place between two groups within the balance sheet, or within the same balance sheet group.

The total picture of all possible effects will be as follows:

1 A (+)   = E + L (+)

2 A (−)   = E + L (−)

3 A (+)   = E (+) + L

4 A (−)   = E (−) + L

5 A   = E (−) + L (+)

6 A   = E (+) + L (−)

7 A (+) (−) = E + L

8 A   = E + L (+) (−)

9 A   = E (+) (−) + L

5.4 Period-end accounting

We have mentioned that, theoretically, a balance sheet could be made after every transaction. This would, however, be inefficient. Let us therefore see how period-end accounting is done in a rational way. The basics for constructing the profit and loss account and the balance sheet are the balance sheet at the beginning of the period and the transactions recorded during the period.

Although we have not explicitly considered the profit and loss account, it should be relatively easy to see the connection between what we described above and the profit and loss account. In the examples, we recorded wages and sales in separate accounts and later on we placed them into a more general account, namely E (−) and E (+) respectively. These examples are both illustrations of items in a profit and loss account: the first one is an expense, and the second one a revenue. Instead of looking at these items directly as equity, it is practical to put all expenses and all revenues into one statement. This is what we do in the profit and loss account, as we have seen in Chapter 3. We emphasize that each individual account, and the total, influence the equity position. This fact we proved and underlined at the end of Chapter 3, where the net profit of the period explained the change in equity.

Again, we return to the case of James Super:

James Super is naturally enough eager to know the result for the month of January, and he wants to see his position at January 31. The balance sheet at the end of the period and the profit and loss account for January will give him the answers.

We know the position at January 2:

Assets

Equipment	500
Bank account, Local Bank	100
	600

Equity and liabilities

Equity (James Smith)	200
Loan, Local Bank	400
	600

Further, James has recorded the following data during January:

Accounts	Debit	Credit
Cash	30	25
Bank	250	280
Purchases of goods	400	0
Wages	30	0
Rent	20	0
Trade suppliers	275	400
Interest	4.5	0
Sales	0	300
Loan, Local Bank	0	4.5
	1009.5	1009.5

Additionally, James finds that the stock now on hand was purchased for 160 000, and that office expenses for this month, but not paid, are 5000. He wants to have all expenses included in the profit and loss account for January, so therefore he also calculates one-twelfth of the annual depreciation on the equipment, which amounts to 4.2. This information gives the following recordings:

	Debit	Credit
Office expenses (expense)	5	
Office expenses, not paid (liability)		5
Depreciation of equipment (expense)	4.2	
Equipment (asset, reduction)		4.2

Again we see the double effect: office expenses should be included in this period even if they have not been paid; compare E (–), L (+). And, when an asset (equipment) has been used, it is logical to record the depreciation in this period, and this means an expense. A reduction in the asset must then be a consequence; compare E (–), A (–).

We can now make the technical period-end entries, as shown in Table 5.1.

Table 5.1 Period-end accounts for James Super Market – working schedule

Account for:	Equipment Deb.	Equipment Cred.	Bank Deb.	Bank Cred.	Cash Deb.	Cash Cred.	Equity Deb.	Equity Cred.	Loan Local Bank Deb.	Loan Local Bank Cred.	Stock Deb.	Stock Cred.	Trade suppliers Deb.	Trade suppliers Cred.	Sales Deb.	Sales Cred.	Wages Deb.	Wages Cred.	Rent Deb.	Rent Cred.	Office expenses Deb.	Office expenses Cred.	Interest Deb.	Interest Cred.
Balance, January 2	500		100					200			400													
Transactions in January			250	280	30	25				400 / 4.5			275	400		300	30		20				4.5	
Profit and loss account		4.2					3.7*					240			300			30		20		5		4.5
Balance, January 31		495.8		70		5	196.3*		404.5			160	125								5			
Total	500	500.0	350	350	30	30	200	200	404.5	404.5	400	400	400	400	300	300	30	30	20	20	5	5	4.5	4.5
Balance	495.8		70		5			196.3		404.5	160			125								5		

* The profit for the month is the difference between revenues and expenses. In January, the expenses are higher than the revenues. This means that the equity is reduced by 3.7 and is now 196.3.

Profit and loss account, January 19XX

	Debit	Credit
Sales		300
Cost of goods sold	240	
Wages	30	
Rent	20	
Office expenses	5	
Interest expense	4.5	
Equipment (depreciation)	4.2	
Loss (transferred to Equity)		3.7
	303.7	303.7

Balance Sheet, January 31, 19XX

	Debit balances	Credit balances
Equipment	495.8	
Stock	160	
Bank account	70	
Cash	5	
Equity		196.3
Office expenses unpaid		5
Trade suppliers		125
Loan, Local Bank		404.5
	730.8	730.8

47

In a total bookkeeping system the balance sheet at the beginning of a period, the transactions in the period and the use of the accrual principle give the data for the balance sheet at the end of the period and the profit and loss account for the period. We see that all accounts have been closed and the net figure either transferred to the balance sheet or the profit and loss account. There are just these two alternatives and, as we have seen, the profit and loss account is in fact a specification of increases and decreases in equity. Once again, we underline that there is always balance in what we do: balance in the sum of the debit and credit when we started, balance in the sum of transactions in the period, and balance in what we do at the end of the period. Therefore, there must be balance in the balance sheet at the end of the period.

The technical period end of each single account underlines this balance. When, for example, the cash account shows debits (inflows) of 30 000 and credits (outflows) of 25 000, the net figure, 5000, is found as an increase in the balance at the end of the period. This is the situation as far as the cash is concerned.

As far as goods are concerned, this is a little more complicated, but the logic behind it should be clear enough. The stock, 160 000, at the end of the period is a balance item. When the purchases have been 400 000, the cost of goods sold must be 240 000. This is a profit and loss item and is found in this statement.

We can now present the following financial accounts for James Super:

Profit and loss account, January 19XX   (000s)

Sales	300.0
Cost of goods sold	240.0
Wages	30.0
Rent	20.0
Office expenses	5.0
Depreciation on equipment	4.2
Total operating costs	299.2
Operating profit	0.8
Interest	4.5
Loss	−3.7

Balance sheet, January 31, 19XX   (000s)

Assets
Equipment   495.8
Stock   160.0
Bank account, Local Bank   70.0
Cash   5.0
                                                    730.8

Equity and liabilities
Equity   196.3
Loan, Local Bank   404.5
Trade creditors   125.0
Unpaid office expenses   5.0
                                                    730.8

James is satisfied with the fact that the profit and loss account for the first month shows a positive operating profit. But we have to add that he has received no salary himself, despite his long working days. In the future, though, he feels quite sure that there will be an improvement in business sufficient to secure himself a reasonable salary.

We see the fundamental link between the net profit (loss) according to the profit and loss account and the change in equity. The decrease of 3.70 (200 at January 2, and 196.30 at January 31) is fully explained by the loss in the period.

Questions and answers

1 **Why do you think double-entry accounting was first developed in practice?**

Answer:
It was in practice that business people experienced that a transaction always has two sides. It was therefore logical to keep track of both effects. That was exactly what double-entry accounting did. It was both more rational and gave a better overview than the single-entry bookkeeping system.

2 **Why is it good logic to make use of the T-account?**

Answer:
In the answer to Question 1 above we said that a transaction always has two sides. An account records this fact with two sides, and a T-account underlines this.

3 **Explain debit and credit and their use.**

Answer:
The debit is the left side of the account, credit the right side.
Generally, to debit an asset account means an increase in that asset, to debit a liability account means a decrease in the liability and to debit an equity account means a decrease in equity.

Generally, to credit an account will mean a decrease in assets, an increase in liability or an increase in equity.

4 **In the text we developed the following general connections in bookkeeping:**

(a) A (+)   = E + L (+)
(b) A (−)   = E + L (−)
(c) A (+)   = E (+) + L
(d) A (−)   = E (−) + L
(e) A   = E (−) + L (+)
(f) A   = E (+) + L (−)
(g) A (+) (−) = E + L
(h) A   = E + L (+) (−)
(i) A   = E (+) (−) + L

Give examples of transactions within these alternatives in addition to those mentioned in the text (under (i) we do not expect examples at this point, but in the answer you will also find examples of this alternative).

Answer:
(a) The purchase of a building on credit, bank loan.
(b) Down-payment on mortgage, payment to trade creditors.
(c) Interest income, dividends received on shares, new share capital.
(d) Interest expenses, dividends paid.
(e) Social security costs not paid, taxes not paid, interest not paid.
(f) Long-term debt converted into equity capital.
(g) Purchase of land for cash, sales of investments, payment from customers, cash loan to employees.
(h) Converting of trade creditor liability into long-term liability, converting of long-term liability into short-term liability.
(i) Increase of share capital without payment.

5 **Why is it necessary at the period end to take into consideration unpaid expenses and pre-paid expenses?**

Answer:
Because the goal is to measure the profit for a period by matching the revenues and the relevant expenses for a period. That means that all expenses have to be relevant for this period. This will also give a correct picture of the balance sheet situation.

? Problems

1 Record the following transactions in T-accounts:

(a) Purchase of goods for cash
(b) Cash paid into bank account
(c) Cash payment to a supplier for goods delivered earlier
(d) Sales on credit
(e) Purchase of machinery on credit
(f) Cash received from mortgage loan
(g) Payment of value added tax
(h) From bank account partial repayment on mortgage loan
(i) Cash from trade customers for goods sold earlier
(j) Cash payment to the owner

2 Below you will find information linked to stock. How would you close the accounts at the end of the month?

Stock at January 1	500
Purchases	8 500
Sales	12 000
Stock at January 31	1 000

3 Close the account for machinery on the basis of the following information:

Balance at January 1	800
Purchase of new machinery by cheque during the year	2000
Depreciation of machinery	600

4 Below you will find the balance sheet at December 31 last year, the bookkeeping entries for January and additional information at January 31. What will the balance sheet at January 31 and the profit and loss account look like?

Balance sheet, December 31, last year

Building	400
Stock	300
Trade debtors	200
Postal account	100
Total assets	1000
Equity	400
Debentures	300
Bank overdraft	200
Trade creditors	100
Total equity and liabilities	1000

Entries for January	Debit	Credit
Trade debtors	4 000	4 100
Postal account	1 500	1 350
Bank overdraft	1 850	1 800
Trade creditors	2 900	3 000
Purchases of goods	3 000	
Sales		4 000
Wages	600	
Other operating expenses	400	
	14 250	14 250

Additional information at January 31

Stock valued according to purchase prices is 400, but due to the fact that some of it is old-fashioned, a write down of 50 is necessary. The building was purchased for 1200 and is depreciated over 20 years with an equal yearly amount. An operating expense relevant for this month of 20 has not been recorded until now.

6 Basic measurement problems

2 + 2 = ?
The mathematician:	*2 + 2 = 4.000*
The strategist:	*2 + 2 = 5*
The financier:	*2 + 2 = 3.8*
The accountant:	*What would you like it to be?*

LEARNING OBJECTIVES

After studying this chapter, you should be able to:

- see the measurement problems of stock, both the measurement of stock in the balance sheet, and the measurement of cost of goods sold in the profit and loss account;
- discuss the valuation of trade debtors;
- understand what depreciation means in accounting and know the different methods of depreciation;
- know the problem area of goodwill;
- see how accounting figures will vary when items are expensed, compared with being capitalized;
- understand how investments in other firms are accounted for in accounting;
- know the problems when assets and liabilities in foreign currencies have to be translated into your currency.

We have said that the most important function of accounting is to measure the financial consequences of decisions made in the firm. The objective of this chapter is not to go very deeply into the many measurement problems we find within financial accounting. However, in order to use accounting data and also to be able to ask the relevant questions, we need a basic understanding of the main measurement problems within the field and of how these problems are usually solved in financial accounting.

When discussing the different problems we will look at them in relation to both the measurement in the balance sheet and that in the profit and loss account. That should give the best understanding.

At the end of most of the main measurement problems we discuss, you will find examples from annual reports. The examples are from the following companies:

- Marks & Spencer (UK);

- Volkswagen (Germany);

- Danisco (Denmark);

- Volvo (Sweden);

- Bergesen (Norway);

- Coca-Cola (USA).

6.1 Recognition of revenue and income

The determination of income involves relating revenues, expenses, gains and losses for appropriate accounting periods. A key question is the timing of income or revenue recognition.

Two conditions must be met before revenue can be recognized: it must be realized or realizable and it must be earned.

Typically, revenue is recognized when the critical event takes place. This event can be anywhere in the chain of business events from production through sale to the receipt of cash from the sale.

The alternatives for recognizing revenue and income are illustrated in Fig. 6.1 (production company).

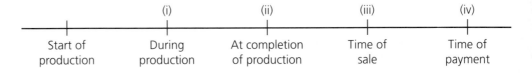

Figure 6.1 Recognizing revenue and income

The time of sale (iii) is the most common method of revenue recognition. At that point the customer has agreed to buy the goods and the price is settled. There will be a risk if payment is to take place later, but allowances for bad debts will take care of this risk.

Alternative (i), recognition during production, is the preferable accounting policy for long-term contracts. The accounting method used in such cases is the percentage-of-completion method. Revenue and income are recognized as the work on the contract progresses. If, for example, a construction company enters into a contract to build a tunnel for 110 million, and the company estimates the total cost at 100 million, that it will take three years to complete and the cost for each year will be 20 million, 30 million and 50 million respectively, then the recognition of revenue and income will be (millions):

	Year 1	Year 2	Year 3	Total
Revenue	22	33	55	110
Income	2	3	5	10

This way of recognizing revenue and income seems more adequate and more logical than the alternative: to wait until the contract is completed, 'the completed contract method' (in our case, to recognize a revenue of 110 and an income of 10 in year 3).

The difficulty in using the percentage-of-completion method is to make estimates of the ultimate costs.

Related to the reporting of revenue during production is the recognition of increased value arising from natural growth or an ageing process. Examples include growing timber, livestock, fish farming and the ageing of certain wines and alcoholic drinks.

Alternative (ii), recognition at completion of production, can, as mentioned above, be used in a long-term contract, but also in some extractive industries where the market is ready to buy the products.

Alternative (iv), recognition of time at payment, has the advantage that there is no longer a risk of non-payment. But as we have seen before, the accrual principle is basic in financial accounting, so this alternative is generally not used. In small companies, in non-profit organizations and in some governmental organizations, this way of recognition is, however, quite normal.

6.2 Stocks/inventories

We have seen many examples already of problems with the measurement of stock, both in connection with the balance sheet and the profit and loss account. We underline this fundamental connection:

stock at the beginning of the period
+ purchases during the period
= goods available for sale
- stock at the end of the period
= cost of goods sold

The pricing of stock is one of the most debated and also most important problems in accounting measurement. The value of stock directly influences the profit for the period, often with considerable effect.

We emphasize that the basis for valuation is the purchase price of the goods in hand. But the prudence principle must also be taken into account. In this case it means the lower of cost or market value. Cost includes the net invoice price, i.e. less purchase discounts, cash rebates, freight and transportation costs and applicable taxes or tariffs. Pricing stock at cost raises the problem of assumed cost flow. Assumed flow means that the flow does not necessarily have to be the same as the actual flow of goods. Usually, the pricing of stock is made according to one of the following alternative flows:

- specific identification;

- average cost;

- first-in, first-out (FIFO);

- last-in, first-out (LIFO).

Specific identification means that the units in stock at the end of the period can be identified to a specific purchase. Usually, this method is used when the stock consists of few and big pieces.

Average cost is computed by dividing the total value of goods available for sale by the total units. This gives the weighted average unit costs, and this amount also applies to the stock at the end of the period. The following example illustrates the average cost method:

January 1	Opening stock	200	units	@	100	20 000
January 10	Purchase	1000	units	@	105	105 000
January 20	Purchase	500	units	@	110	55 000
January 30	Purchase	200	units	@	125	25 000
January 31	Cost of goods sold	1700	units	@	107.90	183 400
January 31	Closing stock	200	units	@	107.90	21 600

FIFO is based on the assumption that the first items acquired should be assigned to the first items sold. This means that the goods on hand at the end of a period are assumed to be from the latest purchases. In our example we will have the following:

January 1	Opening stock	200	units	@	100		20 000
January 10	Purchase	1000	units	@	105		105 000
January 20	Purchase	500	units	@	110		55 000
January 30	Purchase	200	units	@	125		25 000
January 31	Cost of goods sold	1700	units				180 000
January 31	Closing stock	200	units	@	125		25 000

In the example, we see that the stock at the end of the period is lower when we use the average method compared with the FIFO method. The effect of the valuation of stock at the end of the period means that the cost of goods sold is higher when we use the average method compared with the FIFO method. We have to underline that in our example the prices are going up all the time. If the prices are decreasing, then the stock at the end of the period will be higher when we use average cost and that means lower cost of goods sold compared with the FIFO method.

Internationally, the average cost method and the FIFO method are the most widely used. We mention, however, that *LIFO* (last-in, first-out) also occurs, especially in the US. When using this method and assuming increasing prices, the stock at the end of the period will be relatively low and cost of goods sold relatively high.

As we have mentioned, cost will be the most appropriate valuation of stock, but we have to test this value against the market, since lower of cost or market value is the application of the prudence principle. If the market price is lower, the stock has to be written down to market value. The market value may mean either current replacement cost or sales value less necessary sales cost. Internationally, both alternatives are used.

The next problem we will discuss in connection with stock concerns manufacturing firms. First we show that stock in such a firm comprises three types: raw material, work in progress/process and finished goods. The first type is materials and supplies and can be looked upon as parallel to stock in a trading firm. Work in progress is not relevant in a non-manufacturing organization, but finished goods are equivalent to stock in a trading firm.

Let us use some figures in order to illustrate the accounts and the presentation in such a case:

A manufacturing firm has a stock of raw material at January 1, of 100 and at December 31 of 80. The purchase of raw material during the year was 500. Labour and other operating costs were 2000 during the year. At January 1, work in progress was 200, and at the end of the year, 300. The stock of finished goods was 400 at January 1 and 200 at December 31.

The accounts will include the following:

Balance sheet	Dec. 31, this year		Dec. 31, last year	
Raw material	80		100	
Work in progress	300		200	
Finished goods	200	580	400	700

Profit and loss account	This year
Raw material	520
Salaries and other operating cost	2000
Decrease in work in progress and finished goods	100
Cost of goods sold	2620

We stress that in the profit and loss account sales must be compared with cost of goods sold, which follows from the matching principle. Therefore, we must make corrections for changes in all categories of stock. Let us check the total first:

We learn from the figures that the purchase of raw material during the year was 500 and that wages and other operating costs were 2000, which means 2500 altogether. We also see that total stock has decreased by 120, which means that 2620 must be the cost of goods sold. This is the amount we find in the profit and loss account. From the balance sheet we can see which of the three categories of stock have changed.

Another valuation problem is also met in a manufacturing firm, namely which costs should be included in the stock of work in progress and finished goods. One view is just to include the direct or variable costs, another also to include part of the factory overhead costs. Of course, the valuation in the balance sheet will be lower when using the first alternative, the direct costing method, than the second alternative, the full cost method or absorption costing. The effect on the profit for the year, however, will also depend on the change in the volume of the work in progress and finished goods.

The general rule for the recognition of revenue is the time of sale. But in some industries, for example the building and construction industry, *long-term contracts* occur. In such cases, the profit should reflect the proportion of the work carried out at the accounting date. This means that work in progress on long-term contracts will include part of the profit.

EXAMPLES

Stocks

Stocks and work in progress are valued at the lower of cost and net realizable value using the retail method. **(Marks & Spencer)**

Inventories

Raw material and supplies as well as merchandise are valued at average acquisition cost or the lower replacement cost. In addition to direct materials, the values given for work in progress and finished goods also comprise direct labour, material overheads including depreciation and commensurate administration expenses incurred in connection with production operations. Provision is made for all discernible storage and inventory risks by way of adequate value adjustments. **(Volkswagen)**

Stocks

Stocks are valued at the lower of cost on a first-in, first-out basis and net realizable value. Cost is based on purchase cost and production cost. Production cost includes cost of material and direct labour. Write downs are effected for obsolete items, including slow-moving items. **(Danisco)**

Inventories

Inventories are shown at the lower of cost, in accordance with the first-in, first-out method (FIFO), or replacement value. Adequate provision has been made for obsolescence. **(Volvo)**

Work in progress, bunkers and other inventories

Inventories are stated at cost or market value, whichever is the lower. Allowance has been made for obsolete inventory. Work in progress includes direct materials and payroll with the addition of indirect expenses. **(Bergesen)**

Inventories

Inventories are valued at the lower of cost or market. In general, cost is determined on the basis of average cost or first-in-first-out methods. However, for certain inventories cost is determined on the last-in-first-out (LIFO) method. The excess of current costs over LIFO stated values amounted to approximately .... million and .... million at December 31, 19XX and 19XX, respectively. **(Coca-Cola)**

6.3 Debtors/accounts receivable

Here we will discuss the problem arising from sales on credit to customers, often called trade credit. Sales on credit carry a risk of non-payment. When valuing trade debtors at the end of the year, the prudence principle means that this item must not be overvalued. Uncollectable or doubtful receivables must therefore be written down to a realistic value. Further, it follows from the matching principle that a loss on trade debtors should be matched against the sales. It will, of course, be impossible to know at the time of sale which sale will not be collected. But the expected loss should be estimated and expensed in the relevant period.

One way to find the necessary write down on debtors is to value each debtor separately. In the case of bankruptcy, the claim might have to be written down to zero, if any doubt exists the amount has to be reduced, and there will be no write down when the full amount is expected to be paid. It is also possible to look at debtors as a total and write down the amount by a certain percentage. This percentage has to be based on experience.

In both these alternatives we used a balance sheet view, as we started with evaluation of the asset (debtors). We could also have used a profit and loss account view. Then credit sales of the period would have been the basis for the calculation and again a realistic percentage would be found by experience.

Since the calculated loss on debtors is an estimated figure, the realized amount will differ from the *ex ante* figure. This 'mistake' we have to take into consideration in the next accounting period.

As far as reporting is concerned, most firms will give just one figure for debtors in the balance sheet and then give details in the notes to the accounts of the amount of the reduction for doubtful accounts. In situations with few items in the balance sheet, this amount may be given directly on the face of the balance sheet.

6.4 Tangible fixed assets/property, plant and equipment

Within the fixed asset group we distinguish between tangible and intangible assets. Tangible fixed assets have physical substance. Land, buildings, machinery and equipment are examples of such assets. Some of these assets have a limited life and must therefore be depreciated. Land, however, has no limited life and is not subject to depreciation.

The main questions in connection with depreciable tangible fixed assets are:

1 What is the cost of the asset?

2 How should the cost be allocated against revenues over time?

3 How should repairs, maintenance and additions to the assets be treated?

4 How should the disposal of fixed assets be recorded?

We will concentrate on Question 2, giving short comments on the other questions.

The acquisition cost includes all expenditures necessary to get the asset ready for use. That means that freight, transportation, installation, etc. should be included. Interest on borrowed money is usually not included but expensed.

Depreciation is a systematic distribution of cost, less scrap value, over the estimated useful life of the asset. We stress that, in accounting, depreciation is an allocation process not a valuation.

In earlier chapters we have seen examples where the cost of a fixed asset has been spread evenly over the lifetime of the asset. This method of depreciation is called the *straight-line method*. It is by far the most commonly used method. It is easy both to use and to understand. It seems logical in a way to have the same expense in every period during the life of the depreciable asset. Internationally, this method dominates.

The most common method within *accelerated* depreciation methods is the *reducing-balance method*. Here the same percentage is used, but on book value, so that the yearly amounts of depreciation decrease over time. The arguments for this type of depreciation are that the asset is assumed to be more efficient in the first years, that change in techniques can lead to rapid loss in value for some assets and that the repair expenses will often be greater in the later years.

The *unit of production method* is based on the philosophy that the use of the asset is what explains the decreasing value, not the passage of time. This means that every unit will have the same amount of depreciation. This method is usually applied in oil and gas industries and in mineral explorations.

We will illustrate the straight-line method and the reducing-balance method by the following example:

Machinery is bought for 100. The expected economic life is five years, with no scrap value. Using the two methods we will have the following book values of assets and depreciation costs:

	Straight-line method, 20%		Reducing balance method, 30%	
	Balance, Dec. 31	P&L, depreciation	Balance, Dec. 31	P&L, depreciation
Year 0	100		100	
Year 1	80	20	70	30
Year 2	60	20	49	21
Year 3	40	20	34	15
Year 4	20	20	24	10
Year 5	0	20	17	7

We see that the reducing-balance method means higher depreciation in the early years, lower in the later.

In the discussion above, the cost of fixed assets has been the basis for depreciation. This is a new example of the basic accounting assumption of historical cost. However, we also have to apply the principle of prudence in connection with fixed assets. Again the test must be the market. This means that it can be necessary to *write down* fixed assets. Such a write down must be seen over a longer time horizon, so usually the condition for writing down must be that the fall in value is assumed to be permanent. It seems logical to classify a necessary write down as an operating cost, since such a write down will influence the ordinary depreciation later on.

We also mention that *writing up* of assets may be possible, but this varies between countries; in some countries it is permitted, and in other countries, for example the US, it is prohibited. Where it is permitted, the practice varies; in some countries, for example the UK, it must be done in a systematic way; in other countries, for example in Scandinavia, it is up to the firm itself to decide whether to write up, which asset to write up and by what amount. We must stress that writing up is alien to the concept of historical cost.

EXAMPLES

Fixed assets

(a) *Capitalized interest.* Interest is not capitalized on the cost of land and buildings.

(b) *Depreciation.* Depreciation is provided to write off the cost or valuation of tangible fixed assets by equal annual instalments at the following rates:

Freehold and leasehold land and buildings over 50 years – 1 per cent or nil.
Leasehold land and buildings under 50 years – over the remaining period of the lease.
Fixtures, fittings and equipment – 6.66 per cent to 33.33 per cent according to the estimated life of the asset.

(c) *Repairs and renewals.* Expenditure on repairs, renewals and minor items of equipment is written off in the year in which it is incurred. Certain major items of fixed plant and structure are incorporated within the cost of buildings when purchased. When replaced, these are fully expensed as repairs and renewals in the profit and loss account. **(Marks & Spencer)**

Tangible assets

These are valued at acquisition or manufacturing cost minus depreciation. The regular depreciation is based on the following useful lives:

Buildings 25–50 years
Building and site utilities 10–18 years
Technical equipment and machinery 5–8 years
Power generators 14 years

Factory and office equipment 4–8 years
Special tools, jigs and fixtures are amortized using unit rates based on expected production quantities. **(Volkswagen)**

Tangible fixed assets

Land and buildings are entered at cost plus revaluation less accumulated depreciation and write-downs.

Depreciation is provided according to the straight-line method based on the useful lives of the assets to expected residual value. The lifetimes of major assets are fixed individually, the lifetimes of other assets are fixed in respect of groups of uniform assets. Expected lifetimes are:

Buildings 20–40 years
Plant and machinery 10–20 years
Fixtures, fittings, tools and equipment 3–7 years

Assets with a short lifetime, small assets, and minor improvement costs are entered as expenses in the year of acquisition.

Finance loan assets, chiefly computer hardware, are capitalized and depreciated according to the straight-line method over their useful lives. The remaining capitalized lease obligations are included under creditors. **(Danisco)**

Depreciation and amortization

Depreciation is based on the historical cost of the assets, reduced in appropriate cases by write downs, and estimated economic life. The depreciation period for leasing vehicles and company vehicles is normally 3 to 10 years. Machinery is depreciated over 5 to 10 years and buildings over 25 to 50 years, while the greater part of land improvements are depreciated over 20 years. **(Volvo)**

Fixed assets and depreciation

Depreciable fixed assets have been stated in the balance sheet as cost less accumulated ordinary depreciation. Ordinary depreciation is charged on a straight-line basis over the economic life of the assets.

Vessels are estimated to have a total economic life of 20 years. Ordinary depreciation on real estate is provided at 3 per cent per annum. **(Bergesen)**

Property, plant and equipment

Property, plant and equipment are stated at cost, less allowances for depreciation. They are depreciated principally by the straight-line method over the estimated useful lives of the assets. **(Coca-Cola)**

Leasing

Usually a company will own property, plant and equipment for use in its business activities. But a company may also acquire the use of property for specific periods of time with stipulated payments through contractual arrangements called leases.

Short-term leases will cover only a portion of the economic life of the assets. Such leases are referred to as *operating* leases. The accounting treatment of such leases is simple: the rental payments are part of the operating expenses, and they are reported as they are paid.

Long-term leases, however, can in fact be economically equivalent to purchase, with financing by the lessor. Such leases are referred to as *capital* leases or *finance* leases. When the situation is that a lease is in fact equivalent to a purchase, then the asset should be capitalized and depreciated over its economic life. The lease payments should be treated as interest and repayments of a loan.

The decision of whether the lease agreement is an operating lease or a finance/capital lease should be based upon economic reality ('substance over form'). Generally the following four criteria are used for classifying a lease as a capital lease:

● the lease transfers ownership of the asset to the lessee at the end of the lease term;

● the lease contains an agreed purchase possibility;

● the lease term covers the major portion of the asset's life;

● the present value of the minimum lease payments should be almost the fair market value.

Any one of the criteria above is sufficient to classify a lease as a capital lease.

The following example will illustrate how a capital lease is accounted for:

Purchase price of a machine:	400 (no scrap value)
Economic life:	4 years
Lease term:	4 years
Yearly rental:	126

In this case we see that the lease term covers 100 per cent of the economic life of the machine. The net present value of the yearly rentals is 400 when we use 10 per cent interest, or if the internal rate of interest is 10 per cent. We have the following calculation:

Year	Machine	Depreciation (straight-line)	Interest	Liability
Jan. 1, year 1	400			
Dec. 31, year 1	300	100	40 (10% of 400)	314
Dec. 31, year 2	200	100	31 (10% of 314)	219
Dec. 31, year 3	100	100	22 (10% of 219)	115
Dec. 31, year 4	0	100	11 (10% of 115)	0

In the financial statements the reporting will be as follows:

	Year			
	1	2	3	4
Profit and loss account				
Depreciation	100	100	100	100
Interest expense	40	31	22	12
Balance sheet				
Machine	300	200	100	0
Liabilities	314	219	115	0

This treatment is exactly as if the machine was bought and financed 100 per cent by loan. Compared with the treatment as an operating lease (yearly expense of 126), this means substantial differences for the operating income in each of the four years. In the balance sheet nothing would have been reported if the transaction were treated as an operating lease.

EXAMPLES

Valuation

Leasing and rental assets are valued at acquisition or manufacturing cost minus depreciation. **(Volkswagen)**

From the balance sheet

Tangible fixed assets			
Leased equipment and plant	xx	xx	
Creditors	xx	xx	
Capitalized lease obligations	xx	xx	**(Danisco)**

Leasing of ships, where the leasing agreement in fact represents a financing of the vessel, is treated as finance lease. **(Bergesen)**

6.5 Intangibles

Intangible assets have no physical substance but still represent values for the firm. In many cases they are linked to legal rights, for example patents, copyright and trade marks. Other categories of intangible assets are research and development costs and goodwill.

Normally intangible assets will have the following characteristics:

- no physical substance;
- future value, but the value is often difficult to calculate;
- limited economic life, difficult to stipulate;
- usually acquired or invested for operating activities, not for investment purposes.

The accounting problem we meet when measuring intangible assets is that although they undoubtedly represent future value, this value is uncertain and hard to document. According to the prudence principle it can be argued that they should be expensed in the same period they occur. But economic theory should lead to quite another conclusion, namely to allocate the cost of intangible assets to the periods that benefit from them; in other words, to capitalize and depreciate. In accounting we often use the word amortization for this.

When an intangible item is expensed, there will never be an asset in the balance sheet. From a balance sheet point of view, therefore, it is a conservative principle to expense intangible items, when compared to capitalization. This has an effect on the yearly profit, however, due to the fact that over time capitalization and depreciation/amortization have an accumulative effect. Let us illustrate this effect with an example linked to research and development (R&D) expenses.

Compare company A and company B. They spend exactly the same yearly amount in R&D. Company A, however, has a policy of expensing such costs, while Company B will capitalize and depreciate over five years. Over a period of five years, the amounts used for R&D are:

Year 1	200	
Year 2	300	
Year 3	400	
Year 4	200	
Year 5	100	1200

Company A and Company B will report the following amounts as cost for the different years:

	Year 1	Year 2	Year 3	Year 4	Year 5	Total
Company A	200	300	400	200	100	1200
Company B	40	100	180	220	240	780

We see that the R&D cost shows big differences between the two companies for each single year, but Company A does not always report a higher cost. As we see, the opposite happens in the last two years.

We also see that over the five-year period, the total differs. The difference (420) is the undepreciated part of the R&D over the last four years (80 per cent of R&D in year five, 60 per cent of R&D in year four and so on).

Accounting for goodwill has attracted intellectual attention over many years. In 1980 a researcher estimated that almost one thousand books and articles had been written since 1880 on this subject. The figure is much higher now!

Goodwill is the excess of the cost of a group of assets over the individual assets. Usually goodwill will arise in connection with the acquisition of a firm as a whole. Goodwill in accounting is only discussed in connection with acquisitions, as internal goodwill which is generated in the firm is never taken into account. This follows on from the fundamental principle of transaction.

When acquiring another firm, it seems logical to compare the purchase amount with the sum of the individual assets. It also seems logical to value the individual assets at market values at the time of acquisition, and then draw the following conclusion: since a buyer is willing to pay more than the sum of the individual assets there must be an expected higher benefit. The total value of the firm has a higher value than the sum of its individual assets. There are many reasons for the willingness to pay more for a firm than for the individual parts: an established firm has a market position and an organization. The reason can also be that there would be a synergy effect as a result of combining the acquired firm with one's own firm.

The treatment of goodwill is a controversial issue in accounting. Theoretically, there can be little doubt of the accounting solution: the reason for paying more than the sum of individual assets is expected extra profit. Therefore, goodwill should be reported as a long-term asset and depreciated over its expected economic life. It will of course be difficult to say for how long goodwill will last, but this fact should not give rise to the conclusion that goodwill should be expensed in the same period as the acquisition took place. The motives for doing so are said to be the prudence principle, but we emphasize again that, theoretically, this principle should not be used in such a way.

Internationally, the accounting solution to the goodwill problem varies. In most countries goodwill will be capitalized and amortized over time. This time horizon varies from up to 40 years (in the US) down to five years according to EU rules. In some cases the whole amount of goodwill is written down against the equity, i.e. not reporting any cost of goodwill at all.

EXAMPLES

Intangible assets

Shown at acquisition cost and depreciated pro rata temporis. **(Volkswagen)**

Intangible fixed assets

Intangible fixed assets are valued at cost less accumulated amortization and write downs. Amortization is provided according to the straight-line method based on the estimated useful lives of the assets which are 2–5 years depending on the actual circumstances. **(Danisco)**

Research and development costs

Research and development costs include costs, salaries and depreciation attributable to the research and development activities of the group. Research and development costs are charged to the profit and loss account as incurred. **(Danisco)**

Research and development and warranty expenses

Research and development costs are charged to cost of sales as incurred. Estimated costs related to product warranties are charged against cost of sales at the time the products are sold. **(Volvo)**

Goodwill and other intangible assets

Goodwill and other intangible assets are stated on the basis of cost and are being amortized, principally on a straight-line basis, over the estimated future period to be benefited (not exceeding 40 years). **(Coca-Cola)**

6.6 Investment in other firms

There are many motives for a firm to have financial interests in other firms. One reason is that such an investment is looked upon as a better alternative than keeping the money in the bank. In such cases the investment will normally be classified as a current asset. There may be cases where such an investment is looked upon as a long-term investment and classified accordingly. In these cases the valuation of the investment will comply with the general valuation rules in accounting.

If the investment is of a size representing a substantial influence over another firm, the accounting treatment could be different from the treatment described above. Such investments are often made for strategic reasons. It is hard to say how big an investment should be in order to have substantial influence, but usually in accounting this is more than a 20 per cent stake. If the investment is more than 50 per cent, a parent–subsidiary relation exists, and then consolidated group accounts are prepared. We will return to such accounts in Chapter 9.

With an investment of 20–50 per cent the accounting treatment is usually according to the *equity* method. Here, the investment in the balance sheet will show at any time the amount in the net balance sheet invested in the firm, and the profit and loss account will show the firm's percentage of net profit.

We can summarize the different types of investments in other firms and the accounting treatment of such investments as in Table 6.1.

Table 6.1 Accounting treatments of investments

Types of investment	Influence / Ownership	Accounting treatments by investor				
		Cost	Market value	Pro-rata (gross) method	Equity (net) method	Group accounts
Small, often short-term financial investments	No influence Small part of the total equity capital	X	X			
Associated companies	Substantial influence 20–50% ownership			X	X	
Subsidiaries	Dominating influence Over 50% ownership	X Parent company			X Parent company	X
Partnership	Variable influence and ownership			X	X	
Joint ventures	Variable influence and ownership, non-permanent business			X	X	

Comments

More than one cross means that various alternatives are in use – from an international perspective. In the first type of investment (small financial investments), the market value alternative will be limited to investments in quoted companies.

Types of investment

The first type of investment is classified either as a current (liquid) asset or as a fixed (financial) asset. This classification is made by the company itself, depending on the purpose of the investment.

Investments in *associated (affiliated) companies* have an upper limit of 50 per cent. This is logical, as passing this level makes the investment an investment in a subsidiary. The lower limit of 20 per cent is a practical way of under-lining a substantial investment.

Investments in *subsidiaries* have a logical lower limit of ownership: in normal circumstances more than 50 per cent (of the voting capital) will give control over a company.

Partnership exists when two or more persons carry on a business in common (with a view to profit) based on an agreement as to the contribution which each will make towards the capital of the business and the share of the profit or loss each will bear. The 'persons' are usually individuals; however, they could be corporations or other partnerships.

A corporate *joint venture* is a corporation owned and operated by more than one person or an association of persons jointly undertaking a non-permanent business (contrast with partnership). No single part in a joint venture has a dominating influence.

Accounting treatments

Cost means the purchase price of the investment.

Market value means a valuation of the investment at current prices. Such a valuation seems both relevant and realistic for shares in quoted companies.

The *pro-rata* or *gross method* means that the relevant parts of revenues, expenses, assets and liabilities are taken into the accounts, either item by item or in groups. If a company has a 40 per cent investment in another company, the treatment will be as follows: 40 per cent of sales, 40 per cent of expenses for the year, 40 per cent of the assets, 40 per cent of the liabilities. Thus the net effect will be 40 per cent of the net income and 40 per cent of the equity.

The *equity* or *net method* (in contrast to the gross method) means that the investment is measured as the percentage of the equity at any time. The profit part for the year thus increases the investment, while the dividend received reduces the investment.

Group accounts are relevant when a company (the parent company) has a controlling interest in another company (subsidiary). The best economic information in such a case is to present a group financial statement.

EXAMPLES

Current asset investments

Current asset investments are stated at market value. All profits and losses from such investments are included in net interest income or in Financial Activities turnover as appropriate. (**Marks & Spencer**)

Affiliates are now (in Volkswagen Group) valued on the basis of the proportionate stockholders' equity.

Joint ventures in the consolidated financial statements are included on the basis of the proportionate stockholders' equity. Six joint ventures are valued at acquisition cost. (**Volkswagen**)

Financial fixed assets

Participating interests in subsidiary undertakings are valued at net asset value in the accounts of the parent company according to the equity method.

Participating interests in associated undertakings are valued in the accounts of the parent company and the consolidated accounts according to the equity method. (**Danisco**)

Associated companies are companies in which Volvo has long-term holdings equal to at least 20% but not more than 50% of voting rights. Holdings in associated companies are reported in accordance with the equity method. (**Volvo**)

Vessels that are not wholly owned are owned through investments in Norwegian general and limited partnerships. The investments in these companies represent either joint ventures or means of financing, and are included on a pro-rata basis. Investments in associated companies are presented according to the equity method, other investments are included in accordance with the cost method.

Our investments in companies in which we have the ability to exercise significant influence over operating and financial policies are accounted for by the equity method. Our investments in other companies are carried at cost or fair value as appropriate. (**Bergesen**)

6.7 Transactions and translation of foreign activities

When a firm has activities abroad, there will usually be amounts in the accounts stated in foreign currencies. Such items will have to be translated into the firm's national currency, as all accounts have to be measured in this.

The activities in the international market could be the selling and buying of goods or services, stem from loan transactions, or refer to capital investment, for example in a subsidiary abroad.

The problems here usually involve both the profit and loss account and the balance sheet. In the balance sheet, cash, bank accounts, trade debtors, loan debtors and investments are examples of assets. The liabilities in foreign currency could be trade creditors or loan creditors. In the profit and loss account, items that it is necessary to translate can be both operational and financial in nature. We start with an uncomplicated example:

On January 5, a company sells 100 000 units for 1 FC (Foreign Currency) each of a certain merchandise to a company abroad. The company invoices in foreign currency (FC), and the amount is to be paid within two weeks. At the time of the sale the exchange rate is 1 FC = 1.5 DC (Domestic Currency). The bill is paid, on January 20 when the exchange rate is 1 FC = 1.6 DC.

In this case the entry on January 5 will be a sale of 150 000 DC and this will be the amount owed by the trade debtor. On January 20 the payment will be 160 000 DC. Then the entry will show a gain on foreign exchange of 10 000 DC. Since the gain is realized in the same period, there is no accounting problem involved, we just have to register the gain as a profit in the profit and loss account.

However, where the transaction is not completed at the time of drawing up the balance sheet, we will be facing an accounting problem. The solution to this problem is much debated. As a basic rule unrealized gains should not be accounted for, but a loss should be taken into account at the end of the period. This follows from the prudence principle and illustrates once more the lower of cost or market value rule. But there are exceptions to this general rule. First of all, many firms, for practical reasons, will use the exchange rate at the balance sheet date for current assets and current liabilities. Second, the risk of exchange rate changes can be taken care of by means of a forward contract, i.e. a fixed rate of exchange, where it seems reasonable to use the rate of exchange agreed upon. Third, the firm may have assets and liabilities in the same foreign currency. This can happen simply because the firm both sells and buys in the same country, but it can also be a strategic decision in order to reduce the risk of exchange losses. In such cases it seems both reasonable and logical to look upon assets and liabilities in the same currency as a total. Here a portfolio principle is used. Such a principle could also be used for more foreign currencies but then as a total plan in order to reduce risk.

For long-term liabilities a special measurement problem arises. Basically, the cost of a loan in foreign currency must consist of an interest component and a component relating to the change in the rate of exchange. For example, if a loan in foreign currency has a very low nominal interest, it must be expected that the rate of exchange in that currency will increase. If we assume perfect financial markets it would be reasonable to say that the cost of the loan should be the same as a corresponding loan in the home country. Therefore, at the end of an accounting period the interest cost should be the nominal interest of the foreign loan, plus or minus the effect of the change in the foreign exchange rate during the year, up to the same cost as if it had been a loan in the home country. If this is not done, a loss will occur in the future, a loss which will become steadily greater over time (the so-called snowball effect). The upper limit here is found by using the interest parity hypothesis.

The problems of translating foreign subsidiaries will be discussed in Chapter 9 concerning consolidated group accounts.

Questions and answers

1 **What does FIFO mean as a cost flow principle?**

   Answer:
   FIFO means first-in, first-out and the assumed cost flow then is that the goods which are bought first are sold first. This means that the stock at the end of a period is assumed to be the last purchased.

2 **Which items of stock will you find in the balance sheet of a manufacturing firm?**

   Answer:
   Raw material, work in progress, finished goods.

3 **How would you apply the prudence principle for stock in a manufacturing firm?**

   Answer:
   Raw material according to the purchase price today or realizable value if damaged, work in progress and finished goods tested against expected sales value, less costs to make good and sell.

4   How is the expense 'Loss on trade debtors' in the profit and loss account calculated?

Answer:
Realized loss during the year, plus or minus the change in expected loss on trade debtors, minus, eventually, amounts paid on previously written-down claims.

5   If a firm uses straight-line depreciation how does it then measure the yearly expense?

Answer:
Straight-line depreciation means an equal amount of depreciation each year. When the acquisition cost, economic life and estimated scrap value are decided, the calculation is just a division.

6   Why can it be necessary to write down a fixed asset?

Answer:
Because the prudence principle says that an asset cannot be overvalued. Therefore, if the situation is that the fixed asset has a lower value than the book value, the book value has to be reduced. The reason for reducing the value is that the loss in value is expected to be permanent.

7   Why is writing up a fixed asset a bad thing to do?

Answer:
Writing up is in conflict with the basic accounting principle, historical cost. All measurements in financial accounting are based on this principle. Write up of an asset is just a partial thing, it is not a systematic alternative. Moreover, when the firm itself decides whether an asset should be written up and with what amount, this causes problems when comparing financial statements.

8   Is it possible to capitalize internally-created goodwill?

Answer:
It is possible but it is not usual to capitalize internally-created goodwill. In practice, only purchased goodwill can be capitalized.

9   What will the valuation of a small investment in another firm be?

Answer:
Basically, the purchase price, but this can be written down if necessary (lower of cost or market value).

10 Why does it seem reasonable to use the equity method in a case of an investment from 20 per cent up to 50 per cent?

Answer:
Because such an investment is normally a long-term investment, often done for strategic reasons. By reporting the percentage of the equity and the profit, the information is much better than in the alternative mentioned under Question 9.

? Problems

1 A firm has the following data for trade debtors and loss on trade debtors: gross debt at December 31 this year, 100; gross debt December 31 last year, 90. Expected loss: 3 at the end of the last year, 5 at the end of this year. Realized loss this year: 2. What is the amount of 'loss on trade debtors' this year?

2 Calculate the cost of goods sold and stock at January 31 according to the FIFO principle:

Stock at January 1:	100 units @ 100
Purchase, January 10:	100 units @ 110
Sales, January 15:	120 units @ 200
Purchase, January 20:	100 units @ 120
Sales, January 31:	110 units @ 210

3 For a manufacturing firm the following data are given: Raw material at January 1: 1000 units at 20; purchased during the year: 5000 units at 21; raw material at December 31: 500 units. Work in progress and finished goods at January 1, 800 000; at December 31, 1 750 000. Other operating costs for the year: 2 400 000. The firm applies the FIFO principle. Which amounts will you find in the profit and loss account?

4 Calculate the yearly depreciation according to the straight-line method and the reducing-balance method, 30 per cent, for this case: purchase price 100, economic life five years, scrap value 20.

5 If the asset mentioned under Question 4 is sold for 30 after five years, what will then be registered in the profit and loss account for the fifth year in each of the two alternatives?

6 Firm A has as an accounting policy to expense R&D currently. The last five years these expenditures have been: 20, 10, 15, 10 and 5 respectively. Firm B has the same R&D expenditures in the same years as A, but it capitalizes these expenditures and depreciates them over five years in equal yearly amounts. What will be the effect on the operating profit for each of the five years for these two firms?

7 Financial accounting and tax accounting

'The tax world is a primitive world.'

Tax expert

LEARNING OBJECTIVES

After studying this chapter, you will:

- have made some reflections about the relationship between financial accounting and tax accounting and alternative solutions;
- understand the idea behind the deferred tax model;
- have seen some typical examples of items which are measured differently within financial accounting and tax accounting.

7.1 An ideal starting point, but ...

As we have said before, accounting tells us about the financial situation of a firm. It should therefore be both logical and rational that the financial accounts could also be the tax accounts. However, in practice, tax rules change according to political goals, and the taxation of firms is an instrument in industrial and fiscal policy. Given this fact, we can conclude that financial accounting built upon tax rules will generally not be as informative as it should be. We find that there are alternative solutions to this conflict when we look at international practice.

7.2 Three alternatives

One obvious solution is to let the tax accounts also be the financial accounts. Such an alternative can be explained in different ways, for example the fact that the dominant user of accounting is the tax authority. This is often the case for small private firms. Another explanation can be that the differences between the tax rules and financial accounting are relatively small, so it does not matter too much. Besides, information can be given in footnotes, so that more correct financial accounting data can be calculated. Still another explanation can be found in the level of financial accounting in a particular country. With no strong profession as a driving force in the development of financial accounting, tax accounting will in fact steer the practice in financial reporting. Germany and many of the south European countries have historically had a close link between tax accounting and financial accounting and are illustrations of this alternative.

Another alternative is to combine financial accounting and tax accounting in the same information system. This idea was originally developed in Sweden and is still used in some Scandinavian countries. In Scandinavian terminology this model can be translated into the 'tax link model'.

The link between financial accounting and tax accounting in this model is technically made in the profit and loss account by a special section at the end of this statement, where the differences between specific items are taken care of. Let us illustrate this with the following example:

In the financial accounts machinery is depreciated on a straight-line basis at 10 per cent. According to the tax rules, 30 per cent reducing balance is accepted. If we take an investment in machinery of 100 this means the following yearly depreciation:

	Year						
	1	2	3	4	5	...	10
Financial accounting depreciation	10	10	10	10	10		10
Tax accounting depreciation	30	21	15	10	7		1
Yearly difference	20	11	5	0	−3		−9

In the model described above, this means the following reporting in the profit and loss account:

	Year						
	1	2	3	4	5	...	10
Depreciation	10	10	10	10	10		
Profit before year-end adjustments	100	100	100	100	100		
Year-end adjustments and taxes:							
Additional depreciation	20	11	5	–	−3		
Taxes (30%)	24	27	29	30	31		
Net profit	56	62	66	70	72		

We see from this example that it is possible to give the profit for the year both according to the principle of financial accounting and according to the tax rules. This is done by the year-end adjustment which takes care of the concrete differences between the two accounts.

In the balance sheet these differences, now on an accumulated basis, are taken care of by a separate item, called 'untaxed equity' or something similar. In this example it is constructed as follows:

	Year						
	1	2	3	4	5	...	10
Equity							
Untaxed equity							
Additional depreciation	20	31	36	36	33		
Liabilities							

We see that in this model the separate item in the balance sheet gives full insight into the accumulated 'reserves' due to the differences between the financial and tax accounts. We also see from the example that the item 'untaxed equity' is placed between equity and liabilities. This seems reasonable, since part of it is a tax liability, part of it equity.

As we mentioned, the Scandinavian countries have been the proponents of this model. But Denmark and Norway have now rejected it, Denmark mainly because of EU membership, Norway mainly because of the consequences of international developments in financial reporting, which brings us to the next alternative.

7.3 The deferred tax model

The third alternative, the deferred tax model, is used in leading countries operating financial reporting, such as the US, the UK, Canada and Australia. We will therefore concentrate on this model.

In this model financial accounting and tax accounting are separate: financial reporting has developed according to sound or generally accepted accounting principles, while the tax rules are often quite different. In this model the consequences of the different objectives are taken into consideration, although a connection still exists, for example the fact that not every field of transaction has clear rules, and in some cases it will be practical to use the tax rules in order to avoid differences on all points. But, more fundamentally, since differences exist between tax accounting and financial accounting, this fact will influence the financial accounts.

As illustrated by the depreciation example, positive differences at the beginning of the investment period will be concealed by negative differences later on. This effect, the timing difference effect, should be taken care of when measuring taxes in financial accounting. That is exactly what is done in the deferred tax model. Let us return to our depreciation example again:

In year 1 depreciation according to the tax rules was 30, but 10 according to the generally accepted method for financial reporting. If we use 30 per cent as the tax rate, an amount of 6 (30 per cent of 20) will be postponed, or deferred to a later period. This deferred payment is taken into consideration when taxes for the year are calculated. In our case that means a tax expense in the first year of 30 (30 per cent of 100), even if some of this expense is going to be paid in later years.

The view developed above fully corresponds with the matching principle which, as we have underlined, is a basic principle within financial accounting. It is just as logical to follow this principle in the case of taxes as for other expenses measured in the profit and loss account. In fact it must be questioned why in many countries the tax expense is treated differently from other expenses. There seem to be several myths here, but it is hard to find real arguments for different treatment of this expense. This is the main reason why leading countries in the field of financial reporting use the deferred tax model. Let us once more go back to our depreciation example and demonstrate what the reporting in this model will look like:

In the profit and loss account taxes will be reported as follows (30 per cent tax rate):

	Year						
	1	2	3	4	5	...	10
Profit before taxes	100	100	100	100	100		100
Taxes	30	30	30	30	30		30
Net profit	70	70	70	70	70		70

In this example, the figures in the profit and loss account show the same tax amount for every year. This seems logical, since the profit was the same every year and the tax rate was also the same. It is a demonstration of the logic behind the matching principle.

Let us now consider the balance sheet. Again we return to our example, and we take the assumption that tax on the profit of one year is payable the next year. We will then have the following reporting of taxes:

	Year						
	1	2	3	4	5	...	10
Equity							
Long-term liabilities							
Deferred taxes	6	9	10	10	9		
Short-term liabilities							
Tax payable	24	27	29	30	31		

We see that tax payable is grouped under short-term liabilities, while deferred taxes are a long-term liability. This is according to the general rules of classifying the balance sheet items.

We see how deferred taxes represent the accumulated amount postponed at any time. Since tax depreciation in years one, two and three is higher than the accounting figures, this means increasing deferred taxes up to year three. In year four the two depreciation accounts are equal, and thus deferred taxes are the same. From year five on, the depreciation for tax purposes is less than in the accounts, and the deferred taxes are reduced. At the end of the period the deferred taxes will be zero.

In the example we have demonstrated the measurement problem of taxes as a *temporary timing difference* since the difference will disappear in the long run. There also exist *permanent* differences between tax accounting and financial accounting, due to the fact that some expenses (or revenues) will not be accepted by the tax authorities. Such differences will, of course, never appear as deferred tax in the balance sheet. They have to be taken care of as a tax expense of the year in the profit and loss account and are included in the tax payable amount in the balance sheet.

We have concentrated the explanation of deferred taxes on an example linked to depreciation. This is a representative example, and perhaps the best example to use as an illustration. But we must stress that differences between financial accounting and tax accounting can also be found in many other areas, for example concerning stock, debtors, R&D, goodwill etc. Where such differences exist, the explanation, as we have mentioned, is due to (industrial) political reasons. It can also be explained from a practical tax authority point of view, namely the need for exact rules, which are easy to follow and indisputable.

Before leaving this section, we have to mention a few important issues in the field of deferred taxes.

The first issue follows from the fact that timing differences could be both positive (higher amount of tax deduction than reported in the financial accounts) and negative. A special case exists when the loss for a year can be carried forward and thus reduces taxable income in later years. This economic benefit represents an asset and can either be set against deferred tax items or be shown as an asset in the balance sheet. Internationally, the rules in these cases vary. In some countries there are restrictions on which items of deferred taxes can be netted against tax claims (assets), in other countries a ceiling is set on the amount that can be shown as an asset (not higher than the sum of deferred taxes).

A second question is the economic reality of the deferred tax amount as a liability. If the tax will arise a long time in the future, the net present value is low. Is it then informative to account for deferred taxes with the full amount? In order to put this issue in perspective, the view of using net present value in financial accounting must be questioned. Until now the standard answer seems to be that since net present value is generally not used in financial accounting, it should not be used in connection with deferred taxes either.

EXAMPLES

Tangible assets
Differences between the values required under commercial law and those permitted under tax law are shown under the special items with an equity portion. **(Volkswagen)**

Allocation and untaxed reserves
The individual group companies (including AB Volvo) report untaxed reserves as a separate balance sheet item. In the statement of income, allocations to and withdrawals from untaxed reserves are reported under the heading allocations to untaxed reserves. The reported tax expense is based on income after allocations.

In the consolidated balance sheet untaxed reserves are divided into deferred tax liability in untaxed reserves, which is reported as a long-term liability, and equity in untaxed reserves, which is included in shareholders' equity. **(Volvo)**

Deferred taxation
Deferred taxation is accounted for at anticipated tax rates on differences arising from the inclusion of items of income and expenditure in taxation computations in periods different from those in which they are included in the financial statements. A deferred tax asset or provision is established to the extent that it is likely that an asset or liability will crystallize in the foreseeable future. **(Marks & Spencer)**

Tax
The expected tax on the taxable income for the year, adjusted for the change in deferred tax for the year, is charged to the profit and loss account. **(Danisco)**

Tax in the income statement comprises both tax which is payable for the period and the change in deferred taxes.

Deferred tax is entered as long-term debt in the balance sheet. Deferred tax has been calculated on the net positive temporary differences between the book value and tax values in the balance sheet after balancing the negative temporary differences and the loss carried forward in accordance with the liability method. **(Bergesen)**

From the balance sheet:	This year	Last year
Liabilities and share-owners' equity		
Current		
Accrued taxes		
Total current liabilities		
Long-term debts		
Deferred income taxes		
Share-owners' equity		
		(Coca-Cola)

7.4 An illustration

We can illustrate the three alternatives for measuring and reporting taxes in Figures 7.1, 7.2 and 7.3.

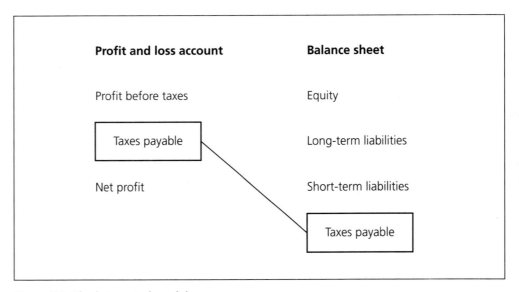

Figure 7.1 The integrated model

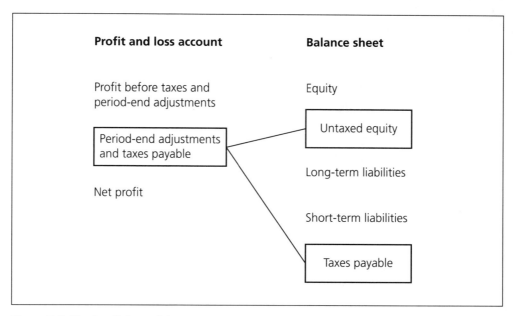

Figure 7.2 The tax link model

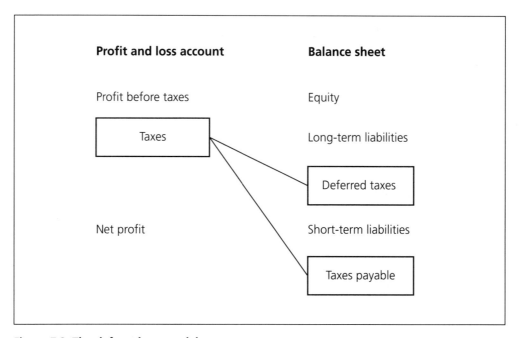

Figure 7.3 The deferred tax model

A NUMERICAL ILLUSTRATION
The most illustrative example of the differences between the three alternatives depicted in Figs 7.1, 7.2 and 7.3 is depreciation. Let us assume the following:

Accounting depreciation (straight-line)	10
Tax depreciation (reducing balance)	30
Profit before depreciation and tax	100

Alternative 1: The integrated model

Profit before depreciation and taxes	100
Depreciation	30
Net profit before tax	70
Taxes (30%)	21
Net profit	49

Alternative 2: The tax link model

Profit before depreciation, year-end adjustment and taxes	100
Depreciation	10
Year-end adjustment	
Additional depreciation	20
Taxes	21
Net profit	49

Alternative 3: The deferred tax model

Profit before taxes	90
Taxes (30%)	27
Net profit	63

Comments
We see that the reported net profit in Alternatives 1 and 2 is the same but the split of depreciation (accounting depreciation and extra for tax purposes) makes Alternative 2 better than 1. Alternative 3 sticks to accounting depreciation only, and the tax expense is measured accordingly.

✓ Questions and answers

1 **Why is it impossible to let the tax accounts be identical to the financial accounts?**

Answer:
Because the tax rules are an (industrial) political issue, so that the rules vary according to political goals. For practical reasons the tax authorities also prefer to have exact, defined rules. And the government/tax authorities may also fear that business firms will try to postpone the tax payable.

2 What will the tax expenses be in 'the integrated model', 'the tax link model' and 'the deferred tax model', respectively?

Answer:

Tax payable on the year's profit, tax payable on the year's profit, taxes based on the accounting profit for the year.

3 How can you read from the balance sheet which of the three models has been used?

Answer:

In 'the integrated model' just one item is found, namely, 'tax payable' as an item among short-term liabilities. In 'the tax link model' the item above is found, but also a special group named 'untaxed equity'. In 'the deferred tax model' there will be two tax items: the first as in the two other models, 'tax payable', the second is 'deferred taxes'.

4 Give examples of permanent and non-permanent timing differences.

Answer:

Permanent: business representation (in some countries) and goodwill (in some countries) are expenses not deductible for tax purposes; special grants etc. and tax-exempt investment income are examples of income not taxed.

Non-permanent: depreciation, stock, R&D, goodwill.

5 What are the most common methods used in financial accounting and for tax depreciation purposes, respectively?

Answer:

Straight-line method for financial accounting, declining-balance method for tax depreciation.

6 What will be the main argument for not discounting the deferred tax amount?

Answer:

Because, generally, this is not done in financial reporting.

? Problems

1 A depreciable asset is purchased for 100. In the financial accounts 20 per cent straight-line depreciation is used, and for tax purposes 40 per cent declining-balance method. What will be the deferred taxes (balance sheet figure) at the end of year two and year three respectively? Assume a 30 per cent tax rate.

2 A firm writes up a fixed asset this year with 100. Which accounts in the balance sheet will that affect? (30 per cent taxes.)

8 How to read – and understand – financial statements and auditors' reports

LEARNING OBJECTIVES

- In the first five chapters we laid the framework for financial accounts. We then discussed the main measurement problems in financial accounting. This was a partial discussion, as each problem was discussed separately. After having studied the relationship between financial accounting and tax accounting, it is time for a concrete illustration. This is the learning objective in this chapter. It will also serve as a summing up so far.

- One very important dimension of this chapter is to give financial statements an international perspective. This is done both in the comments to the statements and by examples from the six international companies we have referred to earlier: Marks & Spencer, Volkswagen, Danisco, Volvo, Bergesen and Coca-Cola.

- We will define the auditor's function and the auditor's report, with examples of different types of reports, in Section 8.4.

- The three basic financial statements will be commented on with reference to specific items in the statements. Here, principles and the most common way of measurement, in an international perspective, will be given with the following references:

  1 the profit and loss account/income statement (from A–Q in Section 8.1);

  2 the balance sheet (from 1–13 in Section 8.2);

  3 the cash flow statement (from i–v in Section 8.3).

8.1 The profit and loss account

		(000 000s)	
		This year	Last year
A	Net turnover	300	250
B	Raw material	100	95
C	Wages	90	85
D	Other operating expenses	46	43
E	Depreciation	21	15
F	Loss on trade debtors	3	2
G	Changes in work in progress and finished goods	10	(5)
	Operating expenses	270	235
H	Operating profit	**30**	**20**
	Dividend income	2	3
	Interest income	3	4
	Interest expenses	10	11
I	Financial expenses, net	5	4
J	Profit before extraordinary items	25	16
K	Gain on sales of land	–	2
L	Net profit before taxes	25	18
M	Taxes	7	5
N	Net profit	18	13
O	Proposed appropriation of profit for the year		
P	Dividend	9	6
Q	Retained earnings	9	7

A glance at the text of the different items assures us that this is a manufacturing company.

A Turnover is the word this company has used. Other companies could use sales or operating revenue. For the six international companies we have referred to before, we get the following picture:

Turnover:	Marks & Spencer
Sales:	Volkswagen, Danisco, Volvo
Operating revenue:	Bergesen, Coca-Cola

Net turnover, or net sales, or net operating revenue(s) means that value-added tax, production duties etc. have been deducted. It is also logical that rebates (quantity and cash rebates) have been deducted.

Since net turnover is normally used as the only revenue (gross) item, revenues from other operating activities will also be included here, for example revenues from leasing premises in addition to the production activities. If the activities are of many different kinds it is normal to specify the revenues from the different activities, or give such specification in the notes on the accounts.

In the notes on the accounts, Coca-Cola gives the following information:

Lines of business

	United States	International	Soft drinks Foods	Corporate	Consolidated
19XX					
Net operating revenues					
Operating income					
Identifiable operating assets					
Equity income					
Investments (principally bottling companies)					
Depreciation and amortization					

Operations in geographic areas

	United States	Africa	European Community	Latin America	Northeast Europe/ Middle East	Pacific & Canada	Corporate	Consolidated
19XX								
Net operating revenues								
Operating income								
Identifiable operating assets								
Equity income								
Investments (principally bottling companies)								
Capital expenditure								
Depreciation and amortization								

B This is the cost of raw material used for production. Since the matching principle is a basic principle, the figure here must be the cost of raw material for goods sold. The calculation of the figure must have been: opening stock plus purchases during the year, minus closing stock. As far as the assumption on the cost flow is concerned, companies in most countries will use the FIFO principle.

C This figure includes all types of wages and salaries, independent of functions (production, administration, distribution and sales). Included in the figure also are all social security, pensions etc.

D All operating expenses not specified above (or below) are included here. Among others, research and development costs, marketing and distribution expenses are included.

E In accounting, this is this year's depreciation in the investment in depreciable fixed assets. Behind this calculation lies a depreciation policy as far as method is concerned. Internationally, the straight-line method dominates, as we have discussed and seen.

All kinds of depreciation are included in this item, including depreciation on goodwill. Also included here are necessary write downs on fixed assets. As we have discussed, such write downs are necessary when a fall in market values is expected to be permanent.

F This expense includes the loss on trade debtors recorded during the year plus or minus the change in estimated loss on trade debtors at the end of the financial year compared with last year. The last part is necessary both because of the prudence principle and also to take into consideration all events influencing this year's activity.

In our example the text indicates that the loss is on trade debtors. Also loss on other debtors will be included here. Loss on financial investment, however, is not included in this item, but in the finance part of the profit and loss account.

G In a manufacturing company changes in work in progress and finished goods will be the normal situation. In order to obtain a correct figure to match the turnover, these changes must come as a plus or minus to the operating cost: as a plus if the stock of those goods has decreased, as this year, as a minus if the stock has increased, as last year.

Many companies do not report this item separately. Of course, this change is taken care of, but it is not specified as a separate item. The correction has, in such cases, been made on the actual expense items (raw material, wages etc., depending on the valuation policy of stock).

In some countries (and in the EU Fourth Directive model, as we will see later on), this change is reported in the revenue section as a correction to revenues. This also takes care of the necessary correction, but in this case we would have an inconsistency as far as the basis for valuation is concerned (sales amount/cost amount).

As we have discussed earlier, most companies internationally will include part of fixed costs when valuing stocks.

H This is the first time we find the word profit in the account. This profit is not influenced by the way a company is financed, since it is before the financial effect. This fact gives an excellent opportunity to contrast companies without taking the financing of the companies into consideration. It is possible to see how the management has taken care of the resources (the assets).

A central question to arise is what 'operating' means. Of course, this classification question must be raised when operating revenues and operating expenses are defined. It depends on the type of activities. With a production company, for example, interest income and interest expense normally will not be operating, but with a bank it is. The final definition must be made by the company itself.

In the six companies we are referring to, the situation is as follows:

Operating profit shown: Marks & Spencer, Danisco, Volvo, Bergesen, Coca-Cola

Operating profit not shown: Volkswagen

I This is a net figure: income from bank accounts, dividends etc., and financial expenses. Usually this figure will be negative, because of the financing structure of a company.

J This item is important for key figures and analytical purposes. It is the profit of ordinary character that counts as far as comparisons are concerned.

K In our example gain on sales of land is reported as an extraordinary item. As we have discussed before, events or transactions must be of unusual nature and infrequent in occurrence in order to be classified as extraordinary. This very restricted view on what should be classified as extraordinary is international. Examples mentioned are uninsured losses from floods, earthquakes, expropriations etc.

The sale of land must, in the company's view, be both so unusual and so infrequent that extraordinary is the right name for it.

This international tendency, not to show any – or at least very few – items as extraordinary raises a very central question: where have the items earlier classified as extraordinary gone? Practice differs here: they can be found among other income or other expenses. In such cases specification in the notes is necessary in order to make a deeper analysis.

L Profit before taxes can be of interest for different types of comparisons, where tax rates differ or between countries.

M The context of this item will differ between countries. In the integrated model, just the amount to be paid on the taxable income for the year is reported. In the tax link model, the amount will be the same as in the first model. In the deferred tax model, however, tax expense is measured on permanent differences, this means financial net income × tax %. Part of this expense is tax payable, with the rest of it being a charge in deferred taxes. In the six international companies the models in use are as follows:

Integrated model:	Volkswagen (for the parent company)
Tax link model:	Volvo (for the parent company)
Deferred tax model:	Marks & Spencer, Volkswagen (group), Danisco, Volvo (group), Bergesen, Coca-Cola

N Net profit is the bottom-line figure and is the figure most referred to in the press.

From the discussion above we can conclude that this figure may differ between countries even if we assume exactly the same events and transactions, according to the law, standards and practice in different countries. International comparative financial accounting research confirms this fact. We will return to this point at the end of this chapter.

O In this case the proposed appropriation of the profit is given in the profit and loss account. The decision lies with the General Meeting of Shareholders, and in many countries the proposed appropriation from the Board is built into the accounts. If not, the profit for the year will be found as a balance sheet item at the end of the financial year.

This is the picture as far as proposed appropriation is given in the profit and loss account of our international companies:

Proposed appropriation given:	Marks & Spencer, Danisco, Bergesen
Proposed appropriation not given:	Volkswagen, Volvo, Coca-Cola

P Dividend to shareholders is a result of the profit for the year and the dividend policy of the company. In our example the dividend proposed at the end of the year, which will be declared and paid in the following year, is recorded as a debt. In other countries, for example the US, equity is reduced when dividends are declared and paid.

Q This is the part of the net profit for the year kept in the company for ensuring the continuance of the company and for expansion.

8.2 The balance sheet

ASSETS	This year	Last year
Fixed assets		
Intangible assets		
1 Research and development costs	1	2
Tangible assets		
2 Land	15	15
3 Buildings	19	20
4 Machinery and equipment	100	50
Financial assets		
Loans	5	8
	140	95
Current assets		
5 Raw material	10	8
Work in progress	20	15
Finished goods	10	25
6 Trade debtors	30	45
Other short-term debtors	10	3
Bonds and shares	20	15
Cash at bank and in hand	10	19
	110	130
Total assets	250	225
OWNERS' CAPITAL AND LIABILITIES		
Capital		
7 Share capital	50	40
Share premium	2	–
8 Retained earnings	27	18
9 Revaluation reserve (land)	3	3
	82	61
Long-term liabilities		
Mortgage loan	83	101
10 Deferred taxes	10	8
	93	109
Short-term liabilities		
11 Dividend	9	6
12 Tax payable	5	4
Other creditors	10	8
13 Bank overdraft (limit 40)	31	13
Trade creditors	20	24
	75	55
Total capital and liabilities	250	225

The *order* of the balance sheet is of interest. In our example the company starts the asset side with fixed assets and ends with current assets. The order on the owners' capital and liabilities side is owners' capital first, then long-term liabilities, and the last group is short-term liabilities. This ordering is also logical between the two sides.

In Europe the order is as reported in our example, since that is the order prescribed in the EU Fourth Directive. We will return to this directive later on in Chapter 11. Internationally, the US and other US-oriented countries report in the opposite order – asset side starting with current assets and ending with fixed assets. This is also the case for many international companies in Europe, especially those listed on the New York Stock Exchange.

In our six international companies the order of the balance sheet is as follows:

Starting with fixed assets: Marks & Spencer, Volkswagen, Danisco
Starting with current assets: Volvo, Bergesen, Coca-Cola

We see that in our case the *groups* are as follows:

Assets
- Fixed assets
  - intangibles
  - tangibles
  - financial
- Current assets

Owners' capital and liabilities
- owners' capital
- long-term liabilities
- short-term liabilities

This grouping is very well suited for analysing the financial statements.

1 This is the only intangible asset in this company. As we have discussed, and also seen examples of, R&D expenditures are either expensed currently, or capitalized and depreciated. Most of the countries accept both, but the most common practice is to expense currently.

From the figures we see that R&D has been reduced by 1 this year. That expense must be included in 'other operating expenses' in the profit and loss account. The accounting policy for this company is obviously to capitalize R&D and depreciate.

2 From the profit and loss account we see that land was sold last year. That gain was measured by comparing the sales amount with the book value.

If we look closer at the items under 'owners' capital', we see that land has been revalued. The amount here must be linked to land still in hand. This means that land reported in the balance sheet has been revalued. In the deferred tax model, this means that 'revaluation reserve' must be after tax. 'Deferred taxes', therefore, also includes the tax part of the revaluation.

3 Buildings must stand for the original purchase price reduced by depreciation over time. From the balance sheet we see that buildings have been reduced by 1. This is the depreciation for the year.

4 Machinery and equipment must also be valued at purchase prices less accumulated depreciation. Since this item is the last one to be depreciated, we see from the profit and loss account that the depreciation of the machinery and equipment this year must have been 20. This means that new machinery and equipment to an amount of 70 must have been purchased this year.

5 These three items are typical for a production company. We see that all of them have changed during the year, two in one direction and the third in the other.

We have discussed why these changes must be taken care of in the profit and loss account earlier. What we should concentrate on now is where these changes can be found, both directly and indirectly in the profit and loss account.

The change in raw material must have been reduced in the item 'raw material', while the changes in the other two are reported separately in one amount. The net change of 10 is easy to find and we also see that this is a net decrease. That is why this net amount has been added to the operating expenses.

6 Trade debtors are reported net. Estimated loss on trade debtors, therefore, is reduced. From the profit and loss account we read that the loss during the year plus or minus the change in expected loss on trade debtors was 3.

7 These items consist of the nominal share capital and payment above the nominal value. We see from the figures that the over par value has been 20 per cent.

8 Here the accumulated amount of that part of the net profit kept in the company over time is shown. The increase of 9 is the retained earnings this year.

9 As we have mentioned before, land still in hand must have been revalued, not this year or last year, but earlier. Such a revaluation is possible in most countries, but forbidden in others, for example in the US.

In the six companies we refer to, the situation is as follows:

| Revaluation: | Marks & Spencer, Danisco |
| No revaluation: | Volkswagen, Volvo, Bergesen, Coca-Cola |

10 Here we find the accumulated difference on assets valued according to the financial accounting rules and the tax valuation. We see that the amount has increased by 2 this year. Tax expenses in the profit and loss account of 7 consist therefore of an increase of 2 in deferred taxes and an amount of tax payable next year of 5. This is confirmed under 'short-term liabilities'.

11 This is the amount to be paid to shareholders after the formal decision has been made by the Annual General Meeting.

12 This is the tax payable next year.

13 The company has classified 'bank overdraft' as a short-term liability. This seems logical, since such a loan is linked to operating activities. The limit is disclosed.

8.3 The cash flow statement

	Operating activities	This year
	Net profit before taxes	25
	Depreciation and other non-cash items	22
	Net change in operating assets and liabilities	14
	Tax paid	4
i	Net cash inflow from operating activities	57
	Investing activities	
	Purchase of machinery and equipment	70
	Reduction in financial assets (loans)	3
ii	Net cash outflow from investing activities	67
	Financing activities	
	New share capital	12
	Reduction in long-term borrowing	18
	Dividend paid	6
iii	Net cash outflow from financing	12
iv	Decrease in cash and cash equivalents	22*

		This year	Last year
* Cash at bank and in hand		10	19
Bonds and shares		20	15
Bank overdraft		31	13
v Net change		22	

The division of the cash flow statement into cash inflows/outflows from operating, investing and financing activities gives an excellent overview of the cash development this year. We will not go into the techniques here, but will concentrate on the analytical aspect of the statement.

i In this case the cash flow from operating activities is constructed according to the indirect or the net method.

The starting point gives an excellent reference to the relevant item in the profit and loss account. The next item underlines the difference between costs and cash, while the final two items illustrate that the change in relevant balance items has to be taken into consideration when we want to show the cash flows.

The definition of operating differs both between countries and between companies. We have included interest income, dividend income and interest expenses. These items could also be looked upon as financial items.

ii In our case this cash outflow is easy to identify. Generally, this section will also include proceeds from disposals of investments and disposal of property, plant and equipment.

iii In this section all items connected with financing activities are included, together with dividend paid. As we have mentioned above, there are good arguments for also including dividend income, interest income and interest expenses in this section.

iv The cash flow effect of the three activities gives the net cash flow change during the year. In our example we have two net cash outflows and the cash inflow from operating activities is not sufficient to compensate for those two outflows. The net cash flow, therefore, is a decrease.

v The analysis of the changes in cash also indirectly gives the definition of cash. We have included bonds and shares as equivalent to cash. We also include the change in the bank overdraft. The alternative would have been to look at this as part of the financing activities, but in a way we then 'hide' the cash decrease.

Internationally, the US has been the country most engaged in the cash flow statement. Statement of Financial Accounting Standards (SFAS) 95, the statement of cash flows from 1987, has been a model for many countries. This standard requires gross rather than net reporting of significant investing and financing activities, thereby providing improved disclosure. For example, the acquisition of property must be shown separately from sales of property.

SFAS 95 defines *investing cash flows* as those resulting from:

- acquisition or sale of property, plant and equipment;
- acquisition or sale of a subsidiary or segment;
- purchase or sale of investments in other firms.

Financing cash flows are those resulting from:

- insurance or retirement of debt and equity securities;
- dividends paid to stockholders.

Cash from operations includes the cost effects of all transactions that do not meet the definition of investing or financing. They are the cash flow consequences of the revenue-producing activities of the firm. They may be reported either directly, using major categories of gross receipts and payments, or indirectly by providing a reconciliation of net income to net cash flow from operating activities. Internationally, and also in the US, the indirect method dominates.

All our six international companies publish a cash flow statement under somewhat different headings:

Cash flow statement, statement of cash flows:	Marks & Spencer, Bergesen, Coca-Cola
Statement of source and application of funds:	Danisco
Statement of changes in financial position:	Volvo
Development of short-term liquidity:	Volkswagen

All, except Volkswagen, make the division between cash from operating, investing and financing. Coca-Cola makes an interesting step combining net cash flows from operations and net cash used for investing activities leading to 'net cash provided by operations after reinvestment'. Just one of the six, Marks & Spencer, uses the direct method when presenting cash flows from operating activities.

8.4 The auditor's report

Audited financial statements are always accompanied by the auditor's report. This is from an independent auditor responsible for seeing that the financial statements issued conform with laws and generally accepted accounting principles. The auditor will also check the accounting systems and the internal control of a company and generally try to confirm that there are no material errors in the financial statements. The auditor is supposed to serve the stockholders and other users of the financial statements and he or she reports to the Annual General Meeting.

We must stress that the responsibility for preparing the financial statements lies with the directors of the company. A good example of this fact is found in the annual report of Marks & Spencer:

Directors' responsibilities for preparing the financial statements

The directors are obliged under company law to prepare financial statements for each financial year and to present them annually to the Company's members in the Annual General Meeting.

The financial statements, of which the form and content is prescribed by the Companies Act 1985, must give a true and fair view of the state of affairs of the Company and the Group at the end of the financial year, and of the profit for that period, and they must comply with applicable accounting standards.

The directors are also responsible for the adoption of suitable accounting policies, their consistent use in the financial statements, supported where necessary by reasonable and prudent judgements.

The directors confirm that the above requirements have been complied with in the financial statements.

In addition, the directors are responsible for maintaining adequate accounting records and sufficient internal controls to safeguard the assets of the Group and to prevent and detect fraud or any other irregularities.

An excellent explanation of what auditing is about can be found in an annual report of Danisco:

The accounts paint a picture of the company

They are the result of the transactions and activities undertaken by Danisco's 11 000 employees during a financial year, and they should show the assets, liabilities and financial position of the company on the last day of the financial year.

The picture is painted by using figures and words which, to ensure comparability with other companies and circumstances, conform with the idiom laid down in the Danish Annual Accounts Act, Danish accounting standards and international accounting practice. The main requirement is that the picture gives a true and fair view of the position of the company.

It is the duty of Danisco's executive board to ensure that the bookkeeping carried out by the company and its subsidiaries provides a basis for giving this view, and that the company has at its disposal the necessary resources and systems for providing the information needed to ensure the profitable operation of Danisco and its subsidiaries.

The executive board is also responsible for ensuring that the company's capital is administered safely.

The board of directors is obliged to supervise that the company's bookkeeping and accounting as well as the executive board's administration of the capital is monitored satisfactorily. The board of directors also has the overall responsibility for the management and operation of the company.

The board of directors and the executive board must make sure that accounts are prepared every year giving a true and fair view of Danisco's financial position and results, and that the specific accounting provisions contained in the law and articles of association are observed in the accounts.

The auditors elected by the General Meeting are called external auditors. Their task is to ensure vis-à-vis the shareholders and other users of financial statements, who as opposed to the executive board and the board of directors do not have direct access to the company's own information, that the accounts prepared by the board of directors and the executive board, do give a true and fair view of the company and of the results of the many activities, and that important risks are shown.

The auditors are not to assess whether the company has transacted its business prudently. However, they must make sure that the shareholders, the financial environment, suppliers, customers, employees and the public in general are given an insight into the activities which enables *them* to assess the way in which the company has conducted its business.

The audit

Danisco's external auditors have to be independent of the company they are auditing in order to make the execution of their duties credible. Therefore, they cannot be employees of the company. They are appointed by the General Meeting to which they report.

Danisco's internal auditing, however, is one of the group's internal control systems, and its purpose is to ensure that the internal management information is valid. The external audit is to an extent based on some of the work carried out by the internal auditors.

The audit of complex accounts such as Danisco's, which also comprise consolidated accounts, including Danisco's many subsidiaries, is a continuous process beginning immediately after the preceding annual accounts have been approved by the Annual General Meeting.

The audit builds on the experience reaped in the previous year, and is planned so that it focuses on the areas where the risk of faults in the accounts is highest. In Danisco's case this might be the valuation of stocks, special risks within financing or activities in new markets.

The audit does not comprise a systematic investigation of all vouchers, but random sampling ensures that the records made by the company can be used in the audit. In a company like Danisco the extensive use of information technology makes it natural to use special resources in this area.

The audit is carried out in such a way that important mistakes and flaws which would give a different overall picture of the accounts are discovered and corrected. In practice, actual criteria of significance are laid down for various parts of the Danisco group.

The audit should convince the auditors that the accounts give a true and fair view, which means that the audit is not planned with a view to revealing malpractice. Mistakes in the accounts due to fraud or irregularities are therefore not necessarily discovered during the audit, partly because such mistakes are often concealed or covered up. But naturally, we are aware of the fact that such abuse may take place. If we detect abuse, we notify the management of the company and special measures are taken with a view to clarification and the prevention of repetition.

The audits of Danish and foreign subsidiaries are carried out by the parent company's external auditors and their international connections according to uniform auditing methods and also we visit the foreign subsidiaries occasionally.

On the completion of the annual accounts some items by nature are not as yet recorded in the company's book of accounts. To ensure that also these items are dealt with correctly in the annual accounts, we obtain statements from the management on these particularly difficult audit areas. Such items might be contingent liabilities, legal actions, or other items to which special risk or uncertainty is attached.

If during our examination of the accounting material we discover flaws in the accounting systems and control functions, we inform the board of directors in a so-called audit report. The report also contains information which we feel the board should know about before taking a position on the prepared accounts. The executive board and heads of business units are notified of less important inexpediencies in procedures and of proposals for their remedy.

Our audit also includes making sure that the duties imposed by the law on the board of directors with regard to keeping books of accounts, records, minutes etc are discharged.

Once the audit has been completed we ask ourselves whether the picture presented by the accounts of the company as a whole gives a true and fair view of its results and state of affairs, i.e. whether the accounts contain the information necessary for a reader of accounts to assess the profit or loss, balance sheets and financial position of the company. Furthermore, we ascertain whether the information provided in the annual report and the notes etc satisfy the requirements of the law. If this is the case and the accounts are deemed to give a true and fair view, we issue an 'unqualified' auditors' report on the annual accounts. However, should there be items which are not in order, we mention them in our report and, if necessary, provide supplementary information.

The annual accounts and consolidated accounts of Danisco A/S for the financial year 1993/94 are provided with an unqualified auditors' report which is reproduced on page 36. The auditors' report implies that:

- the accounts have been audited and submitted in accordance with the requirements of the law and Danisco's articles of association;

- the accounts are set out correctly on the basis of the company's books and computed with due consideration to existing values, rights and obligations;

- the annual report contains the information required, including information about the financial development of the company and the group, and that the annual report is in accordance with the annual accounts;

- the accounts give a true and fair view of the company's and the group's assets and liabilities, financial positions and profit and loss; and

- the audit has not given rise to any qualification on the part of the auditors.

The auditors' report on Danisco's annual accounts for 1993/94 is the result of the efforts of about 125 auditors in many different countries to ensure that the Danisco auditors appointed by Danisco's General Meeting are able to say to Danisco's shareholders: We have done the job for which you appointed us, and audit-wise you may safely approve the accounts.

The external auditors spent about 15 000 hours in all on the audit of the Danisco group's accounts for 1993/94.

On auditing Danisco's annual accounts
by Søren Bjerre-Nielsen, State-Authorized Public Accountant, Schøbel & Marholt

Usually, the auditor's report is unqualified or 'clean', as in the following examples.

EXAMPLES

REPORT OF THE AUDITORS

We have audited the annual accounts and the consolidated accounts 1993/94 for Danisco.

The audit has been performed in accordance with the generally acknowledged auditing principles and has included such auditing procedures as we have deemed necessary.

The accounts for the parent company and the consolidated accounts have been properly prepared in accordance with the requirements of the law and the company's Articles of Association for the submission of accounts. In our opinion the accounts give a true and fair view of the company's assets and liabilities, financial position and profit for the year.

Copenhagen, 30 June 1994

Schøbel & Marholt Revisionsaktieselskab	Ernst & Young A/S
Søren Bjerre-Nielsen	*John Lundin*
HP Møller Christiansen	*Ole Neerup*
State-Authorized Public Accountants	State-Authorized Public Accountants

REPORT OF THE AUDITORS

To the Members of Marks & Spencer plc.

We have audited the financial statements on pages 30 to 52.

Respective responsibilities of directors and auditors
As described above the Company's directors are responsible for the preparation of financial statements. It is our responsibility to form an independent opinion, based on our audit, on those statements and to report our opinion to you.

Basis of opinion
We conducted our audit in accordance with Auditing Standards issued by the Auditing Practices Board. An audit includes examination, on a test basis, of evidence relevant to the amounts and disclosures in the financial statements. It also includes an assessment of the significant estimates and judgements made by the directors in the preparation of the financial statements, and of whether the accounting policies are appropriate to the Company's circumstances, consistently applied and adequately disclosed.

We planned and performed our audit so as to obtain all the information and explanations which we considered necessary in order to provide us with sufficient evidence to give reasonable assurance that the financial statements are free from material misstatement, whether caused by fraud or other irregularity or error. In forming our opinion we also evaluated the overall adequacy of the presentation of information in the financial statements.

Opinion
In our opinion the financial statements give a true and fair view of the state of affairs of the Company and the Group at 31 March 1993 and of the profit, total recognised gains and cash flows of the Group for the year then ended and have been properly prepared in accordance with the Companies Act 1985.

Coopers & Lybrand
Chartered Accountants and Registered Auditors
London
17 May 1993

REPORT OF INDEPENDENT AUDITORS

Board of Directors and Share Owners – The Coca-Cola Company

We have audited the accompanying consolidated balance sheets of the Coca-Cola Company and subsidiaries as of December 31, 1993 and 1992, and the related consolidated statements of income, share-owners' equity and cash flows for each of the three years in the period ended December 31, 1993. These financial statements are the responsibility of the Company's management. Our responsibility is to express an opinion on these financial statements based on our audits.

We conducted our audits in accordance with generally accepted auditing standards. Those standards require that we plan and perform the audit to obtain reasonable assurance about whether the financial statements are free of material mis-statement. An audit includes examining, on a test basis, evidence supporting the amounts and disclosures in the financial statements. An audit also includes assessing the accounting principles used and significant estimates made by management, as well as evaluating the overall financial statement presentation. We believe that our audits provide a reasonable basis for our opinion.

In our opinion, the financial statements referred to above present fairly, in all material respects, the consolidated financial position of the Coca-Cola Company and subsidiaries at December 31, 1993 and 1992, and the consolidated results of their operations and their cash flows for each of the three years in the period ended December 31, 1993, in conformity with generally accepted accounting principles.

As discussed in Note 1 to the consolidated financial statements, in 1993 the Company changed its method of accounting for postemployment benefits. As discussed in Note 14 to the consolidated financial statements, in 1992 the Company changed its method of accounting for post-retirement benefits other than pensions.

Ernst & Young
Atlanta Georgia
January 25, 1994

The examples quoted above are all unqualified reports. But there may be opinions other than unqualified. The reason for that can be classified as follows:

- nature of circumstances;

- uncertainty;

- disagreement.

Depending upon whether or not these circumstances are fundamental, different types of opinions may come out. Below are some examples.

EXAMPLES

Emphasizing an uncertainty

In our opinion ... Without qualifying our opinion we draw attention to Note X to the financial statements. The Company is the defendant in a lawsuit alleging infringement of certain patent rights and claiming royalties and punitive damages. The Company has filed a counter action, and preliminary hearing and discovery proceedings on both actions are in progress. The ultimate outcome of the matter cannot presently be determined, and no provision for any liability that may result has been made in the financial statements.

Qualified opinion – disagreement

As discussed in Note X to the financial statements, no depreciation has been provided in the financial statements which practice in our opinion, is not in accordance with International Accounting Standards. The provision for the year ended December 31, 19XX, should be XXX based on the straight-line method of depreciation using annual rates of 5 per cent for the building and 20 per cent for the equipment. Accordingly, the fixed assets should be reduced by accumulated depreciation of XXX and the loss for the year and deficit should be increased by XXX and XXX, respectively.

In our opinion, except for the effects on the financial statements of the matter referred to in the preceding paragraph, these financial statements ...

Adverse opinion

In our opinion, because of the effects of the matters discussed in the preceding paragraph, the financial statements do not give a true and fair view of (or 'present fairly') the financial position of XYZ Company at December 31, 19XX, and the results of its operations for the year then ended in accordance with International Accounting Standards.

Disclaimer of opinion

Because of the significance of the matters discussed in the preceding paragraph, we are not in a position to, and do not, express an opinion on the financial statements.

9 Understanding consolidated group accounts

LEARNING OBJECTIVES

The objective of this chapter is not to give in-depth coverage of the many problems within the area of consolidated accounts. Consolidation is a comprehensive subject, well worth a separate field of study. We will concentrate on understanding the basic philosophy behind consolidated accounts and how the main problems have been solved when consolidated accounts are presented. In other words, we are users of such accounts, not producers.

After studying this chapter you should:

- know what a group is;
- understand the objective of consolidated accounts;
- have an overview of the main problems within this field of accounting;
- by studying the method of replacing share ownership in another company with the underlying assets and liabilities, have grasped the fundamental idea behind consolidated accounts;
- know what minority interest is;
- have an understanding of the items that differ in the parent company and the consolidated accounts.

Since we are not discussing this subject in great depth, there are no problems at the end of this chapter, but we have given questions and answers.

9.1 What is a group in accounting?

A group is a situation where separate firms together constitute one economic unit. A group can be organized in different ways, but the main criterion is that one firm has control over another. Usually, such control is obtained by ownership. Most groups are organized as companies, so in the discussion we refer to such an organization, but a group can also exist when private persons are in control.

The company controlling another company is called the *parent* company, and the company controlled is a *subsidiary*.

Control is obtained directly, for example, when the parent company P owns the shares in the subsidiaries A, B, C. But it can also be indirect control, for example, when P controls A and B and these companies together have control over company C.

When we refer to a group, or the group, we mean all the companies in the family. If P controls A which again controls B, we have in fact two groups: A and B as one and P + A + B as another. When we in such a case refer to a group, or the group, we mean the total group (P + A + B), consisting of all companies in the group family. Usually, a company has control over another one when ownership is more than 50 per cent of the voting share capital. But control can also exist by a formal agreement between parties, so that in fact there is a control situation. Theoretically, practical control can be obtained with less than 50 per cent ownership, because it is very seldom that all shareholders attend the shareholders' meeting. But normally the controller owns more than 50 per cent of the voting shares.

9.2 The objective of consolidated accounts

We have said that a group is an economic unit. It then seems logical to present that unit financially. Consolidated accounts do so. These accounts give the total economy for all companies within a group, looked upon as one economic unit. If we keep this fact in mind, most of the problems within consolidated accounts will have a logical solution. Our examples will illustrate this.

The first question that might arise is why the accounts of the parent company do not give sufficient information about the group as a whole. In order to answer this question, we will have to look into the accounting treatment of a share ownership. In the balance sheet of the parent company we will find 'investment in subsidiaries' as a long-term investment. According to basic accounting principles, the value of this item in the balance sheet will be the purchase price of the shares or, if a subsidiary is established by the parent company, the share capital. The information value of this amount is very small, since it does not tell us about the situation today; in other words, there is no information about the development of the subsidiary since the time of acquisition. In the profit and loss account, the information value must also be questioned, since only dividends will have been included. This gives no insight into the revenues and expenses and, thus, the profit for the year.

We conclude, therefore, that the accounts of the parent company are not sufficient as a source of financial information. We need accounts which give the total view of all assets and all liabilities, and of all revenues and expenses when looked upon as one single unit. Another question concerns why the accounts for the separate companies have to be put together into one unit. Surely this summary of accounts is only useful for parties interested in having a total picture. The answer here is that it seems practical and rational to present consolidated accounts as part of the accounts instead of leaving that work to outside parties. But, much more importantly, very often there are activities of different kinds among the companies in a group, so a summary would not suffice. Let us illustrate this point with an example: if a company within a group sells goods to another company within the same group, these sales (and corresponding profits) are realized when we look upon the selling company as a separate unit, but the goods are not sold when we look upon the selling and buying companies as a whole. In other words, this part of the sales has to be eliminated, and so no profit can be reported on such a sale.

When we take a total view, looking upon separate companies as one economic unit, it also seems logical that all items in the individual companies' accounts, which have a counterpart within the group must be eliminated, for example, loans between companies, interest on loans, payment for certain services and so on. Although there is nothing wrong in reporting as separate companies, when looked upon as one unit, this information is misleading.

Following on from this, a natural question is whether the accounts of the parent company are necessary. Is it not the consolidated group accounts that the users need? In many ways this is true, and with the main activities in the subsidiaries, the group accounts undoubtedly will be of most interest for all parties. In some countries, for example the US, only group accounts are published. The European tradition is also to publish the accounts of the parent. This tradition has several explanations, the main one being that certain decisions, for example on dividends, are linked to the parent company.

One accounting item (shown in the parent company accounts) gives the best illustration of the idea behind consolidated group accounts, namely 'investment in subsidiaries'. Let us, therefore, look closer at that item and what happens with this item when we want to give a total or comprehensive picture of the group.

9.3 An illustration of consolidation

We will illustrate the problem with the following example:

Balance sheet, December 31, 19XX, Parent Co. Ltd

Assets	(000s)
Fixed assets	
Building	500
Investment in subsidiary, S Ltd	400
	900
Current assets	
Stock	300
Debtors	200
Bank accounts	100
	600
Total assets	1500
Equity and liabilities	
Equity	600
Long-term liabilities	500
Short-term liabilities	400
Total equity and liabilities	1500

This is the situation immediately after company P established the wholly-owned S company. The balance sheet of company S will be as follows:

Balance sheet, December 31, 19XX, Subsidiary Ltd

Assets	(000s)
Bank account	400
Equity	
Share capital	400

(Note: The share capital was fully paid into the bank account.)

There should be no problem in presenting the consolidated group accounts (P + S) in this example:

Consolidated balance sheet, December 31, 19XX

Assets	(000s)
Fixed assets	
Building	500
	500
Current assets	
Stock	300
Debtors	200
Bank accounts	500
	1000
Total assets	1500
Equity and liabilities	
Equity	600
Long-term liabilities	500
Short-term liabilities	400
Total equity and liabilities	1500

We see that we now have a total view of companies P and S looked upon as one economic unit. If we compare the sum of the separate companies with the group accounts, we see that the item 'investment in subsidiary, S Ltd', 400, is taken away, and so is the equity of company S. The equity of the consolidated accounts fully corresponds to the equity of the parent company. We now have a balance sheet showing all the assets and all the liabilities when companies P and S are looked upon as one unit.

The consolidated balance sheet at a later time should be easy to understand in this case: the asset side will consist of the sum of assets of company P and company S, after elimination of internal items, and the same thing applies to the liabilities. The equity in the consolidated balance sheet will consist of the equity of company P, plus retained earnings in company S from the point of establishing the subsidiary. This seems logical, since the investment in the subsidiary has been eliminated against the share capital of that company.

The consolidated profit and loss account at any time will consist of revenues and expenses in both companies, after the elimination of internal items. It is important to see how consolidation affects the profit for the year. The sum of the profit in company P and company S will normally differ from the profit on a consolidated basis. We can think of many explanations of such a difference. One reason is that all unrealized profit is eliminated. We mentioned as an example goods sold from one company in a group to another company in the group but still in hand at the end of the buying subsidiary's year. Here, the profit has to be eliminated, since the stock has not been sold outside the unit. Another reason is that when a company is purchased and the purchase price differs from the book value of the assets, this must be taken into account in the measurements in future years. We will return to this later in this section.

We will now look at a more common situation, the purchase of an existing company, using this example to develop the logical accounting method to treat and follow up such a purchase.

When a company buys an existing company, the purchase price will very seldom be exactly the amount of equity given in the subsidiary's accounts. Accounting data are based on the historical cost principle, which is seldom equivalent to the value of the assets today. Besides, the purchase price will rarely be exactly the sum of the value-based assets (less liabilities). More or less than this amount (market value of tangible assets and liabilities) will be paid, with relevance to the future expectation of earnings. The new situation may alter the old one, so a company may be willing to pay more than the sum of the value of the assets (less liabilities) at the time of purchase.

We discussed this goodwill phenomenon earlier. If the purchase price is less than the sum of the value of the assets (less liabilities), there will be negative goodwill. (Theoretically, negative goodwill should not exist, since the seller will be better off by selling the assets individually. But in practice it does exist, due to practical or non-economic reasons.)

Analysis at the time of purchase will be first to value the individual assets, and then to see what has been paid in addition (goodwill). The consequences of this analysis must be shown in the accounts: the specific assets of the acquired company have to be adjusted to market values, and these values must be used for accounting measurements later on. If, for example, stocks have a value of 120 000 but were valued at 100 000 in the accounts, then 120 000 is the relevant figure to use. That was the amount paid for the stocks. If, for example, a building in the acquired company has a book value of 5 000 000, but a market value (= purchase price) of 7 000 000, then the consequence is that 7 000 000 is the figure to be used both as value and as basis for the depreciation of the building. Also, if a company has paid an extra amount above the sum of the assets (less liabilities), the consequence of this fact must be shown. We have discussed this before, concluding that since the extra payment must be for extra earnings in the future, it seems logical to write off this item in a systematic way.

Let us end this section with an illustration of this reasoning. Assume the purchase price is 4 000 000 and the other figures are as follows:

	Book values (000s)	Market values (000s)	Book values after purchase (000s)
Assets			
Building	5000	7000	7000
Stock	100	120	120
Goodwill	–	–	880
Liabilities	4000		4000
Equity	1100		4000

Under the discussion of goodwill earlier, we mentioned that goodwill has been a subject much debated for more than 100 years. Goodwill has recently become a much more significant part of companies' financial reports than was previously the case. The accounting treatment of goodwill is therefore a major concern for companies and for accounting regulators. The main explanation is the increasing number of takeovers.

The main alternative accounting policies for dealing with purchased goodwill in group accounts are:

● merger accounting;

● immediate write-off against profits;

● immediate write-off against reserves;

● capitalize and amortize.

Under *merger accounting*, or pooling of interests, goodwill does not arise, because the two entities are simply added together. The popularity of merger accounting in some countries seems to be grounded in a desire to avoid the cost of amortizing goodwill. Logically, when a company has been purchased this accounting solution has little meaning. Only when two companies continue as before without one purchasing the other can this method be accepted theoretically.

Immediate write-off against profits (expensing) or *immediate write-off against reserves* have been popular practices in some countries. The company 'gets rid of' goodwill at once and so, from a management point of view, higher profit is reported in the next few years. Again, logically this method must be questioned. When a company purchases another one and pays for goodwill, it changes one asset (cash) for another one (goodwill). The company pays more for the acquired company because of extra anticipated profit in the future.

The basic principle, matching, seems to be fulfilled in a much better way when the last alternative, *capitalize and amortize*, is used. The main problem with

111

the capitalization alternative is the time horizon for amortization, linking uncertainty to goodwill. Consequently, accounting regulators will normally set an upper limit for the period of amortization. As we will see later, EU countries usually have to write off goodwill within a maximum of five years, according to the EU Fourth Directive.

9.4 Minority interests

When a company has control over another, but not full 100 per cent ownership, minority interests will exist. In theory, this could be solved by reporting the majority part of assets, liabilities, revenues and expenses. If, for example, the ownership is 80 per cent, that would mean 80 per cent of all the items in the balance sheet and the profit and loss account. But this solution will not give a total economic picture. Therefore, the consolidated accounts in such a case will include 100 per cent of assets, liabilities, revenues and expenses, showing the minority interests as one item in the profit and loss account and as one item in the balance sheet. So, instead of measuring 80 per cent of all items in the example above, the consolidated accounts present 100 per cent less 20 per cent. This solution not only gives the total but also tells us that we have a situation where a subsidiary (or subsidiaries) is (are) not wholly owned. When reporting in the consolidated profit and loss account, the minority interests are shown as part of net profit:

Profit after taxes

Minority interest

Net profit

In the consolidated balance sheet, the sum of minority interests is usually shown between equity and liabilities as a separate item:

Equity

Minority interests

Long-term liabilities

Short-term liabilities

Is it better to use accounting figures that include or exclude the minority interests? The answer to this depends on the calculations made. In most cases we would be interested in giving the total view, for example the profitability, the equity situation etc., where the minority holding is small. But, in the case of earnings per share, we have to take minority interests into account, since these are separate from the earnings linked to a share in the parent company.

9.5 Subsidiaries abroad

In Chapter 6 we discussed the problems that arise when a company has assets and/or liabilities in foreign currency. When a company has a subsidiary abroad, the figures from that subsidiary will have to be expressed in the currency of the parent company, giving rise to a translation problem. There are two main principles which can be used when translating the amounts of a subsidiary's accounts into the domestic currency: use the current exchange rate, or combine the historical exchange rate(s) and the current exchange rate. With the latter option monetary items (cash, bank accounts, debtors, liabilities) are translated using the current exchange rate, and all other items (the non-monetary items) are translated by using the relevant historical exchange rates. Items in the profit and loss account follow the same basis as the corresponding balance sheet item, for example depreciation will be calculated according to historical exchange rates.

The choice between the two main principles will be based on whether or not the subsidiary operates independently of the parent company. This fact will affect the cash flows between the parent company and the subsidiary abroad, and so should steer the principle of translation and the perception of translation differences. If the subsidiary operates independently, all balance items will normally be translated at the current exchange rate. The translation difference due to the fact that the equity is translated at different exchange rates at the beginning and the end of the period is adjusted directly against the equity capital.

When the subsidiary abroad works closely with the parent company, the monetary items will be translated at the current exchange rate, other items at historical exchange rates. In the profit and loss account the items are translated either at historical exchange rates at the time of the transaction or at the current exchange rate, depending on the corresponding items (if any). Average exchange rates may also be used for transactions which have taken place during the year. The net effect of the translation is a gain or loss element and is reported in the profit and loss account as a financial item.

9.6 An illustration – and summary

A key question in group accounting is the importance of the consolidated accounts compared with the accounts of the individual companies within the group. Consolidated group accounts give the total of all companies looked upon as one unit, and generally such an overall view of the economic situation is of most interest, so the preference will be for consolidated group accounts. We have also mentioned that in many countries, certain decisions, such as dividends, are based on the accounts of the parent company. Here, both the consolidated accounts and those of the parent company are of interest. This means that two sets of accounts will be presented. This can be done in a rational way, as illustrated below. In this example both the parent company and the subsidiaries are active, operating companies, and it is easy to see which items are relevant in the two accounts. This example also sums up the idea behind consolidated accounts and the relationship between the accounts of the parent company and the group.

Profit and loss account 19XX

Parent Ltd			The group	
Current year	Previous year		Current year	Previous year
		Operating revenues and expenses		
		Financial income and expenses		
X	X	Interest from subsidiaries		
X	X	Dividends from subsidiaries		
		Extraordinary income and expenses		
		Profit before taxes		
		Taxes		
		Minority interests	X	X
		Net profit		

Balance sheet, December 31, 19XX

Parent Ltd			Consolidated accounts	
Current year	Previous year		Current year	Previous year
		Assets		
X	X	Share investment in subsidiaries		
X	X	Receivable from subsidiaries		
		Equity and liabilities		
		Equity		
		Minority interests	X	X
		Long-term liabilities		
		Short-term liabilities		
X	X	Payable to subsidiaries		

This example illustrates accounts which are fully relevant for the separate companies, but quite irrelevant for consolidated purposes. We also see that minority interests are items that are only relevant in consolidated accounts. This example does not, of course, cover all the possible differences.

EXAMPLES

Basis of consolidation

The group financial statements incorporate the financial statements of Marks & Spencer PLC and all its subsidiaries for the year ended March 31. **(Marks & Spencer)**

Goodwill

Goodwill arising on consolidation is written off to reserves on acquisition. Goodwill attributable to business disposed of is written back to reserves brought forward, and charged through the profit and loss account. **(Marks & Spencer)**

Scope of consolidation

The fully consolidated Group companies comprise all companies in which Volkswagen AG has a direct or indirect interest of over 50 per cent or which are under management control of the parent company. Apart from Volkswagen AG, this involves 28 German Group companies and 78 foreign Group companies. **(Volkswagen)**

Consolidation principles

The assets and liabilities of the German and foreign companies included in the consolidated financial statements are shown in accordance with the uniform accounting and valuation methods used within the Volkswagen Group. In the case of the associated companies, their own accounts and valuations are used as the basis for determining the proportionate stockholders' equity, except in cases where the figures for foreign Group companies have to be adjusted to bring them into line with German accounting regulations.

Capital consolidation for the companies included in the consolidated financial statements for the first time and determination of figures for associated companies are carried out at the time of acquisition on the basis of the revaluation method.

In contrast to the previous year, goodwill arising from the acquisition of shares in consolidated and associated companies is capitalized and written off over five years, for the sake of greater transparency.

Receivables, liabilities, expenses and income arising between individual consolidated companies are eliminated. Group inventories and fixed assets are adjusted to eliminate intra-Group profits and losses.

Consolidation operations affecting results are subject to apportionment of deferred taxes. Deferred tax liabilities in connection with consolidation operations are set off against the assets-side balance of deferred taxes from the individual companies' financial statements, although these last-mentioned deferred taxes are not shown in the balance sheets. **(Volkswagen)**

Basis of consolidation

The consolidated accounts include Danisco A/S (the parent company) and all undertakings (subsidiary undertakings) in which Danisco, directly or indirectly, holds more than 50 per cent of the voting rights or otherwise has a dominant influence. Companies in which Danisco holds between 20 per cent and 50 per cent of the voting rights without having a dominant influence are regarded as associated companies.

The group accounts consolidate the audited accounts of the parent company and the individual subsidiary undertakings, which have been prepared in accordance with the present accounting policies. Inter-company income and expenditure, shareholdings, balances and dividends as well as unrealized internal profits and losses have been eliminated.

Associated companies, the management of which is undertaken on a unified basis by Danisco and one or several companies, are proportionally consolidated. This implies that the relevant proportion of the companies' items in the profit and loss account and balance sheet is included in the corresponding items of the consolidated accounts and that inter-company items and unrealized profits have been eliminated proportionally.

On the acquisition of new companies the net asset value at the date of acquisition is stated in accordance with the group's accounting policies, and provisions are set aside for any costs resulting from planned restructuring in the acquired undertaking. Where the cost of acquisition exceeds the net asset value computed, the balance is allocated to the extent possible to the assets and liabilities which have a higher or lower value than the book values. Any remaining positive balances are charged directly to capital and reserves as group goodwill in the year of acquisition. Any negative balances (badwill) attributable to future operating losses are recorded under provisions.

Newly acquired subsidiaries and associated companies are included in the profit and loss account at the date of acquisition.

Where a decision to dispose of or sell a subsidiary undertaking has been made, the undertaking's results at the date of decision plus expenses incidental to the disposal are recorded under extraordinary items. Net assets after provisions in such undertakings are recorded under current assets as other debtors or under other provisions.

Comparative figures are not adjusted for undertakings sold, undertakings being disposed of or newly acquired undertakings. **(Danisco)**

Principles of consolidation

The consolidated accounts comprise the parent company, all subsidiaries and associated companies. Subsidiaries are defined as companies in which AB Volvo holds more than 50 per cent of the voting rights. Subsidiaries in which Volvo's holding is temporary are not consolidated, however. Associated companies are companies in which AB Volvo has long-term holdings equal to at least 20 per cent but not more than 50 per cent of the voting rights.

The consolidated accounts are prepared in accordance with the principles set forth in Recommendation of the Swedish Financial Accounting Standards Council.

All acquisitions of companies are accounted for using the purchase method.

Companies that have been divested are included in the consolidated accounts up to and including the date of divestment. Companies acquired during the year are consolidated as of the date of acquisition.

Holdings in associated companies are reported in accordance with the equity method. The Group's share of reported income before taxes in such companies, adjusted for minority interests, is included in the Consolidated income statement, reduced in appropriate cases by amortization of excess values. The Group's share of reported taxes in associated companies, as well as estimated taxes in allocations, are included in the Group's tax expense.

For practical reasons, most of the associated companies are included in the Volvo Group accounts with a certain time lag, normally one quarter. Dividends from associated companies are not included in consolidated income. In the consolidated balance sheet, the book value of shareholdings in associated companies is affected by Volvo's share of each company's income after tax, reduced by amortization of excess values and by the amount of dividends received. **(Volvo)**

The consolidated accounts include the parent company Bergesen d.y. AS and its subsidiaries.

Consistent accounting principles have been applied throughout the Bergesen d.y. Group in the preparation of the consolidated accounts. Intercompany transactions, receivables and liabilities have been eliminated.

The cost of shares in subsidiaries has been eliminated against equity in the subsidiaries at the time of purchase (purchase method). The excess value has been allocated to those assets to which the excess relates. The excess values have been classified as goodwill and depreciated over five years. **(Bergesen)**

Consolidation

The consolidated financial statements include the accounts of the Company and all subsidiaries except where control is temporary or does not rest with the Company. The Company's investments in companies in which it has the ability to exercise significant influence over operating and financial policies, including certain investments where there is a temporary majority interest, are accounted for by the equity method. Accordingly, the Company's share of the net earnings of these companies is included in consolidated net income. The Company's investments in other companies are carried at cost. All significant intercompany accounts and transactions are eliminated. **(Coca-Cola)**

✔ Questions and answers

In this chapter this section will be a mixture of questions and problems. As we explained at the beginning of the chapter, our objective was to get an overview and an insight into the problems of consolidated group accounts as seen from a user's point of view, not to become an expert in the preparation of such accounts – that will need specific training.

1 Which part/words would you recognize as the most important in the definition of a group?

Answer:
As one single unit.

2 Which companies would you include in the group in the following example? Company A owns 100 per cent of the shares in company B and company C; company C owns 40 per cent in company D, and A owns 11 per cent in D; in company E, D owns 25 per cent and B owns 25 per cent.

Answer:
A, B, C and D (51 per cent is sufficient), but not E (50 per cent is not sufficient).

3 Would you say that company Z is controlled by company X in this example? X owns 60 per cent of the share capital in Y, which again owns 60 per cent of the share capital in company Z.

Answer:
Yes, although mathematically the ownership is just 36 per cent (60 per cent of 60 per cent), X controls Y and thus also Z.

4 How many accounts exist in Question 3 above?

Answer:
Five, one for each of the companies X, Y and Z, one for the group consisting of Y and Z and then the real consolidated group account for X, Y and Z, seen as one single unit.

5 Give examples of items you can find in the separate account for a company within a group, but which are irrelevant in consolidated group accounts.

Answer:
In the balance sheet: 'investment in shares in subsidiaries', 'receivable from subsidiaries', 'liability to sister company', 'dividends to parent company'. In the profit and loss account: 'dividends from companies within the group', 'interest to parent company', 'interest from subsidiaries'.

6 A parent company (P) sells machinery at the beginning of this year to a subsidiary (S) at an amount of 100 000. The book value is 80 000, and the expected economic life of the machinery is four years. Which accounts will this transaction affect and what will the relevant figures be in the consolidated accounts for this year?

Answer:
The profit on the sale of the machinery is irrelevant, since this is an internal sale. This profit of 20 000 cannot be reported in the consolidated profit and loss account. Company S will have registered 100 000 as the purchase price of the

machinery. This is not the correct figure in the balance sheet, since we have to regard this machinery as not sold. The balance sheet value will therefore be 60 000, just the same amount as it would have been if not sold (80 000 less depreciation). In addition, Company S will have calculated the depreciation on the basis of the acquisition cost, 100 000, that means 25 000 for this year. This amount must be adjusted down to 20 000 in the consolidated profit and loss account.

7 What would you take into consideration in this example? Company P buys 100 per cent of the shares in Company S. The purchase price is 140 000. The balance sheet items of Company S at the time of purchase are: buildings 200 000; stock 80 000; cash 20 000; equity 100 000; liabilities 200 000.

Answer:
The two assets, buildings and/or stock, might have higher values than the book values. Let us suppose the market values today are 220 000 and 90 000, respectively. Then, 10 000 must be goodwill, which will have to be written off within a limited time horizon.

8 What are 'minority interests', and where do you find these items in the consolidated group accounts?

Answer:
Minority interests exist when not all of the companies within a group are wholly owned by the companies within the group. In the profit and loss account the minority interests will be shown as part of the net profit. In the balance sheet they will be shown separately between equity and liabilities.

9 In the example given in Question 7, which analyses would you make if you bought 80 per cent of the shares in S for 112 000?

Answer:
Since P bought 80 per cent for 112 000, it could logically be argued that the total value of the company must be 140 000. That means the value of the building will be 220 000 in the consolidated balance sheet at the time of purchase and the value of the stock will be 90 000. It could also be argued that the total goodwill will be 10 000, although it can be questioned whether this total calculated amount should be the goodwill in the consolidated account or just the 8000 that really was paid. In the first alternative, the total minority interests will be 28 000, in the second alternative, 26 000.

10 Make an information footnote for this group: The parent company, P, owns 100 per cent of companies A, B, C, D and E, 80 per cent of companies F, G and H, and 60 per cent of companies I and J. The last company is quoted on the stock exchange. Company D owns 90 per cent of companies K and L, and Company F owns 100 per cent of companies M and N. Company I owns 10 per cent of the parent company, P.

Answer:

Shares in subsidiaries

Name		% owned	Book value		Stock exchange value	
			This year	*Last year*	*This year*	*Last year*
A Ltd		100	X	X		
B Ltd		100	X	X		
C Ltd		100	X	X		
D Ltd		100	X	X		
	K Ltd	90	X	X		
	L Ltd	90	X	X		
E Ltd		100	X	X		
F Ltd		80	X	X		
	M Ltd	100	X	X		
	N Ltd	100	X	X		
G Ltd		80	X	X		
H Ltd		80	X	X		
I Ltd		60	X	X		
	P Ltd	10	X	X		
J Ltd		60	X	X	X	X

11 **These extracts show differences in the way goodwill arising from acquisition is treated:**

Goodwill is written off to reserves. (**Marks & Spencer**)

Goodwill is set off against the revenue reserves. (**Volkswagen**)

Charged directly to capital and reserves. (**Danisco**)

All acquisitions of companies are accounted for using the purchase method. Goodwill is amortized on a straight-line basis over 5–20 years. (**Volvo**)

The excess values have been classified as goodwill and depreciated over five years. (**Bergesen**)

Goodwill is amortized principally on a straight-line basis over the estimated future period to be benefited, not exceeding forty years. (**Coca-Cola**)

What are your comments on the treatment of goodwill in these cases?

Answer:

Goodwill in consolidation is one of the most controversial problems internationally within accounting. In our case studies three of the six companies write it off against equity. This means that no cost (as depreciation) is reported in future years. This treatment is not theoretically logical, but as a management policy it can be explained.

10 The EU Fourth Directive

LEARNING OBJECTIVES

After studying this chapter you will understand the requirements of the EU Fourth Directive.

The EU Fourth Directive, dated July 25, 1978, regulates the presentation and content of annual accounts and annual reports for very important types of companies. Some EU companies covered by the Directive are:

- in Germany: die Aktiengesellschaft, die Kommanditgesellschaft auf Ahlien, die Gesellschaft mit beschränker Haftung;
- in France: la société anonyme, la société en commandite par actions, la société à responsabilité limitée;
- in the UK: public companies limited by shares or by guarantee, private companies limited by shares or by guarantee;
- in Denmark: aktieselskaber, kommanditaktieselskaber, anpartsselskaber.

The Seventh Directive of June 1983 deals with consolidated accounts.

In this chapter we concentrate on the Fourth Directive. This Directive is fundamental. It is, however, not possible to go deeply into all of the 12 sections, containing 62 Articles. We will give an overview and concentrate on the most important part of the Directive.

10.1 An overview

Sections and Articles	Comments
Section 1 Article 2 *General provisions* 'The annual accounts shall comprise the balance sheet, the profit and loss account and the notes on the accounts.'	A cash flow statement is not required. The rest of this Article will be discussed in connection with 'true and fair view'.
Section 2 Articles 3–7 *General provisions concerning the balance sheet and the profit and loss account* 'The layout of the balance sheet and the profit and loss account may not be changed from one financial year to the next.' 'The items prescribed must be shown separately in the order indicated.' 'Corresponding items for the preceding financial year must be shown.'	 Departures from this principle can be permitted in exceptional cases. Disclosure in the notes is necessary. As we will see later, the order of the balance sheet is to start with intangibles and end with cash on the asset side. Where the figures are not comparable, the figure for the preceding year must be adjusted or disclosed with relevant comments.
Section 3 Articles 8–14 *Layout of the balance sheet* 'For the presentation of the balance sheet, the Member States shall prescribe one or both of the layouts prescribed by Articles 9 and 10. If a Member State prescribes both, it may allow companies to choose between them.' 'The Member State may permit small companies to draw up abridged balance sheets.'	 The difference between the two models is that the second one (Article 10) presents net current assets/liabilities as the difference between current assets and current liabilities. We will discuss this section in depth later on. Criteria: two of the three following: • balance sheet total < 1 000 000 ECU; • net turnover < 2 000 000 ECU; • average number of employees < 50.
Section 4 Articles 15–21 *Special provisions relating to certain balance sheet items* *Fixed assets* 'Whether particular assets are to be shown as fixed assets or current assets shall depend upon the purpose for which they are intended.'	 The company itself is best placed to define the intended purpose.

Sections and Articles	*Comments*
'Fixed assets shall comprise those assets which are intended for use on a continuing basis for the purpose of the undertaking's activities.'	Indirectly, we also have a definition of current assets here.
'Movements in the various fixed asset items shall be shown in the balance sheet or in the notes on the accounts.'	
'For each fixed asset item there shall be shown separately the purchase price or production cost, the additions, disposals and the cumulative value adjustments at the balance sheet date.'	This is very useful information, normally given in the notes on the accounts.
Participating interest The Directive defines participating interest as: 'rights in the capital of other undertakings intended to contribute to the company's activities'.	
Such interest is defined as a holding exceeding 'a percentage fixed by the Member States which may not exceed 20 per cent'.	Internationally, the 20 per cent limit is the usual criterion. Such an interest will also mean a certain accounting treatment (the equity method).

Sections and Articles	*Comments*
Section 5 Articles 22–27 *Layout of the profit and loss account*	
'For the presentation of the profit and loss account, the Member States shall prescribe one or more of the layouts provided for in Articles 23 to 26. If a Member State prescribes more than one layout, it may allow companies to choose from among them.'	In this section the following alternatives are described:
'The items prescribed must be shown separately in the order indicated.'	Vertical layout: — By type of expenditure, Article 23 / By type of operation, Article 25 Horizontal layout: — By type of expenditure, Article 24 / By type of operation, Article 26
'Corresponding items for the preceding financial year must be shown.'	We will discuss this section in depth later on.

The alternatives table in the Comments column:

In this section the following alternatives are described:	
Vertical layout:	By type of expenditure, Article 23 By type of operation, Article 25
Horizontal layout:	By type of expenditure, Article 24 By type of operation, Article 26

Sections and Articles	*Comments*
Section 6 Articles 28–30 *Special provisions related to certain items in the profit and loss account*	
'Income and charges that arise otherwise than in the course of the company's ordinary activities must be shown under Extraordinary income and Extraordinary charges.'	The international tendency is restrictive as far as extraordinary items are concerned. The distinction from ordinary items, however, is fine, both from an informative and an analytical point of view.
Section 7 Articles 31–42 *Valuation rules*	In this central section both general principles and a number of specific valuation rules are given. We will discuss this section in depth later on.

Sections and Articles	Comments
Section 8 Articles 43–45 *Contents of the notes on the accounts*	As already stated in this Directive, the notes are part of the financial statements. Information in respect of 13 matters is given as a requirement in this section. Again, this section is so important that we will discuss it separately.
Section 9 Article 46 *Contents of the annual report* 'The annual report must include at least a fair review of the development of the company's business and of its position.' The report shall also give an indication of:	This is generally accepted. Still, the obligation to give a fair review is stated.
(a) any important events that have occurred since the end of the financial year;	This means up to the time when the annual accounts are signed.
(b) the company's likely future development;	A very valuable piece of information for all users.
(c) activities in the field of research and development;	This requirement underlines the importance of such activities.
(d) information concerning acquisition of own shares.	Such information is prescribed by Article 22 of Directive 77/91/EC.
Section 10 Articles 47–50 *Publication* 'The annual accounts duly approved, and the annual report, together with the opinion submitted by the person responsible for auditing the accounts, shall be published as laid down by the laws of each Member State in accordance with Article 3 of Directive 68/151/EC.'	The laws of a Member State may permit non-publication of the annual report, instead making it available to the public at the company's office. Member States may permit small companies to publish abridged balance sheets and abridged notes for certain requirements. Member States may relieve small companies from publishing annual accounts and annual reports.
Section 11 Article 51 *Auditing* 'Companies must have their annual accounts audited by one or more persons authorized by national law to audit accounts.' 'The person or persons responsible for auditing the accounts must also verify that the annual report is consistent with the annual accounts for the same financial year.'	
Section 12 Articles 52–62 *Financial provisions*	The Articles in this section are of a more administrative character.

10.2 True and fair view

In the Directive, Section 1, Article 2, we find the following:

> 3 The annual accounts shall give a true and fair view of the company's assets, liabilities, financial position and profit and loss.
>
> 4 Where the application of the provisions of this Directive would not be sufficient to give a true and fair view within the meaning of paragraph 3, additional information must be given.
>
> 5 Where in exceptional cases the application of a provision of this Directive is incompatible with the obligation laid down in paragraph 3, that provision must be departed from in order to give a true and fair view within the meaning of paragraph 3. Any such departure must be disclosed in the notes on the accounts together with an explanation of the reasons for it and a statement of its effect on the assets, liabilities, financial position and profit and loss. The Member States may define the exceptional cases in question and lay down the relevant special rules.

True and fair view (TFV) was brought into the Directive in 1973 when the UK entered the EC (now the EU). It was a previously unknown concept in other European countries. The following quotation (taken from *Principles of Modern Company Law*, Gowers, Sweet & Maxwell, 1992) is worth mentioning:

> We even succeeded in securing the adoption of our basic principle that accounts must present a 'true and fair view', although we were unable to explain precisely what that expression meant.

TFV is not further defined in the Fourth Directive.

TFV has been a controversial issue both in connection with translation into the national languages and also as far as the content is concerned. In fact it is impossible to translate the words literally into any other community language in a meaningful way. The following are some examples of the translation:

Germany: Tatsächlichen Verhältnissen entsprechenden Bild ('According to facts')
France: Une image fidèle ('Faithful')
Denmark: Retvisende bilde ('Right-looking')
Sweden: Rättvisande bild ('Right-looking')
Norway: Pålitelig bilde ('Right-looking')

The concept of a TFV has different meanings in different countries. However, it is an overriding principle which must be observed even if this means that a company has to depart from the national law of its own Member State in order to give a TFV as set out in Article 2.3.

As far as the content is concerned, it is an overriding obligation for a company and its auditor that the accounts shall give a TFV (2.3). Additional information must be given (2.4) and in certain (exceptional) cases the general rules must be departed from in order to give a TFV (2.5). (In Germany, however, this is not the case, as Article 2.5 has not been implemented in national law.)

The Fédération des Experts Comptables Européens (FEE) has made an analysis of those instances where companies, listed and unlisted, provided evidence of a departure from the provisions of national law in order to give a true and fair view. This analysis shows that in only ten out of 341 cases did companies depart from national law in accordance with the overriding TFV concept: five related to listed and five to unlisted companies. These departures occurred not just in Anglo-Saxon-oriented countries, but are spread over six of the nine countries in the first group of EU countries.

We have also seen a few special rules laid down by Member States (Article 2.5). One example is the UK accounting standard for estate agents/real-estate companies stating that they should be valued at market values instead of at historical cost.

10.3 Layout of the balance sheet

Article 8

For the presentation of the balance sheet, the Member States shall prescribe one or both of the layouts prescribed by Articles 9 and 10. If a Member State prescribes both, it may allow companies to choose between them.

Article 9
Assets

A **Subscribed capital unpaid**
of which there has been called _____
(unless national law provides that called-up capital be shown under 'Liabilities'. In that case, the part of the capital called but not yet paid must appear as an asset either under **A** or under **D** (II) (5)).

B **Formation expenses**
as defined by national law, and in so far as national law permits their being shown as an asset. National law may also provide for formation expenses to be shown as the first item under 'Intangible assets'.

C Fixed assets

I Intangible assets

1 Costs of research and development, in so far as national law permits their being shown as assets.
2 Concessions, patents, licences, trade marks and similar rights and assets, if they were:
   (a) acquired for valuable consideration and need not be shown under **C** (I) (3); or
   (b) created by the undertaking itself, in so far as national law permits their being shown as assets.
3 Goodwill, to the extent that it was acquired for valuable consideration.
4 Payments on account.

II Tangible assets

1 Land and buildings.
2 Plant and machinery.
3 Other fixtures and fittings, tools and equipment.
4 Payments on account and tangible assets in course of construction.

III Financial assets

1 Shares in affiliated undertakings.
2 Loans to affiliated undertakings.
3 Participating interests.
4 Loans to undertakings with which the company is linked by virtue of participating interests.
5 Investments held as fixed assets.
6 Other loans.
7 Own shares (with an indication of their nominal value or, in the absence of a nominal value, their accounting par value) to the extent that national law permits their being shown in the balance sheet.

D Current assets

I Stock

1 Raw materials and consumables.
2 Work in progress.
3 Finished goods and goods for resale.
4 Payments on account.

II Debtors

(Amounts becoming due and payable after more than one year must be shown separately for each item.)

1 Trade debtors.
2 Amounts owed by affiliated undertakings.
3 Amounts owed by undertakings with which the company is linked by virtue of participating interests.
4 Other debtors.
5 Subscribed capital called but not paid (unless national law provides that called-up capital be shown as an asset under **A**).
6 Prepayments and accrued income (unless national law provides for such items to be shown as an asset under **E**).

III Investments
   1 Shares in affiliated undertakings.
   2 Own shares (with an indication of their nominal value or, in the absence of a nominal value, their accounting par value) to the extent that national law permits their being shown in the balance sheet.
   3 Other investments.
IV Cash at bank and in hand

E Prepayments and accrued income
(unless national law provides for such items to be shown as an asset under **D** (II) (6)).

F Loss for the financial year
(unless national law provides for it to be shown under **A** (VI) under 'Liabilities').

Liabilities

A Capital and reserves
I Subscribed capital
(unless national law provides for called-up capital to be shown under this item. In that case, the amounts of subscribed capital, and paid-up capital must be shown separately).
II Share premium account
III Revaluation reserve
IV Reserves
   1 Legal reserve, in so far as national law requires such a reserve.
   2 Reserve for own shares, in so far as national law requires such a reserve, without prejudice to Article 22 **(I)** (b) of Directive 77/91/EC.
   3 Reserves provided for by the articles of association.
   4 Other reserves.
V Profit or loss brought forward
VI Profit or loss for the financial year
(unless national law requires that this item be shown under F under 'Assets' or under **E** under 'Liabilities').

B Provisions for liabilities and charges
   1 Provisions for pensions and similar obligations.
   2 Provisions for taxation.
   3 Other provisions.

C Creditors
(Amounts becoming due and payable within one year and amounts becoming due and payable after more than one year must be shown separately for each item and for the aggregate of these items.)
   1 Debenture loans, showing convertible loans separately.
   2 Amounts owed to credit institutions.
   3 Payments received on account of orders in so far as they are not shown separately as deductions from stock.

4 Trade creditors.

5 Bills of exchange payable.

6 Amounts owed to affiliated undertakings.

7 Amounts owed to undertakings with which the company is linked by virtue of participating interests.

8 Other creditors including tax and social security.

9 Accruals and deferred income (unless national law provides for such items to be shown under **D** under 'Liabilities').

D Accruals and deferred income

(unless national law provides for such items to be shown under **C** (9) under 'Liabilities').

E Profit for the financial year

(unless national law provides for it to be shown under **A** (VI) under 'Liabilities').

Article 10

(This article prescribes an alternative layout where **A, B, C, D** and **E** under 'Assets' are the same as in Article 9, but then Creditors becoming due and payable within one year, is deducted, so that 'Total assets less current liabilities' is shown.)

Comments

The first fact we wish to emphasize is the order of the balance sheet. As we have said many times, this order is well known and practised in many European countries, for example the UK and Germany. This order, however, has not been the tradition in the Scandinavian countries, neither is it the order that companies in the US and US-inspired countries present the balance sheet.

From a user's point of view, the grouping of the asset side of the balance is fine.

Fixed assets are divided into three quite different types of assets:

- intangible assets
- tangible assets, and
- financial assets

Current assets are divided into:

- stock
- debtors
- investments, and
- cash

As we shall see in Chapter 13, these are exactly the groups we want to have for analytical purposes.

The share capital/equity and liabilities side of the balance has the heading 'Liabilities'. This can be looked upon as the entity aspect of a firm (compare with the discussion in Chapter 1).

The grouping:

- capital and reserves
- provisions for liabilities and charges, and
- creditors

is, for many users, rather alien. First of all, the second group 'provisions ...' is, up to now at least, uncommon in many countries. Some of the items included in provisions are more uncertain than 'ordinary' creditors, so the separate classification is therefore understandable. However, from an analytical point of view, there exists a danger of building up secret reserves here. This should not be the case in the development of informative financial statements.

In many countries, liabilities are grouped into long-term liabilities and short-term liabilities. In the EU model, creditors are included in both. From the text we see that the one-year horizon should be used and consequences be taken for each item. Thus the possibilities for the users is the same as if it was presented in two different groups.

Of particular interest, and importance, is the division under capital and reserves:

- subscribed capital
- share premium
- revaluation
- reserves, and
- profit and loss brought forward

Worldwide, not all companies acts or accounting acts require such specification, although for analytical purposes this is very important.

10.4 Layout of the profit and loss account

Article 22

For the presentation of the profit and loss account, the Member States shall prescribe one or more of the layouts provided for in Articles 23 to 26. If a Member State prescribes more than one layout, it may allow companies to choose from among them.

Article 23

1 Net turnover.
2 Variation in stock of finished goods and in work in progress.

3 Work performed by the undertaking for its own purposes and capitalized.
4 Other operating income.
5 (a) Raw materials and consumables.
  (b) Other external charges.
6 Staff costs:
  (a) wages and salaries;
  (b) social security costs, with a separate indication of those relating to pensions.
7 (a) Value adjustments in respect of formation expenses and of tangible and intangible fixed assets.
  (b) Value adjustments in respect of current assets, to the extent that they exceed the amount of value adjustments which are normal in the undertaking concerned.
8 Other operating charges.
9 Income from participating interests, with a separate indication of that derived from affiliated undertakings.
10 Income from other investments and loans forming part of the fixed assets, with a separate indication of that derived from affiliated undertakings.
11 Other interest receivable and similar income, with a separate indication of that derived from affiliated undertakings.
12 Value adjustments in respect of financial assets and of investments held as current assets.
13 Interest payable and similar charges, with a separate indication of those concerning affiliated undertakings.
14 Tax on profit or loss on ordinary activities.
15 Profit or loss on ordinary activities after taxation.
16 Extraordinary income.
17 Extraordinary charges.
18 Extraordinary profit or loss.
19 Tax on extraordinary profit or loss.
20 Other taxes not shown under the above items.
21 Profit or loss for the financial year.

Article 24

(This article prescribes an alternative model where the division is between **A** Charges and **B** Income, but the specification of items is the same as in Article 23.)

Article 25

1 Net turnover.
2 Cost of sales (including value adjustments).
3 Gross profit or loss.
4 Distribution costs (including value adjustments).
5 Administrative expenses (including value adjustments).
6 Other operating income.
7 Income from participating interests, with a separate indication of that derived from affiliated undertakings.
8 Income from other investments and loans forming part of the fixed assets, with a separate indication of that derived from affiliated undertakings.

9 Other interest receivable and similar income, with a separate indication of that derived from affiliated undertakings.

10 Value adjustments in respect of financial assets and of investments held as current assets.

11 Interest payable and similar charges, with a separate indication of those concerning affiliated undertakings.

12 Tax on profit or loss on ordinary activities.

13 Profit or loss on ordinary activities after taxation.

14 Extraordinary income.

15 Extraordinary charges.

16 Extraordinary profit or loss.

17 Tax on extraordinary profit or loss.

18 Other taxes not shown under the above items.

19 Profit or loss for the financial year.

Article 26

(This article prescribes an alternative model where the division is between **A** Charges and **B** Income, but the specification of items is the same as in Article 25.)

Comments

The first observation to make, as far as the profit and loss statement is concerned, is of the two main alternative layouts. As seen in Article 22, the Member State shall prescribe one or more models and it may also allow the individual company to choose.

The model presented in Article 23 is by type of expenditure, so the cost of raw material, the cost of employees etc. are shown. The model in Article 25 is by type of operation: cost of sales, distribution costs, administrative expenses.

Worldwide, both models are practised, as you will see from the six examples in Chapter 12. Seen from the user's point of view they both have pros and cons. The essential point is which model is most informative for different kinds of industries. When this is clear, companies in the same industry should keep the same model, again seen from the user's point of view.

Among the specified items in Article 23 we find 'Variation in stock of finished goods and in work in progress'. The item itself is clear enough. Such a correction is necessary in order to reach the correct cost: compare with the matching principle. But two questions must be raised:

1 Is it an item that ought to be specified?

2 Is it logical to report this change as income?

One answer to Question 1 is that the tendency in practice is not to specify the item in the profit and loss account itself, but to give the information in a note.

A starting point to Question 2 is that, although this classification is found in some countries, the dominating practice is to classify these items as a correction to the expenses. The strong argument for this is that the classification is then consistent with the measurement (cost as the valuation principle for finished goods and work in progress).

In both models we recognize that the first item where the word profit is used is 'Profit or loss on ordinary activities'. The natural step 'Operating income' is missing. Although an analyst can make such a calculation him- or herself, many countries have long experience in presenting the profit and loss account just with this first step. Generally, the grouping is weaker in the profit and loss account than in the balance sheet.

10.5 Valuation rules

Article 31

1 The Member States shall ensure that the items shown in the annual accounts are valued in accordance with the following general principles:

   (a) the company must be presumed to be carrying on its business as a going concern;
   (b) the methods of valuation must be applied consistently from one financial year to another;
   (c) valuation must be made on a prudent basis, and in particular:
      (i)   only profits made at the balance sheet date may be included,
      (ii) account must be taken of all foreseeable liabilities and potential losses arising in the course of the financial year concerned or of a previous one, even if such liabilities or losses become apparent only between the date of the balance sheet and the date on which it is drawn up,
      (iii) account must be taken of all depreciation, whether the result of the financial year is a loss or a profit;
   (d) account must be taken of income and charges relating to the financial year, irrespective of the date of receipt or payment of such income or charges;
   (e) the components of asset and liability items must be valued separately;
   (f) the opening balance sheet for each financial year must correspond to the closing balance sheet for the preceding financial year.

2 Departures from these general principles shall be permitted in exceptional cases. Any such departures must be disclosed in the notes on the accounts and the reasons for them given together with an assessment of their effect on the assets, liabilities, financial position and profit or loss.

Article 32

The items shown in the annual accounts shall be valued in accordance with Articles 34 to 42, which are based on the principle of purchase price or production cost.

Article 33

1 The Member States may declare to the Commission that they reserve the power, by way of derogation from Article 32 and pending subsequent coordination, to permit or require in respect of all companies or any classes of companies:

(a) valuation by the replacement value method for tangible fixed assets with limited useful economic lives and for stock;

(b) valuation by methods other than that provided for in (a) which are designed to take account of inflation for the items shown in annual accounts, including capital and reserves;

(c) revaluation of tangible fixed assets and financial fixed assets.

Where national law provides for valuation methods as indicated in (a), (b) and (c), it must define their content and limits and the rules for their application.

The application of any such method, the balance sheet and profit and loss account items concerned and the method by which the values shown are calculated shall be disclosed in the notes on the accounts.

2 (a) Where paragraph 1 is applied, the amount of the difference between valuation by the method used and valuation in accordance with the general rule laid down in Article 32 must be entered in the revaluation reserve under 'Liabilities'. The treatment of this item for taxation purposes must be explained either in the balance sheet or in the notes on the accounts.

For purposes of the application of the last subparagraph of paragraph 1, companies shall, whenever the amount of the reserve has been changed in the course of the financial year, publish in the notes on the accounts *inter alia* a table showing:
   - the amount of the revaluation reserve at the beginning of the financial year;
   - the revaluation differences transferred to the revaluation reserve during the financial year;
   - the amounts capitalized or otherwise transferred from the revaluation reserve during the financial year, the nature of any such transfer being disclosed;
   - the amount of the revaluation reserve at the end of the financial year.

(b) The revaluation reserve may be capitalized in whole or in part at any time.

(c) The revaluation reserve must be reduced to the extent that the amounts transferred thereto are no longer necessary for the implementation of the valuation method used and the achievement of its purpose.

The Member States may lay down rules governing the application of the revaluation reserve, provided that transfers to the profit and loss account from the revaluation reserve may be made only to the extent that the amounts transferred have been entered as charges in the profit and loss account or reflect increases in value which have been actually realized. These amounts must be disclosed separately in the profit and loss account. No part of the revaluation reserve may be distributed, either directly or indirectly, unless it represents gains actually realized.

(d) Save as provided under (b) and (c) the revaluation reserve may not be reduced.

3 Value adjustments shall be calculated each year on the basis of the value adopted for the financial year in question, save that by way of derogation from Articles 4 and 22, the Member States may permit or require that only the amount of the value adjustments arising as a result of the application of the general rule laid down in Article 32 be shown under the relevant items in the layouts prescribed in Articles 23 to 26 and that the difference arising as a result of the valuation method adopted under this Article be shown separately in the layouts. Furthermore, Articles 34 to 42 shall apply *mutatis mutandis*.

4 Where paragraph 1 is applied, the following must be disclosed, either in the balance sheet or in the notes on the accounts, separately for each balance sheet item as provided for in the layouts prescribed in Articles 9 and 10, except for stock, either:
(a) the amount at the balance sheet date of the valuation made in accordance with the general rule laid down in Article 32 and the amount of the cumulative value adjustments; or
(b) the amount at the balance sheet date of the difference between the valuation made in accordance with this Article and that resulting from the application of Article 32 and, where appropriate, the cumulative amount of the additional value adjustments.

5 Without prejudice to Article 52 the Council shall, on a proposal from the Commission and within seven years of the notification of this Directive, examine and, where necessary, amend this Article in the light of economic and monetary trends in the Community.

Article 34

1 (a) Where national law authorizes the inclusion of formation expenses under 'Assets', they must be written off within a maximum period of five years.
(b) In so far as formation expenses have not been completely written off, no distribution of profits shall take place unless the amount of the reserves available for distribution and profits brought forward is at least equal to that of the expenses not written off.

2 The amounts entered under 'Formation expenses' must be explained in the notes on the accounts.

Article 35

1 (a) Fixed assets must be valued at purchase price or production cost, without prejudice to (b) and (c) below.
(b) The purchase price or production cost of fixed assets with limited useful economic lives must be reduced by value adjustments calculated to write off the value of such assets systematically over their useful economic lives.
(c) (i) Value adjustments may be made in respect of financial fixed assets, so that they are valued at the lower figure to be attributed to them at the balance sheet date.
(ii) Value adjustments must be made in respect of fixed assets, whether their useful economic lives are limited or not, so that they are valued at the lower figure to be attributed to them at the balance sheet date if it is expected that the reduction in their value will be permanent.

          (iii) The value adjustments referred to in (i) and (ii) must be charged to the profit and loss account and disclosed separately in the notes on the accounts if they have not been shown separately in the profit and loss account.

          (iv) Valuation at the lower of the values provided for in (i) and (ii) may not be continued if the reasons for which the value adjustments were made have ceased to apply.

    (d) If fixed assets are the subject of exceptional value adjustments for taxation purposes alone, the amount of the adjustments and the reasons for making them shall be indicated in the notes on the accounts.

2 The purchase price shall be calculated by adding to the price paid the expenses incidental thereto.

3 (a) The production cost shall be calculated by adding to the purchasing price of the raw materials and consumables the costs directly attributable to the product in question.

    (b) A reasonable proportion of the costs which are only indirectly attributable to the product in question may be added into the production costs to the extent that they relate to the period of production.

4 Interest on capital borrowed to finance the production of fixed assets may be included in the production costs to the extent that it relates to the period of production. In that event, the inclusion of such interest under 'Assets' must be disclosed in the notes on the accounts.

Article 36

By way of derogation from Article 35 (1) (c) (iii), the Member States may allow investment companies within the meaning of Article 5 (2) to set off value adjustments to investments directly against 'Capital and reserves'. The amounts in question must be shown separately under 'Liabilities' in the balance sheet.

Article 37

1 Article 34 shall apply to costs of research and development. In exceptional cases, however, the Member States may permit derogations from Article 34 (1) (a). In that case, they may also provide for derogations from Article 34 (1) (b). Such derogations and the reasons for them must be disclosed in the notes on the accounts.

2 Article 34 (1) (a) shall apply to goodwill. The Member States may, however, permit companies to write goodwill off systematically over a limited period exceeding five years provided that this period does not exceed the useful economic life of the asset and is disclosed in the notes on the accounts together with the supporting reasons therefore.

Article 38

Tangible fixed assets, raw materials and consumables which are constantly being replaced and the overall value of which is of secondary importance to the undertaking may be shown under 'Assets' at a fixed quantity and value, if the quantity, value and composition thereof do not vary materially.

Article 39

1 (a) Current assets must be valued at purchase price or production cost, without prejudice to (b) and (c) below.

   (b) Value adjustments shall be made in respect of current assets with a view to showing them at the lower market value, or in particular circumstances, another lower value to be attributed to them at the balance sheet date.

   (c) The Member States may permit exceptional value adjustments where, on the basis of a reasonable commercial assessment, these are necessary if the valuation of these items is not to be modified in the near future because of fluctuations in value. The amount of these value adjustments must be disclosed separately in the profit and loss account or in the notes on the accounts.

   (d) Valuation at the lower value provided for in (b) and (c) may not be continued if the reasons for which the value adjustments were made have ceased to apply.

   (e) If current assets are the subject of exceptional value adjustments for taxation purposes alone, the amount of the adjustments and the reasons for making them must be disclosed in the notes on the accounts.

2 The definitions of purchase price and of production cost given in Article 35 (2) and (3) shall apply. The Member States may also apply Article 35 (4). Distribution costs may not be included in production costs.

Article 40

1 The Member States may permit the purchase price or production cost of stock of goods of the same category and all fungible items including investments to be calculated either on the basis of weighted average prices or by the 'first-in, first-out' (FIFO) method, the 'last in, first out' (LIFO) method, or some similar method.

2 Where the value shown in the balance sheet, following application of the methods of calculation specified in paragraph 1, differs materially, at the balance sheet date, from the value on the basis of the last known market value prior to the balance sheet date, the amount of that difference must be disclosed in total by category in the notes on the accounts.

Article 41

1 Where the amount repayable on account of any debt is greater than the amount received, the difference may be shown as an asset. It must be shown separately in the balance sheet or in the notes on the accounts.

2 The amount of this difference must be written off by a reasonable amount each year and completely written off no later than the time of repayment of the debt.

Article 42

Provisions for liabilities and charges may not exceed in amount the sums which are necessary.

The provisions shown in the balance sheet under 'Other provisions' must be disclosed in the notes on the accounts if they are material.

Comments

The valuation rules are very important to study for two main reasons.

- The measurement of the different items presented in the financial statements fully depends on the valuation rules used.
- The variation in the valuation rules is very important, when we compare financial statements between countries. The Directive sets the frame, but in many cases each individual Member State can make a choice and set a narrower frame. Therefore, it is important to know about the variation possibilities.

In *Article 31* many of the general accounting principles are stated:

- the going-concern principle (a);
- the principle of consistency (b);
- the prudence principle (c); here, we notice, almost as a curiosity, that (iii) emphasizes that depreciation is essential, even if the result of the year is a profit or a loss;
- the accrual principle (d).

In *Article 32* the fundamental principle of financial accounting, namely the historical cost principle, is given.

Article 33 considers a basis other than historical cost, full or partial. Here we find detailed rules for how value adjustments should be treated. The most important issue is that a revaluation is defined as a capital adjustment, never as a profit.

Article 34 sets a limit of five years for writing off formation expenses.

Article 35 covers the valuation rules for fixed assets. Here we find a mixture of 'must', 'shall' and 'may be'. It is important to be aware of this when using financial statements. The 'musts' and 'shalls' are:

- a systematic write-off of fixed assets with limited useful economic life (1(b));
- a write-down of fixed assets if the reduction in value is expected to be permanent (1(c)(ii)). Such a write down is a cost (1(c)(iii));
- if an adjustment of fixed assets is for taxation purposes only, the reason for it and the amount of the adjustment shall be given in the notes (1(d));
- the production cost shall include direct and indirect (fixed) costs (3(a) and (b));

The 'mays' are:

- the lower valuation under (1(c)(ii)) is not necessary if the situation has changed (1(c)(iv));
- interest on capital borrowed to finance the production of fixed assets (4).

Article 37 says that research and development costs shall normally be written off within a maximum period of five years. For goodwill, the normal period for write off is also five years.

Article 39 covers the general valuation rules for current assets. Notice the 'shall' rule of lower of cost and market (1(b)). Also that information must be disclosed in the notes if current assets are valued lower for tax purposes (1(e)).

Article 40 regulates the valuation of stock, open for almost every alternative stock-flow assumption: weighted average, FIFO, LIFO or 'some similar method'. It is up to the Member States, eventually, to set limitations on these alternatives.

10.6 The notes on the accounts

As we have mentioned before, the notes are an integral part of the financial statements. The following 13 pieces of information are required to be given in the notes.

1 The valuation method applied to the various items in the annual accounts, and the methods employed in calculating the value adjustments. For items originally expressed in foreign currency, the basis of conversion used must be disclosed.

2 The name of each of the undertakings in which the company holds more than 20 per cent. The proportion of the capital held, the amount of capital and reserves, and the profit or loss.

3 The number and the nominal value of the shares subscribed during the financial year.

4 The number and the nominal value for each class of shares if there is more than one class of shares.

5 Any participation certificates, convertible debentures or similar securities or rights.

6 Amounts owed by the company becoming due and payable after more than five years as well as the company's entire debts covered by valuable security furnished by the company.

7 The total amount of any financial commitments not included in the balance sheet. Commitments concerning pensions and affiliated undertakings must be disclosed separately.

8 Net turnover broken down by categories of activity and into geographical markets.

9 The average number of persons employed during the financial year. Staff costs if not disclosed separately in the profit and loss account.

10 The effect of the profit or loss for the financial year caused by a valuation different from the rules laid down in the Articles, due to tax rules. The influence of such a valuation or future tax charge.

11 The cumulative amount of the difference between tax charged for the financial year payable of those years. This amount may also be disclosed directly in the balance sheet under a separate item.

12 The amount of the emoluments granted in the financial year to the members of the administrative, managerial and supervisory bodies. Any commitments arising or entered into for retirement pensions for former members of those bodies.

13 The amount of advances and credits granted to the members of the administrative, managerial and supervisory bodies, with indications of the interest rates and main conditions. Commitments entered into on their behalf by way of guarantees of any kind.

11 International harmonization

'The market is the driving force in harmonizing financial statements and reporting between countries.'

Top manager at Arthur Andersen & Co.

LEARNING OBJECTIVES

One effect of the EU directives is the harmonization of financial reporting and disclosure that takes place between the EU countries. In this chapter we will take a broader view on the subject of international harmonization of accounting.

After studying this chapter you will:

- understand better the international diversity in financial accounting and reporting practices;
- have studied different ways of grouping countries in order to understand the factors causing differences;
- have reflected on other factors involved in the harmonization drive, directly or indirectly, especially the effects of:
  - the EU directives;
  - the International Accounting Standards Committee (IASC);
  - the Financial Accounting Standards Board (FASB).

11.1 The need for harmonization

Fédération des Experts Comptables Européens (FEE) has defined harmonization in this way:

The process of increasing the consistency and comparability of accounts in order to remove the barriers to the international movement of capital and exchange of information by reducing the differences in accounting and company law. It is not necessary to remove all differences, but only those needed to achieve the above.

Many research reports, investigations and illustrations during the last few decades show significant differences in accounting practices between countries. The following three examples illustrate this:

- Simmonds and Azières (*Accounting in Europe*, Touche Ross, 1989) assembled a single set of accounting data and the accounts were prepared in seven European countries. The profit for the year was as follows:

	ECU m
Spain	131
Germany	133
Belgium	135
Netherlands	140
France	149
Italy	174
UK	192

This produces a difference of nearly 50 per cent between the lowest profit (Spain) and the highest (UK) on the same set of accounting data.

- During the negotiations between SAS, KLM, Swissair and Austrian Airlines in 1993, differing depreciation policies between the airlines came to light. While SAS uses an increasing method of depreciation (2 per cent the first year, 2.33 per cent the second year, 2.66 per cent the third year and so on), KLM uses linear depreciation of 6.7 per cent, while Swissair uses linear depreciation of 8.3 per cent (a time horizon of 12 years, scrap value 10 per cent). The difference in depreciation policies on the same type of aeroplanes led to big differences in the profit between the companies. If SAS, for example, had used the KLM depreciation policy, its profit for 1992 would have been SEK 600m lower than reported.

- The biggest listed company in Norway, Norsk Hydro, reports its accounting figures according to both US GAAP and Norwegian GAAP (N GAAP). For the three years (1991–3) the following differences are reported:

Net income

US GAAP (NOK m)	N GAAP (NOK m)
2996	3406
1763	167
(498)	(675)

A range of factors can be identified to help explain the differences in accounting practice between countries. Blake and Amat (*European Accounting*, Pitman Publishing, 1993) list the following 11 factors that determine national practices, which we have illustrated with examples.

The influence of leading theorists and professional bodies

Examples: Theodore Limperg's 'business economics' approach to accounting (replacement cost system) in the Netherlands (1921); Marti Saario in Finland involving a particular focus on cash flows/depreciation (1945); Edwards and Bell's 'business profit' view in the US (1961).

Economic consequences

Example: Lobbying by a range of interested parties in order to obtain the most favourable outcome.

Economic environment

Example: A high level of inflation may lead to the development of an inflation-accounting system.

Taxation

Examples: The German 'Massblichkeitsprinzip' (principle of bindingness) underlining the legal requirement that the accounts shall be prepared in accordance with the tax law; the US acceptance of the LIFO principle, given that this valuation principle is also used in the financial statements.

Nationalism

Everyone believes, more or less, that their own country's system is the best, and is unwilling to change.

Users and objectives

Different objectives and different user groups in different countries.

Example: Equity investors as the main user group in the US and UK, banks in Germany and other continental countries.

Legal context

Countries with a common law tradition, such as the UK, legislate on broad principles of accounting rules rather than detailed requirements. Countries with a Roman law tradition, such as Germany, have accounting rules and require detailed disclosures.

Sources of finance

A company raising finance from the general public through the stock market might be expected to give higher accounting information than raising capital by private arrangements.

Examples: Many research reports confirm this fact: Singhvi and Desai (*Accounting Review*, 1971) found that the listed companies provided higher levels of disclosure for US companies; Firth (*Accounting and Business Research*, Autumn 1979) found the same for UK companies; and Cooke (*Accounting and Business Research*, Spring 1989) found that Swedish companies listed on the world's stock exchanges showed higher quality of disclosure than those listed only in Stockholm.

Language

Confusion can sometimes arise where regulations are translated into different languages.

Example: 'True and fair view.'

Other country influences

One country may allow accounting practices to be influenced by another country or group of countries.

Examples: Membership of the British Commonwealth has exposed a number of countries to UK accounting influence, and the effect of the EU directives, even outside the EU.

Scandal or crisis

Accounting regulations may emerge in response to a scandal or crisis.

Examples: The requirement of auditing financial statements after bankruptcy in the UK at the end of the 19th century, the foundation of SEC in the US, the Krüger crash in Sweden in 1932 leading to stronger accounting law regulations.

Various researchers have attempted to provide some classifications that can explain some of the accounting diversity in the world. Mueller, a pioneer and still a leading researcher in this field, identifies four elements of differentiation ('Accounting principles generally accepted in the United States versus those generally accepted elsewhere', *International Journal of Accounting*, Spring 1968):

- state of economic development (developed/developing countries);
- state of business complexity (variations in technological and industrial know-how);
- shade of political persuasion (centrally controlled/market oriented);
- reliance on some particular system of law (common-law/code-law system).

In a more recent publication (1991), Mueller provides the following classification:

1 A British–North American–Dutch model with an orientation towards the needs of investors and creditors.

2 A continental model used in continental Europe and Japan, with an orientation towards meeting government-imposed economic, tax or legal restrictions.

3 A South American model with the major focus on accounting for inflation.

4 Various emerging models focusing on theoretical compliance and an international standards model focusing on compliance with accepted international financial accounting standards.

Nobes, another leading researcher in this field, bases his classification of developed Western countries on the general differentiation of micro-based versus macro-uniform as a class, and the importance of the influence of law or economics as a sub-class. This classification is illustrated in Fig. 11.1.

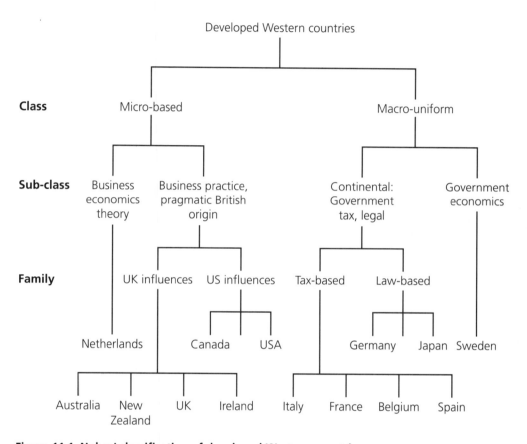

Figure 11.1 Nobes' classification of developed Western countries

Source: Nobes, C., *Interpreting European Financial Standards: Towards 1992* (London: Butterworths, 1989)

In his most recent publication (*A Study of the International Standards Committee*, Coopers & Lybrand, 1994), Nobes makes a very interesting and concrete two-group classification, as shown in Table 11.1 (overleaf).

Table 11.1 Nobes' classification of accounting methods

Type A	Type B
Background	
English law Large, old, strong profession Large stock exchange	Roman law Smaller, younger, weaker profession Smaller stock exchange
General accounting features	
Fair Shareholder-orientation Disclosure Tax rules separate Substance over form Professional standards	Legal Creditor-orientation Secrecy Tax dominated Form over substance Government rules
Specific accounting features	
Percentage of completion method Depreciation over useful lives No legal reserves Finance leases capitalized Cash or funds statements Earnings per share disclosed No secret reserves Few tax-induced provisions Preliminary expenses expensed Taking gains on unsettled foreign currency monetary items	Completed contract method Depreciation by tax rules Legal reserves No leases capitalized No cash or funds statements No earnings per share disclosure Secret reserves Tax-induced provisions Preliminary expenses capitalizable Deferring gains on unsettled foreign currency monetary items
Some examples of countries	
United Kingdom Ireland United States Canada Australia New Zealand Hong Kong Singapore Denmark The Netherlands	France Germany Austria Switzerland Spain Italy Portugal Japan Belgium Greece

Source: Nobes, C., *A Study of the International Standards Committee* (Coopers & Lybrand, 1994)

11.2 The effect of the EU directives

The introductory text of the Fourth Directive specifies, among others, the following important dimensions.

- Coordination of national provisions concerning the presentation and content of annual accounts and annual reports, the valuation methods used and their publication is of special importance for the protection of members and third parties.
- Coordination is necessary in these fields because activities frequently extend beyond national frontiers.

The practical and most important way to fulfil these provisions is to follow these guidelines:

- a minimum equivalent legal requirement of the financial information that should be made available to the public by companies competing with one another;
- a mandatory layout for the balance sheet and the profit and loss account and a minimum content of the notes to the accounts must be laid down;
- coordination of the different methods for the valuation of assets and liabilities.

The differences in financial reporting within the EU have been so great that it has been almost impossible to compare accounts from different European countries without making significant adjustments. There are still differences, but the EU directives have undoubtedly reduced these.

There is, however, a much more far-reaching effect of the provisions contained in the directives, namely the use of these regulations outside the EU. First of all, countries having signed the EEA (European Economic Area) agreement will also have to apply the directives. Also, many of the former Eastern Bloc countries have applied or will apply the directives. So, we shall see the EU directives practised in almost every country in Europe in the near future.

11.3 International Accounting Standards Committee

Another important contribution in the area of harmonization is made by the International Accounting Standards Committee (IASC) and the standards produced by this organization. Active in harmonizing financial reporting, the IASC was founded in 1973 with the following objectives.

1 To formulate and publish in the public interest accounting standards to be observed in the presentation of financial statements and to promote their worldwide acceptance and observance.

2 To work generally for the improvement and harmonization of regulations, accounting standards and procedures relating to the presentation of financial statements.

More than 100 professional bodies from over 80 countries are now members of the IASC. They aim to persuade national standard setters to issue standards in accordance with International Accounting Standards (IAS).

IASC published in 1989, *Framework for the preparation and presentation of financial statements*. This led to the revision of many standards and in particular had the effect of removing as many options as possible. This means a tighter set of standards.

By the end of 1997 the following International Accounting Standards (IAS) had been published:

IAS	1	Disclosure of accounting policies
IAS	2	Inventories
IAS	3	Replaced by IAS 27
IAS	4	Depreciation accounting
IAS	5	Information to be disclosed in financial statements
IAS	6	Replaced by IAS 15
IAS	7	Cash flow statements
IAS	8	Net profit and loss for the period, fundamental errors and changes in accounting policies
IAS	9	Research and development costs
IAS	10	Contingencies and events occurring after the balance sheet date
IAS	11	Construction contracts
IAS	12	Taxes on income
IAS	13	Presentation of current assets and current liabilities
IAS	14	Reporting financial information by segments
IAS	15	Reflecting effects of changing prices (non-mandatory from 1989)
IAS	16	Property, plant and equipment
IAS	17	Accounting for leases
IAS	18	Revenue
IAS	19	Retirement benefit costs
IAS	20	Government grants and disclosure of government assistance
IAS	21	The effects of changes in foreign exchange rates
IAS	22	Business combinations
IAS	23	Borrowing costs
IAS	24	Related party disclosure
IAS	25	Accounting for investments

IAS 26 Accounting and reporting by retirement benefit plans
IAS 27 Consolidated financial statements and accounting for investments in subsidiaries
IAS 28 Accounting for investments in associates
IAS 29 Financial reporting in hyperinflationary economies
IAS 30 Disclosure in the financial statements of banks
IAS 31 Financial reporting of interests in joint ventures
IAS 32 Financial instruments/off-balance-sheet items
IAS 33 Earnings per share

By the end of 1997 the following Exposure Drafts had been issued:

- the IASC framework, the preface to the statement of International Accounting Standards;
- financial instruments;
- intangible assets;
- segment reporting;
- employee benefits.

11.4 Financial Accounting Standards Board

The Financial Accounting Standards Board (FASB) is the standard setter in the US. Statements from FASB immediately become part of the Generally Accepted Accounting Principles (GAAP). This makes FASB the most important organization within the US and US-inspired countries, and also outside those countries, as the US is the leading country in financial accounting literature and financial accounting standard setting. The New York Stock Exchange has to meet the standards set by FASB.

FASB is a non-governmental body with seven full-time members. Most of the members of the Board are auditors; others are from the business world, academia and government service.

FASB was established in 1973; prior to this accounting standards in the US were set by the Accounting Principles Board, a committee of the American Institute of Certified Public Accountants.

The process of developing a new statement of Financial Accounting Standards is as follows. First a Discussion Memorandum on a relevant subject is issued for public comment. Public accountants, representatives from industries, academics, regulators and financial statement users are invited to comment on it.

An Exposure Draft for public comment is then produced. The Securities and Exchange Commission (SEC) is involved.

FASB realized very early in its standard-setting work that creating a conceptual framework was important. Consequently, it has issued six concept standards, or Statements of Financial Accounting Concept (SFACs). SFAC 1, *Objectives of Financial Reporting by Business Enterprises*, focuses on investment decisions:

> Financial reporting shall provide information that is useful to present and potential investors and creditors and other users in making rational investments, credit, and similar decisions. The information should be comprehensible to those who have a reasonable understanding of business and economic activities and are willing to study the information with reasonable diligence.

SFAC 2 is concerned with the quality of accounting information. From an analyst's point of view, relevance and reliability are key characteristics. We give, therefore, definitions of these two dimensions:

> Relevance: the capacity of information to make a difference in a decision.
>
> Reliability: includes verifiability, representational faithfulness and neutrality. The first two elements are connected with whether financial data have been measured accurately and they are what they purport to be. Data without these characteristics cannot be relied upon in making investment decisions.

Unfortunately, relevance and reliability tend to be opposing qualities, and they are also often in conflict with each other. The best example is market value data: highly relevant, but reliable only to a limited extent.

From 1973 to the end of 1997, FASB issued almost 130 statements (some of which amend or replace earlier statements) covering a range of subjects, as will be seen from the following list:

No.
1 Disclosure of Foreign Currency Translation Information
2 Accounting for Research and Development Costs
3 Reporting Accounting Changes in Interim Financial Statements
4 Reporting Gains and Losses from Extinguishment of Debt
5 Accounting for Contingencies

11.5 Example of harmonization – GAAP comparison

We conclude this chapter by presenting the explanatory note regarding the US GAAP and Norwegian GAAP given by Norsk Hydro in its annual report.

Norsk Hydro ASA and subsidiaries
Notes to the consolidated financial statements

**27. SUMMARY OF DIFFERENCES IN ACCOUNTING POLICIES
AND RECONCILIATION OF US GAAP TO N GAAP**

The financial statements prepared in accordance with accounting principles generally accepted in Norway presented on pages 49 to 51, differ in certain respects from US GAAP. A reconciliation of net income and shareholders' equity from US GAAP to Norwegian principles (N GAAP) and a description of these differences follow. The lines with a note reference reflect the variance between the US GAAP balance in that note and the N GAAP balance.

Reconciliation of US GAAP to N GAAP:

Net income

Amounts in NOK million	Notes	1996	1995	1994
Operating income US GAAP		**9,653**	**10,704**	**7,152**
Adjustments for N GAAP:				
Raw materials – Capitalized costs (a)		(538)	(90)	(294)
Depreciation (a) (b) (c)	4, 15	873	822	794
Other operating costs (e)		114	(7)	75
Provision for impairment and losses (a) (c)	5	178	–	–
Operating income – N GAAP		**10,280**	11,429	7,727
Equity in net income of non-consolidated investees		**630**	**744**	**605**
Financial income (expense) US GAAP		**(219)**	**(442)**	**(1,254)**
Adjustments for N GAAP:				
Capitalized interest (c)	7, 15	(545)	(594)	(477)
Foreign exchange gains (d)	7	(87)	(185)	186
Unrealized holding (gain) loss on securities (f)	7	(209)	(90)	160
Other income (expense), net		**213**	**83**	**–**
Extraordinary expense – N GAAP	1	–	(24)	(90)
Income before taxes and minority interest – N GAAP		**10,063**	10,921	6,857
Current income tax expense		**(4,153)**	**(3,096)**	**(1,583)**
Deferred tax income (expense) US GAAP		**100**	**(765)**	**(943)**
Adjusted to N GAAP deferred tax (g)	9	19	147	(128)
Minority interest		**(20)**	**(78)**	**(68)**
Cumulative effect of accounting change		**–**	**(17)**	**127**
Adjusted to N GAAP	1	–	17	(127)
Net income – N GAAP		**6,009**	7,129	4,135

Shareholders' equity

Amounts in NOK million	Notes	1996	1995	1994
Shareholders' equity for US GAAP		**41,547**	**37,154**	**30,866**
Other liquid assets (f)	10	**(405)**	(200)	(110)
Prepaid expenses and other current assets		**(378)**	(230)	100
Investments (f)	12	**(902)**	(883)	(562)
Property, plant and equipment - Capitalized costs (a) (b) (c)	15	**(7,587)**	(7,927)	(8,023)
Dividends payable (b)		**(1,604)**	(1,374)	(974)
Unrealized gains – current and long-term (d) (e)		**(731)**	(568)	(751)
Deferred tax assets and liabilities – current and long-term (g)	9	**6,544**	6,560	6,328
Shareholders' equity for N GAAP		**36,484**	32,532	26,874

155

Norsk Hydro ASA and subsidiaries
Notes to the consolidated financial statements

**EXPLANATION OF MAJOR DIFFERENCES
BETWEEN N GAAP AND US GAAP**

(a) Exploration drilling costs: *Under N GAAP, all explor-ation costs are expensed as incurred.* Under US GAAP, exploration drilling costs are capitalized, provided drilling results in proved reserves, and are amortized as depletion expense when production begins.

(b) Environmental costs: *Under N GAAP, environmental related expenditures were expensed as incurred prior to 1992.* Under US GAAP, environmental related expenditures which increase the life or improve the safety of a facility are capitalized and amortized through depreciation expense. *Beginning in 1992, environmental costs for N GAAP are recorded consistently with US GAAP and the difference represents the amortization of previous years' capitalized costs for US GAAP.*

(c) Capitalized interest: *All interest is expensed as incurred for N GAAP.* Under US GAAP, interest is capitalized for major constructed assets and amortized as part of depreciation expense.

(d) Unrealized exchange gains: *Under N GAAP, unrealized exchange gains on foreign currency assets, liabilities and financial instruments are deferred as current or long-term liabilities. Unrealized gains on non-current assets and long-term liabilities are deferred only to the extent they exceed unrealized losses in the same currency.* All unrealized exchange gains are recognized as financial income for US GAAP. *Unrealized exchange losses are expensed for both N GAAP and US GAAP.*

(e) Commodity contracts: *Under N GAAP, unrealized gains and losses for speculative commodity futures and options contracts are netted for each portfolio and net unrealized gains are deferred as other short-term liabilities.* For US GAAP, gains and losses on speculative contracts are recorded to operating revenue or cost as appropriate, when incurred.

(f) Unrealized holding gain (loss) on securities: *Under N GAAP, Hydro's portfolios of marketable equity and debt securities are carried at the lower of aggregate historical cost or market value.* Under US GAAP, securities are carried at fair value (market) and unrealized holding gains or losses are included in financial income and expense for trading securities and in a separate component of equity, net of tax effects, for available-for-sale securities.

(g) Deferred taxes: *Under N GAAP, deferred taxes are recorded based upon the liability method similar to US GAAP.* Differences occur primarily because items accounted for differently under US GAAP (capitalized exploration drilling costs, capitalized interest, unrealized exchange gains, etc.) also have deferred tax effects. *N GAAP also has more stringent criteria for recognizing deferred tax assets.*

Under N GAAP, offsetting deferred tax assets and liabilities for each tax entity are netted and classified as a long-term liability. Under N GAAP, long-term tax assets relate principally to unfunded pension plans and post retirement benefits. A reconciliation of the current and long-term temporary differences giving rise to the N GAAP deferred tax asset and liability is provided in Note 9. Classification between current and long-term for US GAAP is determined by the classification of the related asset or liability giving rise to the temporary difference. For each tax entity, deferred tax assets and liabilities are offset within the respective current or long-term groups and presented as a single amount. Netting between companies belonging to different tax entities is not allowed.

(h) Dividends payable: *For N GAAP, dividends proposed at the end of the year which will be declared and paid in the following year are recorded as a reduction to equity and as debt.* For US GAAP, equity is reduced when dividends are declared.

12 Six examples of financial reporting

'The annual report is our most important document.'

Norwegian manager

LEARNING OBJECTIVES

The objective of this chapter is to give you practice in the analysis of financial statements. In this chapter you will find six examples of financial statements from the following companies to analyse and comment upon:

- *Marks & Spencer (UK)* The famous department store with over 600 stores worldwide;
- *Volkswagen (Germany)* The world's fourth largest passenger car manufacturer and – in terms of vehicle sales – the market leader both in Germany and in Europe as a whole;
- *Danisco (Denmark)* The largest Danish producer and supplier of products, ingredients and packaging to the international food industry;
- *Volvo (Sweden)* The largest industrial group in the Nordic region, engaged in a broad range of activities in the transport vehicle field. Also known for having one of the most informative annual reports in the world;
- *Bergesen (Norway)* One of the world's largest owners and operators of large tankers and LPG carriers;
- *Coca-Cola (USA)* 'Creating value by refreshing 5.6 billion people.'

All these are listed companies. They are focused on by analysts and professional users of financial statements. The annual reports from these companies are sizable publications: Marks & Spencer, 72 pages; Volkswagen, 79 pages; Danisco, 75 pages; Volvo, 79 pages; Bergesen, 54 pages; and Coca-Cola, 79 pages.

Marks & Spencer – financial statements

Consolidated profit and loss account

FOR THE YEAR ENDED 31 MARCH 1997

	Notes	1997 £m	1996 £m
TURNOVER			
Continuing operations		**7,841.9**	7,211.3
Discontinued operations		**–**	22.4
	2, 3	**7,841.9**	7,233.7
Cost of sales	3	**(5,103.8)**	(4,720.5)
GROSS PROFIT		**2,738.1**	2,513.2
Other expenses	3	**(1,700.2)**	(1,575.8)
OPERATING PROFIT	2, 3	**1,037.9**	937.4
analysed between:			
Continuing operations		**1,037.9**	939.6
Discontinued operations		**–**	(2.2)
Disposal of discontinued operations:			
Loss on disposal		**–**	(15.0)
Goodwill previously written off to reserves		**–**	(10.0)
	4	**–**	(25.0)
Loss on sale of property and other fixed assets		**(1.8)**	(4.2)
Net interest income	5	**65.9**	57.6
PROFIT ON ORDINARY ACTIVITIES BEFORE TAXATION	2	**1,102.0**	965.8
analysed between:			
Continuing operations		**1,102.0**	993.7
Discontinued operations		**–**	(27.9)
Taxation on ordinary activities	6	**(346.1)**	(312.0)
PROFIT ON ORDINARY ACTIVITIES AFTER TAXATION		**755.9**	653.8
Minority interests (all equity)		**(1.3)**	(1.2)
PROFIT ATTRIBUTABLE TO SHAREHOLDERS	7	**754.6**	652.6
Dividends	8	**(368.6)**	(320.9)
UNDISTRIBUTED SURPLUS FOR THE YEAR	22	**386.0**	331.7
EARNINGS PER SHARE (Defined by FRS3)	9	**26.7p**	23.3p
HEADLINE EARNINGS PER SHARE (Defined by IIMR)	9	**26.8p**	24.3p

Consolidated statement of total recognised gains and losses

FOR THE YEAR ENDED 31 MARCH 1997

	Notes	1997 £m	1996 £m
PROFIT ATTRIBUTABLE TO SHAREHOLDERS		**754.6**	652.6
Exchange differences on foreign currency translation	22	**(54.3)**	4.0
Unrealised surpluses on revaluation	22	**10.0**	–
TOTAL RECOGNISED GAINS AND LOSSES RELATING TO THE YEAR		**710.3**	656.6

Balance sheets

AT 31 MARCH 1997

	Notes	THE GROUP 1997 £m	THE GROUP 1996 £m	THE COMPANY 1997 £m	THE COMPANY 1996 £m
FIXED ASSETS					
Tangible assets:					
Land and buildings		**3,056.7**	2,846.2	**2,736.6**	2,540.3
Fixtures, fittings and equipment		**500.1**	531.8	**364.5**	386.0
Assets in the course of construction		**53.1**	50.4	**26.5**	26.4
	12	**3,609.9**	3,428.4	**3,127.6**	2,952.7
Investments	13	**36.6**	46.0	**371.6**	369.3
		3,646.5	3,474.4	**3,499.2**	3,322.0
CURRENT ASSETS					
Stocks		**445.1**	422.8	**310.6**	292.7
Debtors:					
Receivable within one year	14	**819.2**	687.3	**1,456.4**	1,392.5
Receivable after more than one year	14	**906.6**	682.9	**167.4**	131.7
Investments	15	**361.8**	300.0	**–**	–
Cash at bank and in hand	16	**671.5**	782.5	**87.8**	66.2
		3,204.2	2,875.5	**2,022.2**	1,883.1
CURRENT LIABILITIES					
Creditors: amounts falling due within one year	17	**1,775.1**	1,674.9	**1,124.0**	1,160.0
NET CURRENT ASSETS		**1,429.1**	1,200.6	**898.2**	723.1
TOTAL ASSETS LESS CURRENT LIABILITIES		**5,075.6**	4,675.0	**4,397.4**	4,045.1
Creditors: amounts falling due after more than one year	18	**495.8**	497.8	**150.0**	150.0
Provisions for liabilities and charges	19	**31.8**	35.0	**27.9**	27.9
NET ASSETS		**4,548.0**	4,142.2	**4,219.5**	3,867.2
CAPITAL AND RESERVES					
Called up share capital	21	**709.2**	703.9	**709.2**	703.9
Share premium account		**259.8**	221.4	**259.8**	221.4
Revaluation reserve		**456.3**	449.8	**461.9**	458.4
Profit and loss account		**3,104.0**	2,744.5	**2,788.6**	2,483.5
SHAREHOLDERS' FUNDS (all equity)	22	**4,529.3**	4,119.6	**4,219.5**	3,867.2
Minority interests (all equity)		**18.7**	22.6	**–**	–
TOTAL CAPITAL EMPLOYED		**4,548.0**	4,142.2	**4,219.5**	3,867.2

Approved by the Board
19 May 1997

Sir Richard Greenbury, Chairman
J K Oates, Deputy Chairman and Joint Managing Director

Consolidated cash flow information

FOR THE YEAR ENDED 31 MARCH 1997

CASH FLOW STATEMENT

	Notes	1997 £m	1997 £m	1996 £m	1996 £m
OPERATING ACTIVITIES					
Received from customers		7,509.5		7,045.2	
Payments to suppliers		(5,109.8)		(4,737.5)	
Payments to and on behalf of employees		(909.4)		(929.0)	
Other payments		(593.2)		(580.3)	
CASH INFLOW FROM OPERATING ACTIVITIES	25		897.1		798.4
RETURNS ON INVESTMENTS AND SERVICING OF FINANCE	26A		65.4		55.7
TAXATION	26B		(318.6)		(296.8)
CAPITAL EXPENDITURE AND FINANCIAL INVESTMENT	26C		(413.1)		(319.4)
ACQUISITIONS AND DISPOSALS	26D		(0.2)		(4.9)
EQUITY DIVIDENDS PAID			(305.6)		(271.3)
Cash outflow before management of liquid resources and financing			(75.0)		(38.3)
MANAGEMENT OF LIQUID RESOURCES AND FINANCING					
Management of liquid resources	26E	91.3		(127.7)	
Financing	26F	64.7		113.5	
			156.0		(14.2)
INCREASE/(DECREASE) IN CASH			81.0		(52.5)

RECONCILIATION OF NET CASH FLOW TO MOVEMENT IN NET FUNDS (see note 27)

	1997 £m	1996 £m
INCREASE/(DECREASE) IN CASH	81.0	(52.5)
Cash (inflow)/outflow from (decrease)/increase in liquid resources	(91.3)	127.7
Cash inflow from increase in debt financing	(21.0)	(77.3)
Exchange movements	(4.2)	(2.2)
MOVEMENT IN NET FUNDS	(35.5)	(4.3)
Net funds at 1 April	97.0	101.3
NET FUNDS AT 31 MARCH	61.5	97.0

The cash flow information shown above is presented in accordance with the revised version of FRS1 'Cash flow statements'.

The comparative figures have been restated (see note 24).

Accounting policies

The financial statements are prepared in accordance with applicable accounting standards in the United Kingdom. A summary of the more important Group accounting policies, which are applied consistently, is given below.

BASIS OF ACCOUNTING
The financial statements are drawn up on the historical cost basis of accounting, modified to include the valuation of certain United Kingdom properties at 31 March 1988 and the valuation of investment properties. Compliance with SSAP19 'Accounting for investment properties' requires a departure from the requirements of the Companies Act 1985 relating to the depreciation of investment properties as explained below.

BASIS OF CONSOLIDATION
The Group financial statements incorporate the financial statements of Marks and Spencer p.l.c. and all its subsidiaries for the year ended 31 March 1997.

CURRENT ASSET INVESTMENTS
Current asset investments are stated at market value. All profits and losses from such investments are included in net interest income or in Financial Services turnover as appropriate.

DEFERRED TAXATION
Deferred taxation is accounted for at anticipated tax rates on differences arising from the inclusion of items of income and expenditure in taxation computations in periods different from those in which they are included in the financial statements. A deferred tax asset or provision is established to the extent that it is likely that an asset or liability will crystallise in the foreseeable future.

FIXED ASSETS
a Capitalised interest
Interest is not capitalised in the cost of land and buildings.

b Depreciation
Depreciation is provided to write off the cost or valuation of tangible fixed assets by equal annual instalments at the following rates:
Freehold and leasehold land and buildings over 50 years: 1% or nil (see (ii) and c below);
Leasehold land and buildings under 50 years: over the remaining period of the lease;
Fixtures, fittings and equipment: 4% to $33^1/_3$% according to the estimated life of the asset.

(i) Depreciation is charged on all additions to depreciating assets in the year of purchase.

(ii) Given that the lives of the Group's freehold and long leasehold properties are so long and that they are maintained to such a high standard, it is the opinion of the directors that in most instances the residual values would be sufficiently high to make any depreciation charge immaterial. The directors have based their estimates of residual values on prices prevailing at the time of acquisition or revaluation. Where residual values are lower than cost or valuation, depreciation is charged to the profit and loss account. Any permanent diminution in value is also charged to the revaluation reserve or the profit and loss account as appropriate.

c Investment properties
Investment properties are revalued annually and included in the balance sheet at their open market value. In accordance with SSAP 19, no depreciation is provided in respect of investment properties. This represents a departure from the Companies Act 1985 requirements concerning the depreciation of fixed assets. These properties are held for investment and the directors consider that the adoption of this policy is necessary to give a true and fair view.

d Repairs and renewals
Expenditure on repairs, renewals and minor items of equipment is written off in the year in which it is incurred.

Certain major items of fixed plant and structure are incorporated within the cost of the buildings when purchased. When replaced, these are fully expensed as repairs and renewals in the profit and loss account.

LONG-TERM ASSURANCE BUSINESS
The value of the long-term assurance business consists of the present value of surpluses expected to emerge in the future from business currently in force, and this value is included in prepayments and accrued income. In determining their value, these surpluses are discounted at a risk-adjusted, post-tax rate. Changes in the value are included in the profit and loss account grossed up at the standard rate of corporation tax applicable to insurance companies.

OPERATING LEASES
Costs in respect of operating leases are charged on a straight line basis over the lease term.

FOREIGN CURRENCIES
The results of overseas subsidiaries are translated at average exchange rates for sales and profits. The balance sheets of overseas subsidiaries are translated at year-end exchange rates. The resulting exchange differences are dealt with through reserves and reported in the consolidated statement of total recognised gains and losses.

Transactions denominated in foreign currencies are translated at the exchange rate at the date of the transaction. Foreign currency assets and liabilities held at the year end are translated at year-end exchange rates or the exchange rate of a related forward exchange contract where appropriate. The resulting exchange gain or loss is dealt with in the profit and loss account.

GOODWILL
Goodwill arising on consolidation is written off to reserves on acquisition. Goodwill attributable to businesses disposed of is written back to reserves brought forward, and charged through the profit and loss account.

PENSION CONTRIBUTIONS
Funded pension plans are in place for the Group's UK employees and the majority of staff overseas. The assets of these pension plans are managed by third party investment managers and are held separately in trust.

Regular valuations are prepared by independent professionally qualified actuaries. These determine the level of contributions required to fund the benefits set out in the rules of the plans and to allow for the periodic increase of pensions in payment. The contributions and any variations from regular cost arising from the actuarial valuations are charged or credited to profits on a systematic basis over the estimated remaining service lives of the employees.

SCRIP DIVIDENDS
The amount of dividends taken as shares instead of in cash under the scrip dividend scheme is added back to reserves. The nominal value of shares issued under the scheme is funded out of the share premium account.

STOCKS
Stocks are valued at the lower of cost and net realisable value using the retail method.

TRADING RESULTS
The trading results include transactions at stores up to and including the nearest Saturday to 31 March. All other transactions are included up to 31 March each year.

Marks & Spencer

Comments

Perhaps your first observation is that the financial year-end is March 31. In most countries the financial year follows the calendar year, but not in the UK. There it varies between companies. There is no restriction on the date of the financial year-end in the relevant laws of the UK.

Only consolidated (group) figures are presented in the profit and loss account and in the cash flow statement, but in the balance sheet you will also find the figures for the parent company ('the company'). This is not so common; for example, in the US only group accounts are presented, but in most European countries financial statements also include all parent accounts, as well as group accounts. You will find examples of these practices later on.

In the *profit and loss account* you find a division between continuing and discontinued operations. This presentation is in accordance with *Reporting Financial Performance* from the Accounting Standards Board (ASB). You will see that this split continues all the way down.

You will notice the underlining of ordinary activities (also as far as tax is concerned). Finally, we notice that profit for the year is defined after minority interests and that the disposition of profit is shown in the profit and loss account.

The *consolidated statement of total recognized gains and losses* shows the link between the profit for the year and (part of) the change in capital and reserves in the balance sheet.

The *balance sheet* presents the figures for the group and the parent company.

Note the ordering of the balance sheet and the way M&S is grouping and defining 'Net assets'.

The notes on 'Shareholders' funds' indicate that fixed assets have been revalued in the financial statements at up-to-date valuations rather than at historic cost. The notes state that a chartered surveyor has valued the company's freehold and leasehold properties. This valuation was made on the basis of 'open market value for existing use'.

The *cash flow statement* is divided into the three activities of operating, investing and financing, but is not as clear as it could be. It is, however, easy to calculate the amounts of the three activities.

M&S reports 13 *accounting policies*. Two are bases of accounting and consolidation, the others are principles of valuation for the most important items. Some of these we have referred to in previous chapters, namely, deferred taxation, fixed assets (depreciation) and stocks. We do not comment on the others; they should be self-explanatory.

We underline the treatment of goodwill arising on consolidation: written off to reserves on acquisition.

Volkswagen – financial statements

Volkswagen Group
Financial Statements for the Fiscal Year Ended December 31, 1996

Balance Sheet of the Volkswagen Group, December 31, 1996 – DM million –

Assets	Note	Dec. 31, 1996	Dec. 31, 1995
Fixed assets	(1)		
Intangible assets		120	91
Tangible assets		20,631	18,271
Financial assets		3,274	3,198
Leasing and rental assets		12,118	10,297
		36,143	**31,857**
Current assets			
Inventories	(2)	10,368	9,392
Receivables and other assets	(3)	31,205	27,248
Securities	(4)	3,499	2,156
Cash on hand, deposits at German Federal Bank and Post Office Bank, cash in banks		13,080	13,174
		58,152	**51,970**
Prepaid and deferred charges	(5)	**273**	**250**
Balance-sheet total		**94,568**	**84,077**

Stockholders' equity and liabilities	Note		Dec. 31, 1996	Dec. 31, 1995
Stockholders' equity				
Subscribed capital of Volkswagen AG	(6)		1,825	1,714
Ordinary shares		1,387		
Non-voting preferred shares		437		
Potential capital	346			
Capital reserve	(7)		4,946	4,557
Revenue reserves	(8)		4,378	4,038
Net earnings available for distribution			318	209
Minority interests			468	472
			11,935	**10,990**
Special items with an equity portion	(9)		**1,374**	**1,649**
Special item for investment subsidies	(10)		**11**	**15**
Provisions	(11)		**36,026**	**31,742**
Liabilities	(12)		**41,996**	**37,823**
Deferred income			**3,226**	**1,858**
Balance-sheet total			**94,568**	**84,077**

Statement of Earnings of the Volkswagen Group for the Fiscal Year Ended December 31, 1996 – DM million –

	Note	1996	1995
Sales	(13)	**100,123**	**88,119**
Cost of sales		90,504	80,699
Gross profit		**+ 9,619**	**+ 7,420**
Selling and distribution expenses		8,301	7,089
General administration expenses		2,660	2,368
Other operating income	(14)	7,487	6,811
Other operating expenses	(15)	5,760	4,659
Results from participations	(16)	+ 509	+ 229
Interest results	(17)	+ 1,209	+ 979
Write-down of financial assets and securities classified as current assets		131	210
Results from ordinary business activities		**+ 1,972**	**+ 1,113**
Taxes on income		1,294	777
Net earnings	(18)	**+ 678**	**+ 336**

Development of short-term liquidity of the Volkswagen Group million DM

	1996	1995
Net earnings	+ 678	+ 336
Depreciation and write-up of tangible assets	+ 4,780	+ 6,345
Depreciation and write-up of leasing and rental assets	+ 4,042	+ 3,479
Change in medium and long-term provisions	+ 2,294	+ 1,307
Other expenses and income not affecting payments	– 706	– 1,067
Cash flow	**+ 11,088**	**+ 10,400**
Change in short-term provisions	+ 2,070	+ 2,038
Change in inventories and trade receivables	– 4,973	– 3,111
Change in liabilities (excluding liabilities to banks and customer deposits)	+ 4,146	+ 2,085
Change in other items	– 263	+ 175
Inflow of funds from current operations	**+ 12,068**	**+ 11,587**
Inpayments from disposal of fixed assets	+ 2,433	+ 2,344
Outpayments for additions to fixed assets	– 15,279	– 13,072
Outflow of funds in respect of capital investments	**– 12,846**	**– 10,728**
Inpayments in respect of capital increases	+ 500	+ 294
Outpayments to stockholders (dividends)	– 220	– 137
Change in medium and long-term liabilities to banks	– 1,135	– 341
Outflow of funds in respect of financing operations	**– 855**	**– 184**
Change in funds	**– 1,633**	**+ 675**
Funds at start of period	**+ 2,392**	**+ 1,717**
Funds at end of period	**+ 759**	**+ 2,392**

Notes on the Financial Statements of the Volkswagen Group for the Fiscal Year Ended December 31, 1996

Financial statements in accordance with commercial law

The consolidated financial statements of the Volkswagen Group have been prepared in accordance with the provisions of the German Commercial Code, with due regard to the provisions of the Corporation Act.

In order to improve clarity, we have combined certain items in the balance sheet and statement of earnings. These items are shown separately in the notes on the financial statements. In the interest of improved international comparability, the statement of earnings has been prepared according to the cost of sales method.

Scope of consolidation

The fully consolidated Group companies comprise all companies in which Volkswagen AG has a direct or indirect interest of over 50 % or which are under management control of the parent company. Apart from Volkswagen AG, this involves 28 German Group companies and 78 foreign Group companies.

Three previously consolidated companies in Germany and one abroad have been omitted from the scope of consolidation, since they conduct little business. They are now entered at acquisition cost. A further four companies have ceased trading and are therefore no longer consolidated. Seven companies previously valued at equity and two non-consolidated affiliated companies are now fully consolidated. One newly established company in Germany is likewise consolidated.

One newly established affiliated company is now incorporated in the Volkswagen Group on the basis of the proportionate stockholders' equity. One company is omitted from consolidation after being liquidated. Accordingly, seven domestic and seven foreign affiliates are now valued on the basis of the proportionate stockholders' equity.

14 German and 23 foreign subsidiaries are not consolidated. The companies in question are subsidiaries which are omitted under the provisions of § 296 subsection 1 item 2 or subsection 2 of the German Commercial Code.

Six joint ventures in Germany and 16 abroad are included in the consolidated financial statements on the basis of the proportionate stockholders' equity. A further six joint ventures are valued at acquisition cost.

25 German and eight foreign companies in which participations are held and on which Volkswagen AG or other Group companies exert a significant influence are included in the consolidated financial statements as associated companies.

A list detailing all interests held by the Volkswagen Group is deposited in the Wolfsburg register of companies under HRB 215. It can also be obtained direct from Volkswagen AG*.

Consolidation principles

The assets and liabilities of the German and foreign companies included in the consolidated financial statements are shown in accordance with the uniform accounting and valuation methods used within the Volkswagen Group. In the case of the associated companies, their own accounts and valuations are used as the basis for determining the proportionate stockholders' equity, except in cases where the figures for foreign Group companies have to be adjusted to bring them into line with German accounting regulations.

Capital consolidation for the companies included in the consolidated financial statements for the first time and determination of figures for associated companies are carried out at the time of acquisition on the basis of the revaluation method.

In contrast to the previous year, goodwill arising from the acquisition of shares in consolidated and associated companies is capitalized in the amount of five million DM and written off over five years, for the sake of greater transparency.

Receivables, liabilities, expenses and income arising between the individual consolidated companies are eliminated. Group inventories and fixed assets are adjusted to eliminate intra-Group profits and losses.

Consolidation operations affecting results are subject to apportionment of deferred taxes. Deferred tax liabilities in connection with consolidation operations are set off against the assets-side balance of deferred taxes from the individual companies' financial statements, although these last-mentioned deferred taxes are not shown in the balance sheets.

Translation of currencies

For the purpose of the consolidated financial statements, additions to tangible assets in the individual financial statements of foreign companies and the amounts brought forward in respect of companies consolidated for the first time are translated at the average rates for the months of acquisition. Depreciation and disposals are translated at middle rates weighted in line with the monthly additions (historical rates).

With the exception of loans, financial assets are translated at the rates applying on the date of acquisition and are carried forward on this basis. Loans are translated at the middle rate for the balance-sheet date.

Short-term leasing and rental assets, together with the related liabilities, are translated at the middle rate for the balance-sheet date.

In countries with high inflation, the raw materials and supplies, work in progress, finished goods and merchandise shown under inventories are translated into DM at historical rates.

The other assets and liabilities are translated at the middle rate for the balance-sheet date.

The change in currency translation differences which results from the exchange rate development in the current year is treated as having an effect on the result. Exchange rate profits are assigned to a provision for currency risk.

Average monthly rates are used for the most part in the statement of earnings. However, write-downs of financial assets are taken over on a historical basis. The depreciation of tangible assets which is included in cost of sales, selling and distribution expenses and general administration expenses is

likewise translated at historical rates. The net earnings/losses of foreign subsidiaries are determined by translating the relevant amounts in local currency at the rate applying on the balance-sheet date, taking into account the balance-sheet currency translation with an effect on results.

The inventory consumption incorporated in cost of sales in the financial statements of companies in countries with high inflation is included in the statements of earnings of the Group in the form of historical values. To improve the information value of the financial statements, the inflation-related components of interest expenses and interest income have been set aside and combined with the exchange rate differences and translation differences under "Other operating expenses" and "Other operating income".

Accounting and valuation principles

The accounting and valuation methods used in the previous year have been retained, with the exception of the changes indicated.

Intangible assets are shown at acquisition cost and written down over 3 years as regular straight-line depreciation.

Tangible assets and **leasing and rental assets** are valued at acquisition or manufacturing cost minus depreciation. Investment subsidies are always deducted or depreciated. Manufacturing cost is determined on the basis of the directly attributable cost of materials and labour cost as well as proportionate material overheads and production overheads including depreciation. Administration expenses are not taken into account.

The regular depreciation is based on the following useful lives:

Buildings 25–50 years

Buildings and site utilities 10–18 years

Technical equipment and machinery 5–8 years

Power generators 14 years

Factory and office equipment including special tools, jigs and fixtures 3–8 years

To the extent permissible for tax purposes, Group companies in Germany charge regular depreciation on movable assets using the declining-balance method with a scheduled changeover to the straight-line method at a later date, taking account of multi-shift operation. For the first time, Group companies abroad also charge regular depreciation on additions to movable assets using the declining-balance method with a scheduled changeover to the straight-line method at a later date, as in Germany. This change of method has a negative effect on Group results amounting to 170 million DM. The straight-line method is applied to assets on which special depreciation is charged.

Additions to special tools, jigs and fixtures up to and including 1995 are depreciated by the straight-line method as from the model launch. Additions as from 1996 are subject to depreciation using the declining-balance method as from date of manufacture, with a scheduled changeover to the straight-line method at a later date. This change of method reduces the profit for 1996 by 218 million DM.

Notes on the Financial Statements of the Volkswagen Group for the Fiscal Year Ended December 31, 1996

Low-value assets are fully depreciated and deleted from the accounts in the year of acquisition.

Differences between the values required under commercial law and those permitted under tax law are shown on the stockholders' equity and liabilities side of the balance sheet under the special items with an equity portion.

Holdings in affiliated and associated companies – if not valued on the basis of the equity method – and other **participations** are shown at acquisition cost or the lower applicable value.

Long-term financial investments are shown at acquisition cost or, in the event of a probably permanent reduction in value, at the lower applicable value.

Non and low-interest-bearing **loans** are stated at cash value; interest-bearing loans at the nominal value.

Within **inventories**, raw materials and supplies as well as merchandise are valued at average acquisition cost or the lower replacement cost.

In addition to direct materials, the values given for work in progress and finished goods also comprise direct labour, proportionate material overheads and production overheads including depreciation, to the extent permissible by law for the parent company.

Provision is made for all discernible storage and inventory risks by way of adequate value adjustments.

Receivables and other assets are stated at the nominal amount. Provision is made for discernible individual risks and general credit risks by way of

appropriate value adjustments. In contrast to the principle applied in the financial statements of Volkswagen AG, receivables in foreign currencies are valued at the middle rates applying on the balance-sheet date or the rates agreed in respect of these receivables.

Securities classified as current assets are stated at acquisition cost or at the lower applicable value on the balance-sheet date, unless the retention of lower values from previous years is permissible.

Provisions for pensions and similar obligations up to December 31st, 1995 are based on actuarial computation and the going-value method in accordance with § 6a of the Income Tax Act for German companies, taking an interest rate of 6 %; and on comparable principles for foreign companies.

In order to establish more effective provision for the future financial burden arising from pension payments, an interest rate of 5 % – in contrast to the principle applied in the financial statements of Volkswagen AG – has been applied as from January 1st, 1996. This adjustment reduces profit by 1,489 million DM. Provisions for long-service gratuities are discounted at 5.5 %, taking account of regulations governing valuation for tax purposes.

The **provisions** for warranty obligations are based on historical and estimated loss in relation to vehicles sold.

Allowance is made for discernible risks and uncertain liabilities by way of adequate allocations to provisions. The provisions cover all risks arising from future claims.

Liabilities are shown at the amount at which they must be repaid or the amount required for fulfillment of the obligation in question. In contrast to the principle applied in the financial statements of Volkswagen AG, liabilities in foreign currencies are valued at the middle rates applying on the balance-sheet date or the rates agreed in respect of these liabilities.

The figures given for **contingent liabilities** correspond to the extent of the liability.

In the statement of earnings, expenses are allocated to the fields of production, selling/distribution and general administration on the basis of cost-accounting rules.

Cost of sales comprises all expenses relating to production and material procurement, all expenses relating to merchandise, research and development costs and expenses in connection with warranties and product liability. The difference between full cost and the lower limit for tax balance sheet entry in valuation of inventories is also stated here.

Selling and distribution expenses comprise labour cost and cost of materials for our selling and distribution departments as well as costs in connection with freight, advertising, sales promotion, market research and service.

General administration expenses comprise the labour cost and cost of materials for the administration departments.

Other taxes totalling 371 million DM (1995: 340 million DM) are allocated to the individual functional areas.

Structure of the VOLKSWAGEN AG balance sheet

Assets	million DM	31.12.1996	%	31.12.1995	%
Fixed assets		17,515	43.7	17,196	43.7
Inventories		3,059	7.6	2,892	7.4
Receivables		11,505	28.7	13,079	33.3
Liquid funds		7,993	20.0	6,146	15.6
Total assets		**40,072**	**100.0**	**39,313**	**100.0**

Stockholders' equity and liabilities	million DM	31.12.1996	%	31.12.1995	%
Stockholders' equity		11,755	29.3	11,248	28.6
Long-term liabilities		8,666	21.6	9,381	23.9
Medium-term liabilities		7,252	18.1	6,862	17.4
Short-term liabilities		12,399	31.0	11,822	30.1
Total capital		**40,072**	**100.0**	**39,313**	**100.0**

**Structure of the VOLKSWAGEN AG statement of earnings
January 1 – December 31, 1996**

	million DM	1996	%	1995	%
Sales		**49,891**	**100.0**	**44,598**	**100.0**
Cost of Sales		46,969	94.1	42,202	94.6
Gross profit		**+ 2,922**	**5.9**	**+ 2,396**	**5.4**
Selling, distribution and administration expenses		4,040	8.1	3,940	8.8
Other operating income and expenses		+ 448	0.9	+ 2,197	4.9
Financial results		+ 1,798	3.6	– 93	0.2
Results from ordinary business activities		**+ 1,128**	**2.3**	**+ 560**	**1.3**
Taxes		498	1.0	150	0.4
Net earnings		**+ 630**	**1.3**	**+ 410**	**0.9**

Volkswagen

Comments
The financial statements consist of:

- balance sheet of the Volkswagen Group;
- statement of earnings of the Volkswagen Group;
- development of short-term liquidity of the Volkswagen Group;
- structure of the Volkswagen AG balance sheet and statement of earnings.

We learn from the figures that the group's accounts are of much more interest than the parent company's accounts; compare the total assets figures (94 568/ 40 072) (DM million) and the sales figures (100 123/49 891) (DM million).

In the *balance sheet* the order is, of course, as prescribed by the EU Fourth Directive. In specific items we notice that 'Leasing and rental assets' are accounted for as fixed assets.

In the stockholders' equity section we find 'Capital reserve' and 'Revenue reserves'; the first comprises premiums on capital increases, whereas the second is retained earnings. Of special interest is the item 'Special items with an equity portion'. The note to this item tells us that the Volkswagen Group has reserves in accordance with the Income Tax Act, especially depreciation for investments in specific areas in Germany. The huge amount in 'Provisions' covers pensions and similar obligations, provisions in respect of taxes and other provisions.

The *statement of earnings* follows the functional model of reporting. In the last part of the accounting policy section cost of sales, selling and distribution expenses and administration expenses are defined and explained.

The *development of short-term liquidity* is a cash flow statement divided into the three sections: current operations, capital investments and financing operations.

The *Volkswagen AG financial statements* are presented also as 'common size'. Not surprisingly, 'Fixed assets' counts for a high percentage of the total assets. The main item is 'Investment in subsidiaries'.

In the *notes to the financial statements* we find Volkswagen's accounting policies and principles. Of special interest are the sections 'Scope of consolidation' and 'Consolidation principles'. In the latter we find a change in the policy of the treatment of goodwill arising from the acquisition of shares in consolidated and associated companies: from direct reduction in equity to capitalization and write off over five years.

Danisco – financial statements

Accounting policies

The accounts of the parent company and the consolidated accounts have been drawn up in accordance with the provisions of the Danish Company Accounts Act, Danish accounting standards and the requirements of the Copenhagen Stock Exchange relating to the accounts of listed companies.

The accounting policies are unchanged compared with last year.

Basis of consolidation

The consolidated accounts include Danisco A/S (the parent company) and all undertakings (subsidiary undertakings) in which the parent company, directly or indirectly, holds more than 50 per cent of the voting rights or otherwise has a dominant influence. Undertakings in which the group holds between 20 per cent and 50 per cent of the voting rights without having a dominant influence are regarded as associated companies. Page 74 gives an overview of the subsidiary undertakings of the group.

The group accounts consolidate the audited accounts of the parent company and the individual subsidiary undertakings, which have been prepared in accordance with the group's accounting policies. Inter-company income and expenditure, shareholdings, balances and dividends as well as unrealised internal profits and losses have been eliminated.

Associated undertakings the management of which is undertaken on a unified basis by Danisco and one or several undertakings are proportionally consolidated. This implies that the relevant proportion of the undertakings' items in the profit and loss account and balance sheet is included in the corresponding items of the consolidated accounts, and that inter-company items and unrealised profits have been eliminated proportionally.

On the acquisition of new undertakings the net asset value at the date of acquisition is stated in accordance with the group's accounting policies, and provisions are set aside for any costs resulting from planned restructuring in the acquired undertaking. The tax effect is taken into consideration. Where the cost of acquisition exceeds the net asset value computed, that balance is allocated to the extent possible to the assets and liabilities which have a higher or lower value than the book value. Any remaining positive balances are charged directly to capital and reserves as goodwill or group goodwill in the year of acquisition. Any negative balances (negative goodwill) attributable to future operating losses are recorded under provisions.

Newly-acquired subsidiary undertakings and associated undertakings are included in the profit and loss account at the date of acquisition.

Where a decision to dispose of or sell a subsidiary undertaking has been made, the undertaking's result at the date of decision plus expenses incidental to the disposal are recorded under extraordinary items. Net assets after provisions in such undertakings are recorded under current assets as other debtors or under provisions.

Comparative figures are not adjusted for undertakings sold, undertakings being disposed of or newly-acquired undertakings.

Foreign currency translations

Danisco's Danish undertakings translate their transactions in foreign currency (eg purchase/sale) into Danish krone at monthly average rates of exchange or at forward rates. The monthly average rates of exchange are used for practical reasons, as these reflect approximately the rates of exchange at the date of the transaction.

The differences in exchange rates arising between the average monthly rate and the rate at the date of payment are included in the profit and loss account as a financial item.

The debtors and creditors of Danisco's Danish undertakings in foreign currency are translated at the exchange rates ruling at the balance sheet date or in some cases at forward rates. The difference between the rate of exchange at the balance sheet date (or the forward rate as the case may be) and the rate of exchange at the time when the debtor or the creditor was incurred is included in the profit and loss account as a financial item.

Tangible fixed assets purchased in foreign currency by Danisco's Danish undertakings are included at the rate of exchange at the date of purchase. On the writeup or writedown of assets the value of which are computed on an continuous basis in foreign currencies, the values are translated into Danish krone at the exchange rate on the date of the writeup or writedown.

The profit and loss accounts of independent foreign subsidiary undertakings are translated into Danish krone according to a monthly average rate of exchange, and the balance sheets are translated at the exchange rate at the balance sheet date. Exchange rate differences occurring on the translation of opening net investments of foreign subsidiary undertakings at the rate of exchange ruling at the balance sheet date are entered under capital and reserves. The same applies to the exchange rate differences following the translation of the profit and loss accounts at a monthly average rate of exchange and the translation of the balance sheets at the exchange rate at the balance sheet date.

With regard to foreign subsidiary undertakings which are integrated in the parent company to the effect that each transaction made by a subsidiary undertaking affects the currency flow of the parent company, another method will be employed which implies the transaction of each transaction as though they were carried out by a Danish undertaking.

At this point in time Danisco does not have any large integrated undertakings and, therefore, all subsidiary undertakings are considered to be independent.

Undertakings in countries with high inflation rates present accounts for consolidation purposes in USD.

Financial instruments

Financial instruments used for hedging current assets and amounts falling due within one year are usually valued at market price at the balance sheet date. Realised as well as unrealised exchange gains and losses are included in the profit and loss account. However, the exchange gains and losses of financial instruments contracted in order to hedge income and expenditure of future years are deferred until such income and expenditure are realised.

With regard to forward exchange contracts entered into to hedge short-term debtors and creditor in foreign currencies the forward rate of exchange is used for valuation of the hedged transactions and therefore, forward exchange contracts are not valued as independent items.

Financial instruments contracted for hedging interest of long-term financing are entered at cost.

The results of financial instruments contracted for hedging new capital investments are included in the cost of the investment.

Profit and loss account
Net sales

Net sales comprise sales invoiced during the year less returned goods and discounts granted in connections with sales. Refunds received from the EU are included in net sales.

Cost of sales

Costs of sales includes costs, depreciation, wages and salaries incurred to achieve the net-sales of the year. Production levies to the EU are included in this item.

Research and development costs

Research and development costs include costs, salaries and depreciation attributable to the research and development activities of the group. Research and development costs are charged to the profit and loss account as incurred.

Distribution and sales costs

Distribution and sales costs comprise costs incurred on the distribution and sales of the products of the group, salaries for sales personnel, advertising and exhibition costs, depreciation, etc.

Administrative expenses

Administrative expenses comprise the costs of the administrative staff and the management, including offices etc, salaries and depreciation.

Other operating income

Other operating income comprises income of a secondary nature in relation to the activities of the group.

Income from subsidiary undertakings and associated undertakings

The relevant proportion of each subsidiary undertaking's profit or loss less unrealised inter-company profits is recorded in the parent company's profit and loss account. The proportion of the subsidiary undertaking's tax is charged to current tax on the profit for the year.

The relevant proportion of each associated company's profit or loss less the relevant proportion of inter-company profits is recorded in the profit and loss accounts of both the parent company and the group. The proportion of tax is charged to current tax on the profit for the year.

Financial items

Interest receivable and payable are included in the profit and loss account with the amounts relating to the accounting year. In addition, financial items comprise realised and unrealised capital gains and losses from exchange and price adjustments of investments and items in foreign currencies.

Extraordinary items

Extraordinary items comprise significant income and expenditure deriving from non-recurring events, activities clearly falling outside the ordinary activities of the group as well as the profit or loss from discontinued activities.

Tax

In Denmark Danisco A/S is taxed jointly with certain wholly owned Danish and foreign subsidiary undertakings. The parent company provides for and pays the aggregate Danish tax of the taxable income of these undertakings, just as provision for deferred tax for these undertakings is made by the parent company.

The expected tax on the taxable income for the year, adjusted for the charge in deferred tax for the year, is charged to the profit and loss account. Withholding taxes relating to repatriation of dividends from foreign subsidiary undertakings are charged in the year in which the dividend is declared. The tax charged is recorded under tax on profit on ordinary activities and tax on extraordinary items.

Deferred tax is provided under the liability method for timing differences between accounting and taxation treatment of fixed assets other that those relating to depreciation on fixed assets. Owing to the group's capital expenditure policy the tax on timing differences concerning fixed assets is not expected to crystallise as current tax within a foreseeable future. Deferred tax for which there is no provision in the accounts is stated in a note.

Furthermore, deferred tax is provided for reversal of tax benefits arising from losses in foreign production and sales undertakings that will crystallise as tax if they are sold or leave joint taxation.

Provisions for tax becoming liable on any sale of assets, including shares of subsidiaries, at booked values are not made in the balance sheets.Deferred tax is provided at the nominal Danish tax rate which is 34 per cent. Changes in deferred tax resulting from changes of the Danish tax rates are dealt with in the profit and loss account.

Balance sheets

Intangible fixed assets

Intangible fixed assets are valued at cost less accumulated depreciation and writedowns. Depreciation is provided according to the straight line method based on the estimated useful lives of the assets which are 2-5 years depending on the actual circumstances.

Tangible fixed asset

Land and building are entered at cost plus revaluation less accumulated depreciation and writedowns.

Plant and machinery and other fixtures, fittings, tools, and equipment are entered at cost less accumulated depreciation and write-downs.

Depreciation is provided according to the straight line method over the estimated useful lives of the assets to expected residual value. The lifetimes of major assets are fixed individually, the lives of other assets are fixed in respect of groups of uniform assets. Expected lifetimes are:

Buildings	20-40 years
Plant and machinery	10-20 years
Fixtures, fittings, tools and equipment	3-7 years

Assets with a short lifetime, small assets and minor improvement costs are entered as expenses in the year of acquisition.

Finance lease assets are capitalised and depreciated according to the straight-line method over their useful lives. The remaining capitalised lease obligations are included under creditors.

Financial fixed assets

Participating interests in subsidiary undertakings are valued at net asset value in the accounts of the parent company according to the equity method. This implies that participating interests are recorded in the balance sheets at the relevant proportion of their net asset value, and that the parent company's share of the profit is included in the profit and loss account less unrealised inter-company profits.

Subsidiary undertakings with a negative net asset value are recorded at zero and amounts owed by these subsidiary undertakings are written down with the parent company's share of the negative net asset value. Should the negative net asset value exceed the amounts owed, the remaining amount is recorded under provisions.

Participating interests in associated undertakings are valued in the accounts of the parent company and the consolidated accounts also according to the equity method, however, with the deduction of the relevant proportion of unrealised inter-company profit.

Under capital and reserves net revaluation of participating interests in subsidiary undertakings and associated undertakings are transferred to undistributed profit in subsidiary undertakings to the extent the revaluation exceeds the dividend received from the companies.

The value of other investments and capital participation, mainly comprising shares and mortgages, is fixed at cost less writedowns due to a permanent reduction of value. All writedowns are included in the profit and loss account.

Own shares are recorded at cost and an equivalent amount is entered under reserve for own shares.

Stocks

Stocks are valued at the lower of cost on a first in first out basis and net realisable value. Production costs include materials and direct labour. Writedowns are effected for obsolete items, including slow-moving items. Indirect production costs, such as maintenance and depreciation of production plant, and factory management, are calculated for the group and stated in a note.

Debtors

Debtors are recorded after an individual evaluation of potential risk.

Investment and capital participation

Investments and participating interests recorded under current assets mainly comprise bonds which are entered at market price at the balance sheet date. Realised as well as unrealised gains and losses from price adjustments are included in the profit and loss account.

Cash flow statement

The cash flow statement of the group which is prepared according to the indirect method shows the group's cash flows from operating activities, investing activities and financing activities as well as the group's cash position at the beginning and the end of the year.

The cash flows from operating activities are computed as a Danisco proportion of the group's profit for the year adjusted for non-cash operating items, change in working capital and paid corporate tax.

The cash flows from investing activities comprise payments made on the purchase and sale of undertakings and activities and the purchase and sale of tangible and financial fixed assets adjusted for changes in debtors concerning the items in question.

The cash flows from financing activities comprise loans, repayments on interest bearing debt and payment of dividends.

Cash comprises deposits with banks, etc. and securities with immaterial currency exposure, whereas securities and capital participation recorded under current fixed assets in the balance sheet are not regarded as cash, in that these have longer terms and thus represent currency exposure.

Profit and loss account 1.5.1996 - 30.4.1997

DKK million

Parent company				Group	
1995/96	1996/97	Notes		1995/96	1996/97
6,289	8,923	1	Net sales	16,186	17,002
3,767	5,341	2	Cost of sales	9,553	9,762
2,522	3,582		Contribution margin	6,633	7,240
845	1,197	2-3	Fixed production costs	2,196	2,405
247	279	2-3	Research and development costs	296	321
1,430	2,106		Gross profit	4,141	4,514
601	828	2-3	Distribution and sales costs	1,481	1,631
436	560	2-4	Administrative expenses	996	1,025
77	71		Other operating income	132	94
470	789		Operating profit	1,796	1,952
1,152	1,036	5	Income from participating interests in subsidiary undertakings	-	-
1	2		Income from associated undertakings	1	2
51	17	6	Income from other capital participation, etc.	51	20
94	107	7	Interest receivable and similar income	188	128
167	164	8	Interest payable and similar charges	432	313
1,601	1,787		Profit on ordinary activities before taxation	1,604	1,789
381	397	9	Tax on profit on ordinary activities	388	405
5	-	9	Adjustment of tax for previous years	-2	-8
1,215	1,390		Consolidated profit for the year	1,218	1,392
-	-		Profit attributable to minority shareholders	3	2
1,215	1,390		Danisco's share of the consolidated profit	1,215	1,390

Proposed appropriation of profit for the year

Dividend DKK 5.00 per share (25%)	301
Reserves	1,089
	1,390

Balance sheets at 30.4.1997   Assets

DKK million

Parent company				Group	
30.4.1996	30.4.1997	Notes		30.4.1996	30.4.1997
			Fixed assets		
3	2	10	*Intangible fixed assets*	6	4
			Tangible fixed assets		
1,301	1,715	10	Land and buildings	3,237	3,328
1,695	2,153	10	Plant and machinery	5,172	5,323
142	213	10	Fixtures, fittings, tools and equipment	334	367
68	249	10	Prepayments for tangible fixed assets and assets under construction	250	455
-	-	10	Leased equipment and plant	32	63
3,206	4,330		Total	9,025	9,536
			Financial fixed assets		
4,800	3,993	11	Participating interests in subsidiary undertakings	-	-
58	51	11	Loans to subsidiary undertakings	-	-
4	3	11	Participating interests in associated undertakings	4	3
84	54	11	Other investments and capital participation	88	55
1	2		Other receivables	12	13
-	52	12	Own shares	-	52
4,947	4,155		Total	104	123
8,156	8,487		Fixed assets total	9,135	9,663
			Current assets		
			Stocks		
310	440		Raw materials and consumables	973	1,033
54	103	13	Work in progress	157	161
1,195	1,409	13	Finished goods and goods for resale	2,325	2,456
5	8		Prepayments for goods	57	58
1,564	1,960		Total	3,512	3,708
			Debtors		
715	1,034	14	Trade debtors	2,493	2,735
1,637	2,028		Amounts owed by subsidiary undertakings	-	-
228	215		Other debtors	354	443
28	34		Prepayments	84	83
2,608	3,311		Total	2,931	3,261
4	5		*Investments and capital participation*	8	332
200	244		*Cash at bank and in hand*	1,024	826
4,376	5,520		Current assets total	7,475	8,127
12,532	14,007		Assets total	16,610	17,790

Balance sheets at 30.4.1997   Liabilities

DKK million

Parent company				Group	
30.4.1996	30.4.1997	Notes		30.4.1996	30.4.1997
			Capital and reserves		
1,107	1,202		Share capital	1,107	1,202
341	1,404		Share premium account	341	1,404
-	-		Revaluation reserve	91	83
-	52		Reserve for own shares	-	52
983	872		Undistributed profit in subsidiary undertakings	-	-
5,309	6,476		Other reserves	6,201	7,265
7,740	10,006		Capital and reserves total	7,740	10,006
-	-		*Minority interests*	11	10
			Provisions		
179	205	15	Provisions for deferred tax	172	209
207	138		Other provisions	569	455
386	343		Provisions total	741	664
			Creditors		
			Amounts falling due after more than one year		
1,146	-		Convertible bonds	1,146	-
308	376	16	Mortgage debts	441	478
-	-	16	Bank debts	1,361	1,272
55	77	16	Other creditors	229	130
-	-	18	Other debts	225	217
1,509	453		Total	3,402	2,097
			Amounts falling due within one year		
14	15		Mortgage debts	43	19
108	75		Bank debts	1,194	1,307
18	22		Other creditors	102	102
340	532		Trade creditors	1,133	1,226
-	1		Capitalised lease obligations	32	63
1,362	1,102		Amounts owed to subsidiary undertakings	-	-
-	-	17	Corporation tax	33	55
818	1,151	18	Other debts	1,917	1,910
5	6		Accruals	30	30
232	301		Dividend for the accounting year	232	301
2,897	3,205		Total	4,716	5,013
4,406	3,658		Amounts owed to creditors total	8,118	7,110
12,532	14,007		Liabilities total	16,610	17,790
		19	Guarantees and other financial commitments		
		20	Security and pledge		

Cash flow statement 1.5.1996 - 30.4.1997

DKK million

1995/96	Notes	Group	1996/97
		Cash flow from operating activities	
1,215		Profit for the year	**1,390**
1,325	22	Adjustment	**1,377**
-99	23	Change in working capital	**-246**
2,441		Cash flow from operating activities before financial items total	**2,521**
1		Income from associated undertakings	**2**
2		Income from other capital participation, etc.	**2**
148		Interest receivable and similar income	**75**
-262		Interest payable and similar charges	**-248**
2,330		Cash flow from ordinary activities	**2,352**
-634		Paid corporate tax	**-336**
1,696		Cash flow from operating activities total	**2,016**
		Cash flow from investing activities	
-851	24	Purchase of undertakings and activities	**-63**
-	24	Sale of undertakings and activities	**2**
-975	25	Purchase of tangible fixed assets	**-1,240**
72	25	Sale of tangible fixed assets and investment grants	**81**
266		Sale of financial assets, net	**-**
-		Purchase of financial assets	**-325**
-1,488		Cash flow from investing activities total	**-1,545**
208		Net cash outflow/inflow from operating and investing activities	**471**
		Cash flow from financing activities	
-424	26	Change in interest bearing debt	**-386**
-		Received employee shares	**21**
-		Employee shares and costs convertible bonds	**-71**
-177		Dividend paid	**-232**
-601		Cash flow from financing total	**-668**
-393		Decrease/increase in cash and cash equivalents total	**-197**
1,417	27	Cash at 1.5	**1,023**
1,024	27	Cash at 30.4	**826**

Danisco

Comments

In the section on *accounting policies* presented before the financial statements, this international Danish company underlines that its accounting policies are unchanged compared with last year. This is a good piece of information for the user, because if there had been any changes in the policies they would have also been mentioned.

The 'Basis of consolidation' repeats the consolidation philosophy and the accounting treatment of investments in associated undertakings. We learn that Danisco treats goodwill very conservatively: it is charged directly to capital. Any negative goodwill (badwill) is recorded under provisions.

The accounting principles on the most important items in the profit and loss account and the balance sheet give a great deal of important information and are very well explained.

From the financial statements we see that Danisco does not follow the calendar year, but presents the profit and loss account for the period May 1–April 30 and the balance sheet at April 30.

The figures for the parent company and the group are presented together. The cash flow statement is given only for the group

The reporting model of the *profit and loss account* follows the functional view. We recognize 'Contribution margin', followed (in the next line) by 'Fixed production costs'. This is a typical Danish presentation where the division between fixed and variable costs is essential. This way of thinking – and reporting – has a relatively long tradition in Denmark, with its roots in the teaching philosophy at the Copenhagen Business School.

We find a very good specification of the income from investments and notice also that the tax on profit on ordinary activities is specified. The net profit for the year is the same for the parent company as for the group (Danisco's share). You should spend a few minutes reflecting on this fact.

In the *balance sheets* we find a good grouping and specification of items. We notice the specification (between fixed assets and creditors) and the treatment of leased equipment and plant (a puzzle to think about: how would you explain that the amounts are the same for both items?).

From the section 'Capital and reserves' we see that some fixed assets must have been revalued. From the text in connection with taxes we learn that Danisco uses the deferred tax model. The division of creditors with amounts falling due after more than one year and within one year is good for analytical purposes.

The *cash flow statement* follows the indirect method. We notice the working capital step in the presentation. From the cash flow statement we can analyse as follows:

> The cash decreased both in 1995/6 and 1996/7, altogether by 590 (DKK million). This is due to a generated positive cash flow from operating activities for the two years of 3712 (DKK million), a negative cash outflow of 3033 (DKK million) from investing activities and a negative cash outflow of 1269 (DKK million) from financing activities.

Volvo – financial statements

Consolidated income statements

	1996	1995	1994
Net sales	**156,060**	171,511	155,866
Cost of sales	**(121,249)**	(128,529)	(115,092)
Gross income	**34,811**	42,982	40,774
Research and development expenses	**(8,271)**	(7,343)	(4,652)
Selling expenses	**(14,895)**	(17,418)	(15,737)
Administrative expenses	**(6,685)**	(7,399)	(7,711)
Other operating income	**5,086**	4,168	3,317
Other operating expenses	**(6,336)**	(5,966)	(6,620)
Operating income before nonrecurring items	**3,710**	9,024	9,371
Nonrecurring items	**–**	1,215	–
Operating income	**3,710**	10,239	9,371
Income from investments in associated companies	**314**	2,119	5,861
Income from other investments	**9,007**	788	1,667
Interest income and similar credits	**4,817**	3,996	3,051
Interest expenses and similar charges	**(3,271)**	(3,757)	(3,608)
Other financial income and expenses	**(374)**	(337)	36
Income after financial items	**14,203**	13,048	16,378
Taxes	**(1,825)**	(3,741)	(2,783)
Minority interests	**99**	(45)	(365)
Net income	**12,477**	9,262	13,230

Statements of changes in consolidated financial position

		1996		1995		1994
Year's operations						
Net income		**12,477**		9,262		13,230
Depreciation and amortization		**5,351**		5,656		5,107
Write-down of shareholdings and fixed assets		**–**		1,817		574
Income from equity method investments after taxes		**(222)**		(730)		(1,274)
Dividends received from associated companies		**119**		404		160
Gain on sales of securities		**(8,169)**		(1,180)		(4,243)
Gain on sales of subsidiaries		**–**		(3,032)		–
Minority interests after taxes		**(99)**		45		365
Increase in current operating assets:						
Receivables	**(4,777)**		(962)		(3,538)	
Inventories	**(547)**		(516)		(2,687)	
Increase (decrease) in current operating liabilities	**(618)**		570		5,915	
Increase (decrease) in deferred tax liabilities	**23**	**(5,919)**	(267)	(1,175)	(1,373)	(1,683)
Net financing from year's operations		**3,538**		11,067		12,236
Investments (increase)						
Property, plant and equipment, etc:						
Capital expenditures for property, plant and equipment	**(8,200)**		(6,491)		(4,274)	
Investment in leasing and company vehicles	**(3,851)**		(2,585)		(2,495)	
Disposals	**1,958**		1,351		1,460	
Investments in shares, net	**14,080**		1,953		8,182	
Long-term receivables, net	**(2,804)**		(1,953)		(1,563)	
Acquisitions and sales of companies	**(878)**	**305**	(4,420)	(12,145)	–	1,310
Remaining after net investments		**3,843**		(1,078)		13,546
Financing, dividends, etc						
Increase (decrease) in short-term bank loans and other loans	**5,151**		(3,993)		(6,233)	
Increase (decrease) in long-term loans	**(1,844)**		6,166		(2,011)	
Increase (decrease) in minority interests	**45**		(37)		145	
Dividends paid to AB Volvo shareholders	**(1,854)**		(1,512)		(601)	
Dividends paid to minority shareholders	**(33)**		(3)		(132)	
Settlement of loans to Renault	**(1,536)**		–		(1,422)	
Other	**(121)**	**(192)**	46	667	23	(10,231)
Increase (decrease) in liquid funds excluding translation differences		**3,651**		(411)		3,315
Translation differences on liquid funds		**(296)**		(732)		(308)
Increase (decrease) in liquid funds		**3,355**		(1,143)		3,007
Liquid funds, January 1		**23,306**		24,449		21,442
Liquid funds, December 31		**26,661**		23,306		24,449

In the Statement of changes in financial position, the effects of major acquisitions and divestments of subsidiaries in each year, including the distribution of the shareholding in Swedish Match in 1996, have been excluded from other changes in the balance sheet. The effects of changes in foreign exchange rates at translation of foreign subsidiaries have been excluded, since they do not affect cash flow.

Notes to Consolidated financial statements

Amounts in SEK M unless otherwise specified. The amounts within parentheses refer to the two preceding years; the first figure is for 1995 and the second figure is for 1994.

1 Accounting principles

Principles of consolidation
The consolidated accounts comprise the Parent Company, all subsidiaries and associated companies. Subsidiaries are defined as companies in which Volvo holds more than 50% of the voting rights. Subsidiaries in which Volvo's holding is temporary are not consolidated, however. Associated companies are companies in which Volvo has long-term holdings equal to at least 20% but not more than 50% of the voting rights.

The consolidated accounts are prepared in accordance with the principles set forth in Recommendation RR01:91 of the Swedish Financial Accounting Standards Council.

All acquisitions of companies are reported in accordance with the purchase method.

Companies that have been divested are included in the consolidated accounts up to and including the date of divestment. Companies acquired during the year are consolidated as of the date of acquisition.

Holdings in associated companies are reported in accordance with the equity method. The Group's share of reported income before taxes in such companies, adjusted for minority interests, is included in the consolidated income statement, reduced in appropriate cases by amortization of excess values. The Group's share of reported taxes in associated companies, as well as estimated taxes in allocations, are included in Group tax expense.

For practical reasons, most of the associated companies are included in the consolidated accounts with a certain time lag, normally one quarter. Dividends from associated companies are not included in consolidated income. In the consolidated balance sheet, the book value of shareholdings in associated companies is affected by Volvo's share of company's income after tax, reduced by amortization of excess values and by the amount of dividends received.

Foreign currencies
In preparing the consolidated financial statements, all items in the income statements of foreign subsidiaries (except subsidiaries in highly inflationary economies) are translated to Swedish kronor at the average exchange rates during the year (average rate). All balance sheet items except net income are translated at exchange rates at the respective year-ends (year-end rate). The differences in consolidated shareholders' equity arising as a result of variations between year-end exchange rates are charged or credited directly to shareholders' equity and classified with restricted or unrestricted reserves. The difference arising in the consolidated balance sheet as a result of the translation of net income in foreign subsidiaries to Swedish kronor at average rates is charged or credited to unrestricted reserves. Movements in exchange rates change the book value of foreign associated companies. This difference affects restricted reserves directly.

When foreign subsidiaries and associated companies are divested, the accumulated translation difference is reported as a realized gain/loss and, accordingly, affects income.

Financial statements of subsidiaries operating in highly inflationary economies are translated to Swedish kronor using the tem-

poral method. Monetary items in the balance sheet are translated at year-end rates and nonmonetary balance sheet items and corresponding income statement items are translated at rates in effect at the time of acquisition (historical rates). Other income statement items are translated at average rates. Translation differences are credited to, or charged against, income in the year in which they arise.

In the individual Group companies as well as in the consolidated accounts, receivables and liabilities in foreign currency are valued at year-end exchange rates. In the individual Swedish Group companies, unrealized exchange gains on long-term receivables and liabilities are allocated to an exchange reserve. In the consolidated accounts, this is divided into a Deferred tax liability and Equity in untaxed reserves.

When valuing outstanding forward exchange contracts, provision is made for unrealized losses to the extent that the latter exceed unrealized gains. In calculating the size of unrealized losses, a portion of the amounts secured through forward contracts is excluded; this consists of amounts for which there is substantial assurance that the currency flow from commercial transactions will cover forward contracts. Unrealized gains in excess of unrealized losses are not credited to income.

In valuing loans whose original currency denomination has been changed as a result of currency swap contracts, the amount of the loans in Swedish kronor is calculated based on the currencies in which the loans are to be repaid.

Exchange differences on loans and other financial instruments in foreign currency, which are used to hedge net assets in foreign subsidiaries and associated companies, are offset against translation differences in the shareholders' equity of the respective companies.

Exchange gains and losses on payments during the year and on the valuation of assets and liabilities in foreign currencies at year-end are credited to, or charged against, income before taxes and minority interests in the year they arise.

The more important exchange rates employed are shown on the following page.

Inventories
Inventories are posted at the lower of cost, in accordance with the first-in, first-out method (FIFO), or net realizable value. Adequate provision has been made for obsolescence.

Capital expenditures for property, plant and equipment
Capital expenditures for property, plant and equipment includes investments in buildings, machinery and equipment, as well as in long-term intangible assets. Investments in leasing and company vehicles are not included.

Depreciation and amortization
Depreciation is based on the historical cost of the assets, reduced in appropriate cases by write-downs, and estimated economic life. Capitalized type-specific tools are generally depreciated over 2 to 5 years. The depreciation period for leasing vehicles and company vehicles is normally 3 to 5 years. Machinery is generally depreciated over 5 to 10 years, and buildings over 25 to 50 years, while the greater part of land improvements are depreciated over 20 years. In connection with its participation in aircraft engine projects with other companies, Volvo Aero in certain cases compensates these companies for part of the development costs incurred before Volvo Aero entered the project. These costs are capitalized and depreciated over 5 to 10 years.

Exchange rates

Country	Currency	Average rate			Year-end rate		
		1996	1995	1994	1996	1995	1994
Belgium	BEF	0.217	0.242	0.231	0.215	0.226	0.235
Denmark	DKK	1.158	1.274	1.216	1.156	1.200	1.226
Finland	FIM	1.463	1.636	1.484	1.482	1.529	1.573
France	FRF	1.312	1.430	1.394	1.312	1.360	1.395
Italy	ITL	0.00436	0.00439	0.00480	0.00451	0.00421	0.00459
Japan	JPY	0.0618	0.0765	0.0757	0.0593	0.0648	0.0749
Netherlands	NLG	3.982	4.447	4.252	3.941	4.150	4.301
Norway	NOK	1.040	1.126	1.095	1.066	1.052	1.103
Great Britain	GBP	10.486	11.281	11.821	11.605	10.330	11.650
Germany	DEM	4.462	4.981	4.768	4.423	4.644	4.817
United States	USD	6.712	7.140	7.717	6.872	6.672	7.463

The difference between depreciation noted above and depreciation allowable for tax purposes is reported by the parent company and in the individual Group companies as accumulated extra depreciation, which is included in untaxed reserves. Consolidated reporting of these items is described below under the heading Allocations, deferred tax liability, untaxed reserves.

Goodwill is included in intangible assets and amortized on a straight-line basis over 5 to 20 years. The goodwill amounts pertaining to Volvo Construction Equipment and Prévost are being amortized over 20 years, due to the holdings' long-term and strategic importance. The goodwill amounts pertaining to Swedish Match were amortized, as planned, over periods of 20 years up to the date of the divestment in May 1996.

Research and development costs and warranty expenses
Research and development expenses are charged to operating expenses as incurred.

Estimated costs for product warranties are charged to cost of sales when the products are sold.

Nonrecurring items
Nonrecurring items are reported separately in the income statement. They pertain mainly to income and expenses attributable to major changes in the composition of the Group. To show the results of the Volvo Group's continuing operations, "Operating income before nonrecurring items" is also reported. This deviates from Recommendation RR4 of the Swedish Financial Accounting Standards Council, which states that such an income/loss term is not compatible with the premise upon which the Recommendation is based.

Allocations, deferred tax liability, untaxed reserves
Tax laws in Sweden and certain other countries allow companies to defer payment of taxes through allocations to untaxed reserves.

The individual Group companies (including AB Volvo) report untaxed reserves as a separate balance sheet item. In the income statements, allocations to and withdrawals from untaxed reserves are reported under the heading Allocations to untaxed reserves. The reported tax expense is based on income after allocations.

In the consolidated balance sheet, untaxed reserves are divided into deferred tax liability in untaxed reserves, which is reported as a long-term liability, and equity in untaxed reserves, which is included in shareholders' equity. The deferred tax liability in untaxed reserves is calculated based on the anticipated tax rate for the immediately following year in each country. Calculation of the amount of tax liability takes into account that a portion of the untaxed reserves may be withdrawn without tax consequences by utilizing tax-loss carryforwards. Deferred tax receivables resulting from future tax-loss carryforwards exceeding deferred tax liability are not reported.

No allocations to untaxed reserves are reported in the consolidated statements of income. Group tax expense is calculated as the sum of reported tax expense for each Group company, adjusted for the effect of allocations to, and withdrawals from, untaxed reserves. This adjustment is offset by the annual change in the item Deferred tax liability in untaxed reserves in the consolidated balance sheet. The Group's tax expense is also affected by the Group's share of tax expenses in associated companies and by consolidated adjustments, primarily the elimination of internal profits. The Group's reported tax expense thereby becomes attributable mainly to reported income (loss) before taxes and minority interests.

New Act governing annual reports effective in 1997
A new Annual Report Act (ÅRL) became effective in Sweden on January 1, 1996. As of that date, the act applied to credit institutions and insurance companies. The new regulations became applicable to other companies, including Volvo, effective in the fiscal year beginning January 1, 1997 or later. The act involves the adaptation of Swedish accounting legislation to the accounting rules applied within the European Union. See also pages 70-71.

Definitions of key ratios
Operating margin
Operating income divided by sales.

Return on capital employed
Income divided by average total assets less average noninterest-bearing current liabilities. Income includes operating income, income from equity method investments, dividends received, gain (loss) on sale of securities and interest income.

Return on operating capital
Operating income divided by average operating capital. Operating capital consists of operating assets (inventories, receivables and long-term assets) reduced by noninterest-bearing current liabilities. This ratio is used only for Volvo's operating sectors, not for the Group as a whole.

189

Return on shareholders' equity
Net income divided by average shareholders' equity.

Interest coverage
Income divided by interest expense. Income includes operating income, income from equity method investments, dividends received, gain (loss) on sale of securities and interest income.

Self-financing ratio
Net financing from year's operations (see Statement of Changes in Financial Position) divided by capital expenditures for property, plant and equipment and investments in leasing and company vehicles.

Net financial assets (net debt)
Short- and long-term interest-bearing liabilities (including accruals for postretirement benefits) reduced by liquid funds and long-term interest-bearing receivables. Net debt in Volvo's sales-financing companies is not included since interest expense in these companies is charged against operating income and does not affect consolidated net interest expense.

Percentage of total assets
Shareholders' equity and minority interests divided by total assets.

Percentage of shareholders' equity
Shareholders' equity divided by total assets.

Income (loss) per share
Net income (loss) divided by the weighted average number of shares outstanding during the period.

Cash flow from operations
Operating income charged with a standard tax (28%), increased by depreciation, adjusted for changes in working capital and reduced by net investments. Working capital consists of noninterest-bearing current assets and liabilities, excluding tax claims/liabilities. This key ratio is applied solely to the operating sectors, not to the Group as a whole.

Financial information in accordance with generally accepted accounting principles in the United States (U.S. GAAP)

A summary of the Volvo Group's approximate net income and shareholders' equity, determined in accordance with U.S. GAAP, is presented in the accompanying tables.

Volvo also submits an annual report (Form 20-F) to the Securities & Exchange Commission (SEC) in the United States.

Application of U.S. GAAP would have the following approximate effect on consolidated net income and shareholders' equity of the Volvo Group:

Net income	1996	1995	1994
Net income in accordance with Swedish accounting principles	12,477	9,262	13,230
Items increasing (decreasing) reported net income:			
Foreign currency translation (A)	(89)	5,457	3,432
Income taxes (B)	494	(523)	(234)
Tooling costs (C)	(312)	(633)	(1,028)
Business combinations (D)	(529)	355	(546)
Shares and participations (E)	176	(116)	(97)
Interest costs (F)	15	2	2
Leasing (G)	49	49	41
Debt and equity securities (H)	(147)	368	(129)
Other (I)	(95)	111	82
Minority interests	–	2	2
Tax effect of above U.S. GAAP adjustments	178	(1,399)	(633)
Net increase (decrease) in net income	(260)	3,673	892
Approximate net income in accordance with U.S. GAAP	**12,217**	**12,935**	**14,122**
Approximate net income per share, SEK in accordance with U.S. GAAP	**26.40**	**28.20**	**34.60**
Weighted average number of shares outstanding (in thousands)	463,558	457,984	408,721

Shareholders' equity	1996	1995	1994
Shareholders' equity in accordance with Swedish accounting principles	57,876	51,200	43,332
Items increasing (decreasing) reported shareholders' equity:			
Foreign currency translation (A)	3,660	3,920	(1,537)
Income taxes (B)	1,398	904	1,427
Tooling costs (C)	–	312	945
Business combinations (D)	2,558	6,070	5,715
Shares and participations (E)	(90)	(266)	(151)
Interest costs (F)	503	487	484
Leasing (G)	(91)	(140)	(187)
Debt and equity securities (H)	1,604	10,472	1,296
Other (I)	583	682	548
Tax effect of above U.S. GAAP adjustments	(1,726)	(4,782)	(919)
Net increase in shareholders' equity	8,399	17,659	7,621
Approximate shareholders' equity in accordance with U.S. GAAP	**66,275**	**68,859**	**50,953**

Significant differences between Swedish and U.S. accounting principles.

A. Foreign currency translation. In consolidation, valuation of outstanding forward exchange contracts covering future flows of foreign currencies, Volvo makes a provision for unrealized losses to the extent that such losses exceed unrealized gains. Unrealized gains in excess of unrealized losses are not credited to income. In accordance with U.S. GAAP, these forward exchange contracts are valued at market price through fictive closing. Gains and losses arising therefrom are included in income. Unrealized gains on forward contracts in 1996 were estimated at 3,660 (3,920; loss 1,537).

B. Income taxes. Volvo applies the liability method of accounting for income tax in accordance with U.S. GAAP (SFAS 109). Under the liability method, deferred tax receivables and liabilities are established for the temporary differences between the financial reporting basis and the tax basis of Volvo's assets and liabilities at tax rates expected to be in effect when such amount are realized or settled.

In 1994 and 1995 tax expense calculated in accordance with Swedish principles was lower than in accordance with U.S. GAAP due to the utilization of tax-loss carryforwards and the difference in tax effect of temporary differences that were reported earlier in accordance with U.S. GAAP.

Tax expense for 1996 was lower under U.S. GAAP due to loss carryforwards on the years operations exceeding utilized loss carryforwards under Swedish GAAP.

C. Tooling costs. Up to and including 1992, Volvo expensed all tooling costs in the year incurred. In accordance with U.S. GAAP, all significant tooling costs are capitalized and depreciated over a period not exceeding five years. Effective in the 1993 accounts, Volvo has applied this accounting method and is capitalizing type-specific tools. Adjustments under this point pertain to depreciation of capitalized tooling costs in accordance with U.S. GAAP prior to 1993.

D. Business combinations. There are differences between Swedish reporting and U.S. GAAP in the method of accounting for certain acquisitions, particularly in the recognition and amortization of excess values and accounting for the tax benefits related to utilization of loss carryforwards of purchased subsidiaries.

Volvo's earnings in 1993 include a provision for an excess value related to Volvo Trucks which resulted from the exchange of shares with Renault. In accordance with U.S. GAAP, the corresponding excess value should be reported as a fixed asset (goodwill) which is being amortized over a period of five years.

In accordance with U.S. GAAP, the acquisition of BCP Branded Consumer Products AB (BCP) resulted in a gain, before taxes, of 1,320 in 1993. The gain was attributable to the exchange of Pharmacia shares for BCP shares. The transaction is reported in Volvo's 1993 financial statements as an exchange of shares that did not affect income.

In 1994 Volvo acquired the remaining outstanding BCP shares. For U.S. GAAP purposes, an excess value (goodwill) of 5,280 was recognized, based on the fair value of Volvo shares exchanged for the acquired BCP shares in June 1994. For Swedish GAAP purposes, the acquisition resulted in a smaller excess value amounting to 2,500, based on the fair value of Volvo shares in October 1993. During 1995 Volvo sold some shares attributable to the BCP acquisition. Of original goodwill of 5,280, approximately 20% was charged against the capital gain.

All shareholdings attributable to the BCP acquisition were divested in 1996; through the distribution of Swedish Match.

In 1995 AB Volvo acquired the outstanding 50% of the shares of Volvo Construction Equipment Corporation (formerly VME) from Clark Equipment Company in the U.S. In connection with the acquisition, an excess value (goodwill) of SEK 2.8 billion was reported. The shareholding was written down by SEK 1.8 billion, the portion of the excess value estimated to be attributable to the Volvo brand name at the date of acquisition. In accordance with U.S. GAAP, the excess value of SEK 2.8 billion should be amortized over the economic life (20 years).

E. Shares and participations. In calculating Volvo's share of earnings and shareholders' equity in associated companies in accordance with U.S. GAAP, account has been taken to the differences between the accounting of these companies – in accordance with Volvo's principles – and U.S. GAAP. The differences relate mainly to accounting for and amortization of excess values, accounting for utilized tax-loss carryforwards and, prior to 1992, accounting for tooling costs.

F. Interest costs. In accordance with U.S. GAAP, interest costs incurred in connection with the financing of the construction of property and other qualifying assets are capitalized and amortized over the economic life of the pertinent assets.

G. Leasing. Certain leasing transactions are reported differently in accordance with Volvo's accounting principles, compared with U.S. GAAP. The differences relate to sale-leaseback transactions.

H. Debt and equity securities. Effective January 1, 1994, in connection with accounting in accordance with U.S. GAAP, Volvo adopted the new accounting principle for debt and equity securities (SFAS 115: Accounting for Certain Investments in Debt and Equity Securities). SFAS 115 addresses the accounting and reporting for investments in equity securities that have readily determinable fair values, and for all debt securities. These investments are to be classified as either "held-to-maturity" securities that are reported at cost, "trading" securities that are reported at fair value with unrealized gains or losses included in earnings, or "available-for-sale" securities, reported at fair value, with unrealized gains or losses included in shareholders' equity.

The cumulative effect of adopting SFAS 115 as of January 1, 1994 amounted to 7 and is included in income for 1994.

As of December 31, 1996, unrealized gains after deducting for unrealized losses in "available-for-sale" securities amounted to 1,512 (10,233; 1,425). The increase between 1994 and 1995 pertains mainly to reclassification of the holding in Pharmacia from an associated company, reported in accordance with the equity method, to a marketable security. During 1996 a large part of the interest in Pharmacia & Upjohn was sold, which explains the decrease compared to 1995. Sale of "available-for-sale" securities in 1996 provided approximately SEK 13.6 billion (1.9; 8.5) and the capital gain, before tax, on sales of these securities amounted to approximately SEK 8.3 billion (1.2; 0.7).

I. Other. Includes adjustments pertaining to pension costs.

Consolidated balance sheets

	December 31, 1996		December 31, 1995		December 31, 1994	
Assets						
Non-current assets						
Intangible assets		**2,277**		5,626		4,545
Tangible assets						
Property, plant and equipment	**26,458**		25,094		25,991	
Assets under operating leases	**4,968**	**31,426**	2,847	27,941	2,205	28,196
Financial assets						
Shares and participations	**12,412**		18,087		18,548	
Long-term sales-finance receivables	**5,831**		4,161		3,534	
Other long-term receivables	**7,425**	**25,668**	6,743	28,991	5,385	27,467
Total non-current assets		**59,371**		62,558		60,208
Current assets						
Inventories		**23,148**		23,929		23,380
Short-term receivables						
Sales-finance receivables	**9,721**		6,175		5,817	
Other receivables	**22,258**	**31,979**	22,731	28,906	24,728	30,545
Marketable securities		**21,577**		15,817		15,878
Cash and bank accounts		**5,084**		7,489		8,571
Total current assets		**81,788**		76,141		78,374
Total assets		**141,159**		138,699		138,582
Shareholders' equity and liabilities						
Shareholders' equity						
Restricted equity						
Share capital	**2,318**		2,318		2,220	
Restricted reserves	**14,906**	**17,224**	14,264	16,582	14,545	16,765
Unrestricted equity						
Unrestricted reserves	**28,175**		25,356		13,337	
Net income for the year	**12,477**	**40,652**	9,262	34,618	13,230	26,567
Total shareholders' equity		**57,876**		51,200		43,332
Minority interests		**504**		605		838
Provisions						
Provisions for postemployment benefits	**3,150**		6,890		6,097	
Deferred taxes	**3,055**		3,350		4,107	
Other provisions	**11,933**	**18,138**	11,252	21,492	9,807	20,011
Non-current liabilities						
Bond loans	**7,955**		6,975		4,317	
Other loans	**10,234**	**18,189**	9,910	16,885	7,679	11,996
Current liabilities						
Loans	**14,263**		11,691		21,555	
Trade payables	**11,960**		12,702		13,075	
Other current liabilities	**20,229**	**46,452**	24,124	48,517	27,775	62,405
Shareholders' equity and liabilities		**141,159**		138,699		138,582
Assets pledged		**6,503**		5,434		6,527
Contingent liabilities		**6,188**		7,450		7,581

AB Volvo
balance sheets

		Dec 31 1996	Dec 31 1995	Dec 31 1994
Assets				
Liquid funds	Note 9	6	1,590	5,262
Accounts receivable from subsidiaries		1,971	3,484	897
Other receivables	Note 10	56	113	122
Total current assets		2,033	5,187	6,281
Property, plant and equipment	Note 11	97	82	79
Investments in shares – subsidiaries	Note 12	46,893	42,110	32,683
Other investments in shares	Note 13	7,025	7,317	8,230
Long-term receivables due from subsidiaries		–	158	2,565
Other long-term receivables		105	105	372
Total long-term assets		54,120	49,772	43,929
Total assets		56,153	54,959	50,210
Liabilities and shareholders' equity				
Accounts payable		36	52	31
Loans from subsidiaries		7,067	1,198	530
Other amounts due to subsidiaries		11,322	2,884	1,393
Other loans	Note 14	2	34	1,644
Other current liabilities and provisions	Note 14	396	1,964	2,096
Total current liabilities		18,823	6,132	5,694
Amounts due to subsidiaries	Note 15	8,606	10,958	9,640
Other long-term loans		1	2	36
Accruals for pensions	Note 16	280	487	447
Total long-term liabilities		8,887	11,447	10,123
Untaxed reserves	Note 17	758	739	1,024
Shareholders' equity	Note 18			
Share capital (463,558,252 shares, par value SEK 5)		2,318	2,318	2,220
Legal reserve		7,241	7,241	5,731
Total restricted equity		9,559	9,559	7,951
Retained earnings		17,228	23,906	17,440
Net income		898	3,176	7,978
Total unrestricted equity		18,126	27,082	25,418
Total shareholders' equity		27,685	36,641	33,369
Total liabilities and shareholders' equity		56,153	54,959	50,210
Assets pledged	Note 19	1,217	1,153	1,153
Contingent liabilities	Note 20	64,650	57,441	58,515
Capital expenditures approved		7	14	15

AB Volvo
income statements

		1996	1995	1994
Sales		559	488	440
Cost and expenses		(912)	(863)	(636)
Depreciation	Note 1	(17)	(14)	(12)
Operating loss before non-recurring items		(370)	(389)	(208)
Nonrecurring items	Note 2	–	(1,817)	–
Operating loss		(370)	(2,206)	(208)
Financial income (expense)				
Dividends received	Note 3	904	2,061	3,532
Gain on sales of securities, net	Note 4	–	–	3,569
Interest income	Note 5	233	532	583
Interest expense	Note 5	(1,048)	(1,250)	(1,096)
Other financial income (expense)	Note 6	234	438	(186)
Income (loss) before allocations and taxes		(47)	(425)	6,194
Allocations	Note 7	943	3,601	1,754
Income before taxes		896	3,176	7,948
Taxes	Note 8	2	–	30
Net income		898	3,176	7,978

Volvo

Comments

The focus in the Volvo example is on the consolidated statements. Financial statements for the parent company are also given, but at the end of the annual report.

Volvo's financial reporting is now in accordance with the new Annual Report Act in Sweden. This act has been implemented by Swedish limited liability companies and certain trading companies since 1997. Volvo presents the income statement and balance sheets for the years 1994–6 as they are intended to be presented in 1997, in accordance with the Annual Report Act.

Consolidated *balance sheets* are now presented as prescribed in the EU Directive. That differs substantially from earlier legislation in Sweden, in part because the items are now presented in reverse order of liquidity, and in part because the 'liabilities' item is divided into 'provisions' and 'liabilities'.

The cash flow statement ('*Statements of changes in consolidated financial position*') is presented according to the indirect model and follows the three normal divisions of operations, investments and financing.

In common with many European countries the parent company's statements are also presented in the Volvo case (AB Volvo).

Volvo also presents *Financial information in accordance with US GAAP*. The summary gives a concrete comparison between Swedish GAAP and US GAAP for net income and shareholders' equity and an excellent explanation of the differences (from A–I).

The consolidated financial statements of Volvo cover three years. This is a bonus for users as it gives a longer perspective.

The *statement of income* follows the functional model. We notice 'non-recurring items' defined within the operating loss.

Bergesen Shipping – financial statements

STATEMENT OF INCOME

NOK million	Note	BERGESEN D.Y. GROUP 1996	Pro forma 1995	1994	BERGESEN D.Y. ASA 1996	1995
OPERATING REVENUE (EXPENSES)						
Operating revenue	1	**4,511**	**4,359**	**3,409**	**3,734**	**3,219**
Wages, social security and pensions	1-5	(691)	(803)	(684)	(575)	(561)
Other operating expenses	1-3,6	(2,581)	(2,465)	(1,997)	(2,090)	(1,833)
Operating profit before depreciation		**1,239**	**1,091**	**728**	**1,069**	**825**
Depreciation	1,22	(665)	(814)	(708)	(545)	(713)
Operating profit	1	**574**	**277**	**20**	**524**	**112**
FINANCIAL INCOME (EXPENSES)						
Interest income		77	87	75	80	53
Intercompany interest		-	-	-	9	9
Dividend income		47	40	38	46	40
Profit on securities		23	207	15	23	211
Other financial income	7	2	11	2	5	3
Interest expenses		(361)	(327)	(214)	(326)	(270)
Exchange income (loss)	8	(19)	160	348	(47)	124
Other financial expenses		(10)	(24)	(17)	(10)	(22)
Net financial items		(241)	154	247	(220)	148
PROFIT ON SALE OF LONG TERM ASSETS						
Net profit (loss) on sale of long term assets		(15)	58	(4)	(64)	47
EXTRAORDINARY ITEMS						
Change of accounting principle	P)	61	-	-	48	-
Net profit before tax		**379**	**489**	**263**	**288**	**307**
Tax	9	1,224	(116)	(54)	1,129	(80)
Net profit after tax		**1,603**	**373**	**209**	**1,417**	**227**
Equity transfers and allocations:						
Net profit after tax					1,417	227
Group contribution received					0	73
From temporary restricted funds					116	98
For allocation					1,533	398
Proposed allocation:						
Dividend					76	76
Legal reserve					141	23
Undistributed profit					1,316	299
Total allocations					1,533	398
Earnings per share, NOK	10	21	5.2	3.5		
Cash flow per share, NOK	10	14	18	16		

BALANCE SHEET

ASSETS		BERGESEN D.Y. GROUP		BERGESEN D.Y. ASA	
NOK Million	Note	1996	1995	1996	1995
CURRENT ASSETS					
Bank deposits	26,30	943	1,242	759	788
Bonds, certificates etc.	11	68	82	68	82
Shares	12	829	872	829	848
Receivables, interest bearing	13	10	336	77	301
Receivables, non interest bearing	14	516	615	378	436
Bunkers and other inventories		101	115	73	44
Total current assets		**2,467**	**3,262**	**2,184**	**2,499**
LONG TERM ASSETS					
Shares in subsidiaries	15	-	-	531	402
Shares and holdings in other companies	16,17	11	18	27	26
Net pension assets		38	53	6	6
Other receivables	18	93	155	138	133
Intercompany receivables		-	-	472	1,022
Paid newbuilding instalments	19	380	243	380	243
Periodic maintenance		358	-	284	-
Vessels	20,22	9,962	11,065	8,358	9,487
Equipment, vehicles etc.	22	39	47	39	31
Real estate	21,22	595	640	225	249
Goodwill	22	92	121	92	121
Total long term assets		**11,568**	**12,342**	**10,552**	**11,720**
Total assets		**14,035**	**15,604**	**12,736**	**14,219**

LIABILITIES AND EQUITY		BERGESEN D.Y. GROUP		BERGESEN D.Y. ASA	
NOK Million	Note	1996	1995	1996	1995
CURRENT LIABILITIES					
Unpaid VAT, withholding tax					
social security, holiday pay etc.		86	114	67	72
Tax, payable	9	4	9	4	5
Dividend		76	76	76	76
Other liabilities, ncn interest bearing	24	564	608	470	469
Current portion of mortgage debt	25,26	200	378	123	267
Other liabilities, interest bearing		-	294	-	177
Total current liabilities		**930**	**1,479**	**740**	**1,066**
LONG TERM LIABILITIES					
Intercompany liabilities		-	-	1	99
Net pension obligations	5	76	28	70	22
Mortgage debt	25,26	891	2,867	124	2,306
Other liabilities, interest bearing	25,26	3,840	3,195	4,094	3,195
Deferred tax	9	81	1,322	86	1,226
Total long term liabilities		**4,888**	**7,412**	**4,375**	**6,848**
Total liabilities		**5,818**	**8,891**	**5,115**	**7,914**
SHAREHOLDERS' EQUITY					
Share capital		189	189	189	189
Legal reserve		2,250	2,141	2,127	1,988
Temporary restricted funds		-	126	-	116
Revaluation surplus		68	68	68	68
Undistributed profit		5,710	4,189	5,237	3,944
Total shareholders' equity	27	**8,217**	**6,713**	**7,621**	**6,305**
Total liabilities and equity		**14,035**	**15,604**	**12,736**	**14,219**
Unpaid newbuilding instalments	19	361	287	361	287
Assets charged	28	2,378	6,420	2,333	6,355
Guarantees and joint several liabilities	29	2,215	2,192	2,181	2,151
Off balance sheets items	31	-	-	-	-

Oslo, 12 March 1997
On the Board of Bergesen d.y. ASA

Petter C.G. Sundt   Lars A. Christensen   Ole Lund   Christian Ringnes   Morten Sig. Bergesen

STATEMENT OF CASH FLOW

CASH FLOW FROM OPER. ACTIVITIES	Note	BERGESEN D.Y. GROUP			BERGESEN D.Y. ASA	
		1996	1995	Pro forma 1994	1996	1995
(NOK million)						
Net profit after tax		1,603	373	209	1,417	227
Change deferred tax	9	(1,224)	113	48	(1,129)	80
Depreciation		665	814	708	545	713
Pension costs		28	16	17	13	15
Periodic maintenance		(87)	-	-	(84)	-
Unrealised foreign exchange loss	8	(16)	(29)	(412)	(9)	(23)
Profit/loss on sale of fixed assets		15	(58)	5	64	(47)
Changes in inventories, receivables and						
short term liabilities		362	(200)	8	248	(492)
Deferred capital gains shares, Profit(loss) securities		(23)	(207)	(15)	(23)	(211)
Net cash from operating activities (1)		**1,323**	**822**	**568**	**1,042**	**262**
CASH FLOW FOR INVESTING ACTIVITIES						
Payment for purchase of:						
Vessels bought second hand		(223)	(4,803)	(411)	0	(3,798)
Newbuilding instalments		(137)	(243)	(500)	(137)	(243)
Real estate		(13)	(40)	(95)	0	(11)
Other fixed assets		(26)	(82)	(47)	(151)	(268)
Goodwill		0	(142)	0	0	(142)
Current shares		(33)	(572)	(135)	(57)	(564)
Proceeds from sale of:						
Vessels		447	293	151	303	219
Real estate		51	2	0	28	1
Other fixed assets		62	3	9	49	3
Current shares		99	810	149	99	814
Net cash for investing activities (2)		**227**	**(4,774)**	**(878)**	**134**	**(3,989)**
CASH FLOW FROM FINANCING ACTIVITIES						
Proceeds from new loans		661	2,557	1,770	899	2,196
Loan repayments		(2,448)	(553)	(2,440)	(2,494)	(438)
Intercompany liabilities		0	0	0	452	(171)
New shares issued		0	2,317	(10)	0	2,317
Dividend paid		(76)	(57)	(57)	(76)	(57)
Net cash from financing activities (3)		**(1,863)**	**4,264**	**(737)**	**(1,219)**	**3,847**
Net increase (decrease) in cash (1+2+3)		**(313)**	**312**	**(1,047)**	**(43)**	**120**
Cash as of 1 January		1,324	1,012	2,059	870	750
Cash as of 31 December		**1,011**	**1,324**	**1,012**	**827**	**870**
DETAILS OF CASH AND CASH EQUIVALENTS						
Bank deposits		943	1,242	949	759	788
Bonds, certificates etc.		68	82	63	68	82
Cash as of 31 December		**1,011**	**1,324**	**1,012**	**827**	**870**

ACCOUNTING PRINCIPLES

The annual accounts have been prepared in accordance with the Norwegian Joint Stock Companies Act and generally accepted accounting principles. The main accounting principles followed by Bergesen d.y. ASA are described below.

A) COMPARABLE FIGURES

The general meetings of Havtor ASA and Bergesen d.y. ASA decided in December 1995 to merge the companies. The merger was implemented according to the pooling of interests method which requires that the assets and liabilities of the merging companies are combined at their book values. The comparable consolidated figures for 1994 are pro forma figures for the merged company. Havtor's fleet acquisition from Kværner ASA, Neste OY, International Shipholding Corporation and the shipping partownership Nemo is included from the purchase date, 1 April 1995. Uniform accounting principles have been used.

B) PRINCIPLES OF CONSOLIDATION

The consolidated accounts include the parent company Bergesen d.y. ASA and its subsidiaries (cf. note 15). The consolidated accounts are prepared on the basis of uniform accounting principles that apply to the whole Group. Inter-company transactions, receivables and liabilities have been eliminated. The cost of shares in subsidiaries has been elimi-nated in the consolidated accounts against equity in the subsid-iaries at the time of purchase (Purchase method). The excess values have been allocated to those assets to which the values relate, and are depreciated over the assets' estimated econo-mic life. Excess values not traceable to material assets have been classified as goodwill and are depreciated over five years.

C) SHAREHOLDINGS AND INVESTMENTS IN OTHER COMPANIES

Vessels that are not wholly owned are owned through invest-ments in Norwegian general and limited partnerships, with the exception of Settebello, which is owned through Amazon Transport Inc. The investments in these companies represent either joint ventures or means of financing, and are included in the accounts on a pro rata basis. Thus, assets, liabilities, income and expenses are included with the percentage owned by Bergesen. A number of the company's wholly and partially owned vessels participate in shipping pools which are also included in the accounts on a pro rata basis. Investments in associated companies (including investments in properties in the USA) are presented according to the equity method. Bergesen's share of the profit is included in financial items, while the book value of the investments is reported as shares and holdings in other companies. Other investments are included in accordance with the cost method. Long term shareholdings are written down when the decline in value is considered material and permanent.

D) REVENUE RECOGNITION

Income and expenses related to voyages are accounted for on the percentage of completion basis. Demurrage is recognised as revenue when the claim is considered probable.

E) PERIODIC MAINTENANCE

From 1996, periodic maintenance related to classification and drydocking is capitalised and amortised over the period to the next periodic maintenance. Correspondingly, a part of the cost price of vessels acquired is capitalised as periodic maintenance.

F) OTHER MAINTENANCE

Actual expenses related to ongoing maintenance are charged to expenses when incurred. The franchise to be paid in connection with accidents is charged at the accident date. Expenses related to insurance claims are capitalised and classified as interest-bearing receivables.

G) SHARES, BONDS AND CERTIFICATES

Share investments motivated by financial considerations are classified as current assets, whereas strategic investments are classified as long term assets. Bonds, certificates, short term shareholdings and long term shareholdings are all treated as separate portfolios, and assessed at their cost price or market value at year end, whichever is lower.

H) RECEIVABLES

Receivables are booked at their outstanding value less provisions for probable losses.

I) BUNKERS AND OTHER INVENTORIES

Bunkers and other inventories are reported at cost or market value, whichever is lower.

J) FIXED ASSETS AND DEPRECIATION

Depreciable fixed assets are stated on the balance sheet at cost less accumulated depreciation. Depreciation is charged on a straight line basis over the remaining economic life of the individual assets. As from 1 January 1995, gas carriers are depreciated over 30 years. As from 1 January 1996, tankers and dry bulk vessels are depreciated over 25 years. Real estate is depreciated at three per cent per annum, based on the historical cost.

K) NEWBUILDINGS

Instalments on newbuilding projects are recorded as long term assets as payments are made. Interest incurred during the building period are charged against operations. New vessels are recognised in the balance sheet upon delivery from the shipyard. The cost price comprises total newbuilding instalments based on the rate of exchange at the payment date, plus any additional expenses not included in the new-building contract.

L) LEASING

Financial leases are capitalized in the balance sheet. Operational leases are expensed.

M) FOREIGN EXCHANGE

Bank deposits in foreign currencies are stated at year end rates of exchange. Other current assets and short term liabilities in foreign currencies are stated on a portfolio basis. The same principle has been applied to long term investments, liabilities and forward exchange contracts. Unrealised gains in the same portfolio are not reported as income, while unrealised losses are booked in their entirety. Net unrealised expenses are reversed in the accounts when the unrealised losses are reduced or eliminated.

N) TAX

Deferred tax is calculated with 28 per cent of the temporary differences related to the businesses outside of the shipping tax system.

In 1996, a new tax system for shipping companies was introduced. The changes have the effect that the ongoing income of shipping companies, provided some conditions are met, are not taxed unless the income is distributed as dividend or the company no longer satisfies the conditions. The company must instead pay tonnage tax. Untaxed reserves related to net positive temporary differences when entering the system will be taxed if distributed. The company's board of directors has decided to bring the shipping business into the shipping tax system in 1997. The net present value of deferred tax related to the positive temporary differences to be transferred into the new tax system is evaluated as immaterial, as the company does not expect that the taxable income these temporary differences represent will crystallise in the foreseeable future. The evaluation is based on the company's dividend policy, the liquidity reserves and the retained earnings in those part of the group that will not be covered by the new tax system, and the company's intention of maintaining its shipping activities. The main portion of the deferred tax regarding the part of the shipping business that will be brought into the system is thus taken to income as a separate item. Tonnage tax is classified as other operating expenses. Refer to note 9.

O) PENSIONS

Net pension costs include current service costs (including the effect of expected future salary increases) and interest on the pension obligations less the estimated return on pension plan assets. The losses and gains from changes in actuarial assumptions and pension plans are taken into account when exceeding 10 per cent of gross pension obligations or pension plan assets, whichever is higher. These losses and gains are amortised over the average remaining service period. In the balance sheet, pension plans with net pension obligations are reported as long term liabilities and pension plans with net pension assets are reported as long term assets. Refer also to notes 5 and 27.

P) THE EFFECT OF CHANGES IN PRINCIPLES AND ESTIMATES

As disclosed in item E) above, the company has changed its accounting principle for recognising periodic maintenance. The implementation effect of the change has been booked as a reduction to the net book value of each vessel within the vessel's book values. Reductions beyond the book value are classified as extraordinary income. At the beginning of the year, the estimated unamortised periodic maintenance was capitalised with NOK 322 mill. The change in principle has increased the operating profit before depreciation in 1996 by NOK 26 mill. If the principles had been used in 1994 and 1995, the operating profit before depreciation would have been NOK 21 mill. lower and NOK 2 mill. higher than reported in the accounts for these years. The change has also reduced the depreciation in 1996 by NOK 49 mill. The depreciation period for tankers and dry bulk vessels has been changed from 20 to 25 years. This reduces the depreciation by NOK 137 million for tankers and NOK 16 million for dry bulk.

VALUE ADJUSTED BALANCE SHEET

	Market value NOK Million	%	Book value NOK Million	Excess value NOK Million
ASSETS				
Bank deposits, bonds, certificates etc.	1,011	6	1,011	-
Shares[1]	2,132	12	829	1,303
Other current assets	627	3	627	-
Total current assets	**3,770**	**21**	**2,467**	**1,303**
Gas carriers	8,729	49	6,808	1,921
Crude oil tankers	3,571	20	2,673	898
Dry bulk vessels	585	3	481	104
Total vessels [2]	12,885	72	9,962	2,923
Paid newbuilding instalments	380	2	380	-
Periodic maintenance (dry docking)	-	-	358	(358)
Real estate [3]	791	4	595	196
Other long term assets [3]	181	1	273	(92)
Total long term assets	**14,237**	**79**	**11,568**	**2,669**
Total assets	**18,007**	**100**	**14,035**	**3,972**
LIABILITIES AND EQUITY				
Interest bearing debt	4,858	27	4,931	(73)
Other debt	806	4	806	-
Equity before tax	12,343	69	8,298	4,045
Total liabilities and equity	**18,007**	**100**	**14,035**	**3,972**
Value adjusted equity before tax				
as of 31 December 1996, NOK per share	**163**			

COMMENTS TO THE VALUE ADJUSTED BALANCE SHEET

The purpose of the value adjusted balance sheet is to provide the reader with information about the market value of assets, liability and equity. The valuations are essentially based on external assessments. It is important that the reader evaluates the assumptions on which the market values are based (see notes below). Vessels represent approximately 72 per cent of total balance sheet assets. There is normally a maximum deviation of 10 per cent between the highest and lowest estimates. We have tried to reduce the uncertainty by averaging estimates made by three different brokerage firms. Although the number of vessels sold varies from year to year, there is normally a good second-hand market for tankers. Gas carrier tonnage is bought and sold less frequently, so the brokers' estimates must be based largely on their own evaluations. The valuation of the vessels is based on their market value with no adjustment for any charter parties. It is assumed that charter parties do not have negative values. Vessel prices rose sharply in 1986–1990, then fell back again in 1990–1992. Values remained relatively stable in terms of USD from 1993 to 1995. The tanker fleet showed a marginal increase also in 1996, while the value of the gas- and dry bulk fleet, measured in USD, showed a reduction of 12 per cent. The market value of vessels and the USD exchange rate are the two most important factors affecting value adjusted equity. A 10 per cent change in market value of vessels changes value adjusted equity with NOK 17 per share. A 10 per cent change in USD exchange rate gives a change of NOK 11 per share. Please refer to the segment reports (pages 39–53) for more details.

NOTES TO THE VALUE ADJUSTED BALANCE SHEET

When converting the USD value of vessels, other assets and liabilities in foreign currency, we have used the USD exchange rate as of 31 December 1996, which was NOK 6.44.

1) SHARES

The market value of listed shares is based on the trading prices quoted on the Oslo Stock Exchange 31 December 1996. The market value of unlisted shares has been assessed on the basis of known trading prices and to some extent on our own valuations.

2) VESSELS

The market value of the company's interests in vessels as of 31 December 1996 has been fixed as the average of the valuations regarding unchartered vessels obtained from the ship brokerages Clarkson, Fearnley and Gibson.

3) OTHER ASSETS

The market value in excess of book value concerns real estate in Norway and is based on appraisals carried out by OPAK as of 31 December 1996 and our own estimates. Goodwill is not included in the value adjusted balance sheet.

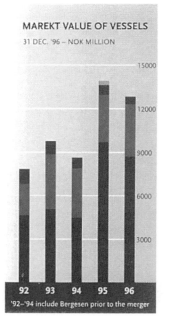

MAREKT VALUE OF VESSELS
31 DEC. '96 – NOK MILLION

15000
12000
9000
6000
3000

92 93 94 95 96
'92–'94 include Bergesen prior to the merger

Other
Dry Bulk
Tankers
Gas

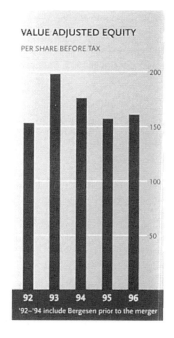

VALUE ADJUSTED EQUITY
PER SHARE BEFORE TAX

200
150
100
50

92 93 94 95 96
'92–'94 include Bergesen prior to the merger

Bergesen

Comments

Bergesen Shipping presents all three basic financial statements both for the parent company (Bergesen d.y. ASA) and for the group (Bergesen d.y. Group) in the same setting. Since the parent company also has the same activity as the subsidiaries, this is a rational and informative way of presentation. In the Bergesen example we see that in 1996 more than 80 per cent of the total operating revenue came from the parent company.

The *statement of income*, where figures are given for three years for the group, is presented according to the expense classification of costs, which is prescribed by the Norwegian Companies Act and Accounting Act.

We see that the proposed allocation (proposed for the shareholders' General Assembly) is linked to the parent company, since this is where this decision lies.

From the *balance sheet* we learn that Bergesen uses the deferred tax model. In a note, very detailed information about the temporary differences is given. They are summarized in this way:

    Current assets
    Long term assets
    Tax loss carried forward
    Net temporary differences
    Deferred tax (28%)

The main part of the temporary differences is linked to vessels (long-term assets).

Bergesen also uses the indirect method for the presentation of the cash flow statement. From this statement it is, analytically, very clear to explain the net decrease in cash this year (1 + 2 + 3).

Perhaps the most interesting part of the Bergesen annual report is the *value-adjusted balance sheet*, where market values are given. The purpose of the value-adjusted balance sheet is 'to provide the reader with information about the market value of assets, liabilities and equity'. It is also said that the valuations are essentially based on external assessments.

From the figures given in the value adjusted balance sheet we see that 'total assets' measured at market value are nearly 30 per cent over book value. The equity is nearly 50 per cent higher!

This is an excellent illustration, underlining the basis of traditional accounting, namely historical cost. The accounting figures do not give market values, and the figures for Bergesen represent one of the few examples internationally where the differences are documented. What can be criticized is the lack of an *income statement* following up the market value philosophy, where both the gross changes in values and the cost consequences of the higher values are taken into consideration.

Coca-Cola – financial statements

Consolidated Balance Sheets

December 31,	1996	1995
(In millions except share data)		

Assets

Current

Cash and cash equivalents	$ **1,433**	$ 1,167
Marketable securities	**225**	148
	1,658	1,315
Trade accounts receivable, less allowances of $30 in 1996 and $34 in 1995	**1,641**	1,695
Inventories	**952**	1,117
Prepaid expenses and other assets	**1,659**	1,323
Total Current Assets	**5,910**	5,450

Investments and Other Assets

Equity method investments		
Coca-Cola Enterprises Inc.	**547**	556
Coca-Cola Amatil Limited	**881**	682
Other, principally bottling companies	**2,004**	1,157
Cost method investments, principally bottling companies	**737**	319
Marketable securities and other assets	**1,779**	1,597
	5,948	4,311

Property, Plant and Equipment

Land	**204**	233
Buildings and improvements	**1,528**	1,944
Machinery and equipment	**3,649**	4,135
Containers	**200**	345
	5,581	6,657
Less allowances for depreciation	**2,031**	2,321
	3,550	4,336

Goodwill and Other Intangible Assets	**753**	944
	$ **16,161**	$ 15,041

December 31,	1996	1995
Liabilities and Share-Owners' Equity		
Current		
Accounts payable and accrued expenses	$ **2,972**	$ 3,103
Loans and notes payable	**3,388**	2,371
Current maturities of long-term debt	**9**	552
Accrued income taxes	**1,037**	1,322
Total Current Liabilities	**7,406**	7,348
Long-Term Debt	**1,116**	1,141
Other Liabilities	**1,182**	966
Deferred Income Taxes	**301**	194
Share-Owners' Equity		
Common stock, $.25 par value		
Authorized: 5,600,000,000 shares		
Issued: 3,432,956,518 shares in 1996; 3,423,678,994 shares in 1995	**858**	856
Capital surplus	**1,058**	863
Reinvested earnings	**15,127**	12,882
Unearned compensation related to outstanding restricted stock	**(61)**	(68)
Foreign currency translation adjustment	**(662)**	(424)
Unrealized gain on securities available for sale	**156**	82
	16,476	14,191
Less treasury stock, at cost (951,963,574 shares in 1996; 919,081,326 shares in 1995)	**10,320**	8,799
	6,156	5,392
	$ **16,161**	$ 15,041

See Notes to Consolidated Financial Statements.

Consolidated Statements of Income

Year Ended December 31,	1996	1995	1994
(*In millions except per share data*)			
Net Operating Revenues	$ 18,546	$ 18,018	$ 16,181
Cost of goods sold	6,738	6,940	6,168
Gross Profit	11,808	11,078	10,013
Selling, administrative and general expenses	7,893	7,052	6,376
Operating Income	3,915	4,026	3,637
Interest income	238	245	181
Interest expense	286	272	199
Equity income	211	169	134
Other income (deductions)-net	87	86	(25)
Gains on issuances of stock by equity investees	431	74	—
Income before Income Taxes	4,596	4,328	3,728
Income taxes	1,104	1,342	1,174
Net Income	$ 3,492	$ 2,986	$ 2,554
Net Income per Share	$ 1.40	$ 1.18	$ .99
Average Shares Outstanding	2,494	2,525	2,580

See Notes to Consolidated Financial Statements.

Consolidated Statements of Cash Flows

Year Ended December 31,	1996	1995	1994
(*In millions*)			
Operating Activities			
Net income	$ 3,492	$ 2,986	$ 2,554
Depreciation and amortization	479	454	411
Deferred income taxes	(145)	157	58
Equity income, net of dividends	(89)	(25)	(4)
Foreign currency adjustments	(60)	(23)	(6)
Gains on issuances of stock by equity investees	(431)	(74)	—
Other noncash items	181	45	41
Net change in operating assets and liabilities	36	(192)	307
Net cash provided by operating activities	3,463	3,328	3,361
Investing Activities			
Acquisitions and investments, principally bottling companies	(645)	(338)	(311)
Purchases of investments and other assets	(623)	(403)	(379)
Proceeds from disposals of investments and other assets	1,302	580	299
Purchases of property, plant and equipment	(990)	(937)	(878)
Proceeds from disposals of property, plant and equipment	81	44	109
Other investing activities	(175)	(172)	(55)
Net cash used in investing activities	(1,050)	(1,226)	(1,215)
Net cash provided by operations after reinvestment	2,413	2,102	2,146
Financing Activities			
Issuances of debt	1,122	754	491
Payments of debt	(580)	(212)	(154)
Issuances of stock	124	86	69
Purchases of stock for treasury	(1,521)	(1,796)	(1,192)
Dividends	(1,247)	(1,110)	(1,006)
Net cash used in financing activities	(2,102)	(2,278)	(1,792)
Effect of Exchange Rate Changes on Cash and Cash Equivalents	(45)	(43)	34
Cash and Cash Equivalents			
Net increase (decrease) during the year	266	(219)	388
Balance at beginning of year	1,167	1,386	998
Balance at end of year	$ 1,433	$ 1,167	$ 1,386

See Notes to Consolidated Financial Statements.

Notes to Consolidated Financial Statements

1. ORGANIZATION AND SUMMARY OF SIGNIFICANT ACCOUNTING POLICIES

Organization
The Coca-Cola Company and subsidiaries (our Company) is predominantly a manufacturer, marketer and distributor of soft drink and noncarbonated beverage concentrates and syrups. Operating in nearly 200 countries worldwide, we primarily sell our concentrates and syrups to bottling and canning operations, fountain wholesalers and fountain retailers. We have significant markets for our products in all of the world's geographic regions. We record revenue when title passes to our customers.

Basis of Presentation
Certain amounts in the prior years' financial statements have been reclassified to conform to the current year presentation.

Consolidation
Our consolidated financial statements include the accounts of The Coca-Cola Company and all subsidiaries except where control is temporary or does not rest with our Company. Our investments in companies in which we have the ability to exercise significant influence over operating and financial policies are accounted for by the equity method. Accordingly, our Company's share of the net earnings of these companies is included in consolidated net income. Our investments in other companies are carried at cost or fair value, as appropriate. All significant intercompany accounts and transactions are eliminated upon consolidation.

Issuances of Stock by Equity Investees
When one of our equity investees sells additional shares to third parties, our percentage ownership interest in the investee decreases. In the event the selling price per share is more or less than our average carrying amount per share, we recognize a noncash gain or loss on the issuance. This noncash gain or loss, net of any deferred taxes, is recognized in our net income in the period the change of ownership interest occurs.

Advertising Costs
Our Company generally expenses production costs of print, radio and television advertisements as of the first date the advertisements take place. Advertising expenses included in selling, administrative and general expenses were $1,437 million in 1996, $1,292 million in 1995 and $1,114 million in 1994. As of December 31, 1996 and 1995, advertising costs of approximately $247 million and $299 million, respectively, were recorded primarily in prepaid expenses and other assets in our accompanying balance sheets.

Net Income per Share
Net income per share is computed by dividing net income by the weighted-average number of shares outstanding.

On April 17, 1996, our share owners approved an increase in the authorized common stock of our Company from 2.8 billion to 5.6 billion shares and a two-for-one stock split. The stated par value of each share remained at $.25 per share. Our financial statements have been restated to reflect these changes.

Cash Equivalents
Marketable securities that are highly liquid and have maturities of three months or less at the date of purchase are classified as cash equivalents.

Cash Equivalents
Marketable securities that are highly liquid and have maturities of three months or less at the date of purchase are classified as cash equivalents.

Inventories
Inventories consist primarily of raw materials and supplies and are valued at the lower of cost or market. In general, cost is determined on the basis of average cost or first-in, first-out methods.

Property, Plant and Equipment
Property, plant and equipment are stated at cost and are depreciated principally by the straight-line method over the estimated useful lives of the assets.

Goodwill and Other Intangible Assets
Goodwill and other intangible assets are stated on the basis of cost and are amortized, principally on a straight-line basis, over the estimated future periods to be benefited (not exceeding 40 years). Goodwill and other intangible assets are periodically reviewed for impairment based on an assessment of future operations to ensure that they are appropriately valued. Accumulated amortization was approximately $86 million and $117 million on December 31, 1996 and 1995, respectively.

Use of Estimates
In conformity with generally accepted accounting principles, the preparation of our financial statements requires our management to make estimates and assumptions that affect the amounts reported in our financial statements and accompanying notes. Although these estimates are based on our knowledge of current events and actions we may undertake in the future, they may ultimately differ from actual results.

New Accounting Standards
We adopted Statement of Financial Accounting Standards No. 123, "Accounting for Stock-Based Compensation" (SFAS 123), in 1996. Under the provisions of SFAS 123, companies can elect to account for stock-based compensation plans using a fair-value based method or continue measuring compensation expense for those plans using the intrinsic value method prescribed in Accounting Principles Board Opinion No. 25, "Accounting for Stock Issued to Employees" (APB 25) and related Interpretations. We have elected to continue using the intrinsic value method to account for our stock-based compensation plans. SFAS 123 requires companies electing to continue using the intrinsic value method to make certain pro forma disclosures (see Note 11).

Statement of Financial Accounting Standards No. 121, "Accounting for the Impairment of Long-Lived Assets and for Long-Lived Assets to be Disposed Of" (SFAS 121), was adopted as of January 1, 1996. SFAS 121 standardized the accounting practices for the recognition and measurement of impairment losses on certain long-lived assets. The adoption of SFAS 121 was not material to our results of operations or financial position. However, the provisions of SFAS 121 required certain charges, historically recorded by our Company in other income (deductions)-net, to be included in operating income.

Coca-Cola

Comments

In order to illustrate the content of an annual report we start with the following résumé of the Coca-Cola report:

1996 annual report

- The Unquenchable Nature of our Business
  - A Message from Roberto C. Goizueta (Chairman, Board of Directors, and Chief Executive Officer)

- Why Share-Owner Value?
  - A Perspective on Value by Roberto C. Goizueta

- Properties of Thirst

- Converting Thirst into Results
  - A Sales, Marketing and Operations Review from the President and Chief Operating Officer

- Financial Review

- Selected Financial Data

- Consolidated Financial Statements

- Notes to Consolidated Financial Statements

- Management and Board of Directors

- Share-Owner Information

- Glossary

If we analyze the 79-page Coca-Cola annual report we find that financial (accounting) figures dominate, either directly or in connection with descriptions of developments of different kinds. But, naturally enough, the PR and advertising aspect is also there (almost a third). In the *selected financial data* section, compound growth rates for five and ten years are given.

The notes to the consolidated financial statements cover 10 pages, with 16 notes altogether.

The *consolidated balance sheet*, presented as the first of the financial statements, starts with 'Current assets', followed by 'Investments and other assets', 'Property, plant and equipment' and 'Goodwill and other intangible assets'. This is a typical US presentation, and has the opposite order to that in Europe (EU directives).

We see that inter-company investments are huge, more than investment in property, plant and equipment.

In a note we are informed that Coca-Cola (Coke) owns approximately 49 per cent of the common stock of Coca-Cola Enterprises (Enterprises). Coke accounts for the investment in Enterprises by the equity method of accounting. Enterprises is the largest bottler of Coca-Cola in the world. The relationship between Coke and Enterprises is complex. Enterprises produces virtually all its products under licence from Coke and buys soft-drinks syrup, concentrates and sweeteners from Coke as well. In effect, Coke controls the products and a substantial portion of the input costs of Enterprises. The Board of Directors is controlled by Coke.

It can be questioned whether Enterprises is in fact a subsidiary and should have been included in the consolidated accounts. If not, it also could be questioned whether a proportionate consolidation would provide a more useful set of financial statements. As mentioned, Coke uses the equity method of accounting. (Take some time to reflect on how the report would look if presented according to the two other alternatives.)

From 'Share-owners' equity' we see that treasury stock (Coca-Cola's own shares) is a huge amount and is deducted from the equity, which is logical.

The *consolidated statements of income* give figures for three years (required for listed companies in the US). Coca-Cola also keeps to the functional model of presentation.

Net interest and equity income are positive, which illustrates the importance of Coca-Cola's financial investments.

The *consolidated statements of cash flows* should be self-explanatory now, but notice the subtraction made, ending up in 'Net cash provided by operations after reinvestment'.

13 Financial analysis

LEARNING OBJECTIVES

In this chapter the objective is to learn how accounting data are used for analytical purposes. Accounting analysis is a specific field within accounting, and part of it is very sophisticated, with mathematical and statistical methods used extensively. We will, however, concentrate on more general analysis.

13.1 What is financial accounting analysis?

Financial accounting analysis is the systematic use of accounting data in order to investigate the financial situation of a firm.

Both the management of the firm and groups outside the firm are interested in a systematic use of accounting data. Such analyses are carried out for many purposes, and they can be either of a continuing character or a one-off phenomenon.

The quality of financial analysis can never be better than the quality of the accounting data themselves. First, remember the basic principles of financial accounting, especially the historical cost principle. Also bear in mind that measurements of accounting events are not always objective. In view of this, we must be aware of the possibility of manipulation of accounting data, and that great creativity can be involved. Finally, very often a user of accounting data can be in doubt about the message and thus also the conclusions to draw from the analysis.

13.2 Comparison is the focal point

Accounting data are produced to be used, generally by comparison of one type or another. It is by comparison that accounting data can tell the economic story and explain it. It is by comparison that signals are found, positive as well as negative. In order to increase the understanding of the different accounting analyses, we will use specific accounting data. The following accounting statements are given:

Profit and loss account, 19XX

	Current year (000s)	Previous year (000s)
Sales	108 500	98 000
Raw material	15 000	12 500
Wages and social expenses	57 500	54 500
Other operating and administration expenses	31 300	24 400
Depreciation	1 400	1 400
(Increases) decreases: work in progress and finished goods	(1 500)	200
Operating income	4 800	5 000
Dividend income	20	20
Interest income	80	60
Interest expense	2 200	1 780
Financial expenses, net	2 100	1 700
Gain from sales of land	1 000	–
Profit before taxes	3 700	3 300
Taxes	1 120	980
Net profit	2 580	2 320
Dividends	1 000	1 000
Retained earnings	1 580	1 320
	2 580	2 320

Balance sheet, December 31, 19XX

	Current year (000s)	Previous year (000s)
Land	6 000	7 000
Buildings	4 000	4 400
Machinery, equipment	8 000	6 000
Long-term debtors	100	100
Prepayment machinery	50	–
Investment in shares	50	50
Long-term assets	18 200	17 550
Finished goods	8 000	6 000
Work in progress	3 000	3 500
Raw material	1 000	1 500
Trade debtors	9 800	8 550
Share investments	200	200
Cash, bank accounts	200	1 400
Current assets	22 200	21 150
Total assets	40 400	38 700
Share capital	5 000	5 000
Capital surplus	1 000	1 000
Revaluation land	3 600	3 600
Retained earnings	3 940	2 360
Equity	13 540	11 960
Mortgage loan	18 000	19 000
Deferred taxes	2 100	1 900
Long-term liabilities	20 100	20 900
Dividends	1 000	1 000
Tax payable	920	700
Other liabilities	2 400	2 200
Bank overdraft, limit 3000	2 440	1 940
Short-term liabilities	6 760	5 840
Total equity and liabilities	40 400	38 700

The operating income in this case is 4 800 000; this tells us something, but relatively little. Is it satisfactory? Compared to last year it is a little lower, but, if the profit in this business sector is generally much lower this year compared with last year, then the income in our example could be good, or very good. On the other hand, if the level of operating income is so low that the company cannot continue in the long run, then we must draw different conclusions. It is therefore necessary to make comparisons in order to draw conclusions.

Comparison is necessary in order to put the accounting data into perspective. Generally, we have three bases for comparison:

- earlier periods (time comparison);
- with other companies (trade comparison);
- with budget (budget comparison).

Since we are concentrating on external analyses, the third basis is of less interest to us.

Most analysts start their analysis of a firm by calculating percentage relations and changes from previous years. This gives an insight into both the structure of the firm and the development of its financial situation. In *vertical analysis* all figures are expressed as a percentage for each year, on a defined basis. In the profit and loss account this basis is normally total revenues. In this way we will have a *common-size profit and loss account*. In the balance sheet, the sum of the assets usually will be the basis for making a *common-size balance sheet*.

In *horizontal analysis* the changes from one period to another are the focus. Then a base year is established for the accounting items.

Let us illustrate these two types of analyses by using the accounting data in our example.

Profit and loss account (millions)

	This year	Last year	Percentage of sales This year	Percentage of sales Last year	Percentage increase (decrease) This year	Percentage increase (decrease) Last year
Sales	108.5	98.0	100	100	10.7	100
Raw materials	14.5	12.5	13.4	12.7	16.0	100
Wages, etc.	57.0	54.6	52.5	55.7	4.4	100
Other operating expenses	32.2	25.9	29.6	26.5	24.3	100
Operating expenses	103.7	93.0	95.5	94.9	11.5	100
Operating income	4.8	5.0	4.5	5.1	(4.0)	100

The accounting data have been calculated in a more concentrated way than that presented in the original profit and loss account. Work in progress and finished goods have been divided between raw materials, wages etc. and other operating and administration expenses. Depreciation has been included in other operating expenses.

Using vertical analysis we can see that two of the cost components have increased from last year, and that the sum of these increases is higher than the decrease in the third component (wages etc.). The net effect is a decrease in operating income from 5.1 per cent of sales to 4.5 per cent.

If we use horizontal analysis we can see that, even if the sales have increased by 10.7 per cent, the operating income is reduced by 4 per cent. This is due to the fact that the operating expenses have increased by 11.5 per cent. Again, we see that it is two components, raw materials and other operating expenses, that have increased more than the sales and that the decrease in the third component, wages, cannot compensate for this increase.

Besides these types of analyses, financial ratio analyses are important. Financial ratios are tools for interpreting financial statements. Generally, such ratios will give an insight into the two most important areas of management: earnings and the soundness of the financial position of the firm.

We can classify financial ratios into four types: ratios measuring profitability, ratios for evaluating funds management, ratios appraising liquidity and ratios for measuring solvency. These are discussed below.

13.3 Profitability

As we have mentioned before, profitability is the most important factor for the firm. In the long run, the firm cannot continue without making sufficient profit. Also, good profitability makes any other financial problems that may occur much easier to handle. But how can we measure profitability? Let us return to our example again:

The operating income this year was 4 800 000, profit before the gain from sales of land 2 700 000, and net profit 2 580 000. If we know the firm well, these absolute figures would reveal a lot, but relatively little to an outside person. For example, the fact that the company earned sufficient money to pay dividends, 20 per cent of the nominal share capital, and also sufficient to increase equity by almost 1 600 000.

These absolute figures, however, give a limited basis for comparison. In order to look at the relative situations, two ratios can be used:

● return on investment ('total capital profitability'); and
● return on equity ('equity capital profitability').

Return on investment shows how well all assets in the firm have been managed. This ratio is considered as the key ratio by analysts. We calculate it in this way:

$$\text{Return on investment} = \frac{\text{Profit before interest expenses and taxes} \times 100}{\text{Average total assets}}$$

Logically, the profit must be before interest expenses, since we want to measure the return on all resources. On the other hand, interest income must be included, since that is part of the disposition of some assets. It also seems reasonable to measure the profit before taxes, because that makes comparison between firms and alternatives more realistic. The average of total assets is used because profit is earned gradually during the year.

In our example, we will have the following data and calculations:

	(000s)
Profit before interest	4 900
Average total assets	39 550
Return on investment:	12.4%

This means that the return on total assets this year has been 12.4 per cent.

When evaluating this return, the natural starting point is the level of interest on alternative investments. If we start with a risk-free investment (for example, government bonds) we will have to add a risk premium since the investment is in a business firm. How much this risk premium should be will depend on the specific risk in the trade of the business. If we say that the risk-free interest is 8 per cent, this means a premium of 4.4 per cent.

Return on equity is calculated in order to see the return on ownership capital. It can be calculated either before or after taxes. In our example we have the following figures and can make the following calculations:

	(000s)
Profit before gain on sales of land	2 700
Net profit	2 580
Average stockholders' equity	12 750
Return on equity (1):	21.2%
Return on equity (2):	20.2%

In the second calculation (2) we have used the profit including gain from sales of land and after taxes. If we exclude the gain from sales of land, we also have to change the tax amount in order to have full correspondence.

In this case the return on equity (1) is much higher than the return on investment. We can compare these figures directly, since both figures are before the gain on sales of land and also before taxes. The return has risen from 12.4 per cent to 21.2 per cent with the following two explanations:

- first, the average interest on debt must be less than the return on investment;
- second, when this is true, the difference between the two must depend directly on the relationship between liabilities and equity.

Let us make a calculation in order to test these explanations:

The interest is 2 200 and the average liability (long- and short-term) 26 800. This gives an average interest of 8.2 per cent, that means 4.1 per cent lower than the return on investment. The liability/equity ratio is 2.1. That equals 8.8 and explains the difference in return on investment compared with the return on equity.

Generally, we will have this connection between return on equity and return on investment:

$$\text{Return on equity, } r = R + \left[(R - i) \times \frac{L}{E}\right]$$

where   r = return on equity
R = return on investment
i = interest
L = liability
E = equity
L/E = gearing/leverage

Therefore, in our example: return on equity $= 12.4 + \left[(12.4 - 8.2) \times \frac{2}{1}\right] \approx 21.2$.

13.4 Funds management

These ratios are very closely linked to profitability, since they can explain low and high profitability and also the change in profitability over time. There are many ratios in this area. Here we will concentrate on a few of them, but at the same time give illustrations of the general idea behind them.

Asset turnover ratio shows how efficiently the management uses the total economic resources of the firm to generate sales. It is calculated by:

$$\frac{\text{Sales}}{\text{Average assets}}$$

In our example this ratio is 2.7. In order to say whether or not this is a good ratio, we have to take into consideration the firm's type of industry, and study the development of the ratio during the last few years.

Stock turnover ratio shows how fast the stock moves through the firm:

$$\frac{\text{Cost of sales}}{\text{Average stock}}$$

In our example this ratio is 9, calculated as the total of all kinds of stock (raw materials, work in progress, finished goods).

The reasoning behind this ratio is that funds are tied up in stock, and higher turnover, therefore, will increase the profit.

Average collection period ratio shows how many days of credit the firm gives its customers:

$$\frac{\text{Trade debtors (average)}}{\text{Sales (on credit)}} \times 365$$

In our example the average collection period is 31 days. This ratio can be evaluated both by comparison with established credit terms and with earlier years.

13.5 Liquidity

Liquidity is the cash generating ability of the firm. The best way to show and to explain the development in the total liquidity is with a cash flow statement, as we discussed earlier in Chapter 4. We can illustrate this using our example:

Grouping into the three main liquidity streams, from operation, from investment and from financing, and using the direct method, we will get the following figures:

	(000s)
Cash from trade debtors	107 250
Cash to suppliers, wages and other operating expenses	103 150
Taxes paid	700
Net cash from operation	3 400
Sales of land	2 000
Investment in machinery	3 000
Net cash to investment	1 000
Repayment on mortgage loan	1 000
Interest paid	2 200
Dividends paid	1 000
Interest received	80
Dividends received	20
Net cash for financing	4 100
Net reduction in cash	1 700

We see from the cash flow statement that this year the company spent more cash than it received. The operating activities gave net positive cash, but the net cash used for investment and the net cash for financing activities are higher. The three elements give a clear explanation of the cash changes during the year.

The use of liquidity ratios does not give the total liquidity picture, but can still be important. The difference between current assets and current liabilities gives the *working capital* and is an interesting factor to examine.

Current ratio and *quick ratio* are ratios that build directly on balance sheet data and are defined as:

$$\frac{\text{Current assets}}{\text{Current liabilities}} \quad \text{and} \quad \frac{\text{Quick assets}}{\text{Current liabilities}}$$

In our example the working capital will be 15 440, the current ratio 3.3 and the quick ratio 1.5.

13.6 Solvency

Solvency ratios tell us about the ability of the firm to meet long-term debt payments. Among the ratios most used are the *equity ratio* and *time interest earned*. These are defined as follows:

$$\text{Equity ratio:} \quad \frac{\text{Equity} \times 100}{\text{Total capital}}$$

$$\text{Time interest earned:} \quad \frac{\text{Operating income}}{\text{Long-term debt interest}}$$

13.7 Example – Danisco

An excellent example of financial analysis showing key figures is in the following annual report of Danisco (overleaf).

Key figures

DKK million

Danisco group

	1992/93	1993/94	1994/95	1995/96	1996/97
Net sales	13,027	12,840	14,193	16,186	17,002
Index	100	99	109	124	131
Operating profit	1,148	1,347	1,638	1,796	1,952
Index	100	117	143	156	170
Profit on ordinary activities before tax	826	1,030	1,331	1,604	1,789
Index	100	125	161	194	217
Profit on ordinary activities after tax	701	830	1,016	1,218	1,392
Index	100	118	145	174	199
Consolidated profit for the year	813	830	1,016	1,218	1,392
Cash flow from operating activities	1,745	1,675	1,775	1,696	2,016
Cash flow from investing activities	-2,228	-1,625	-354	-1,488	-1,545
Cash flow from financing activities	888	584	-1,618	-601	-668
Total assets	14,669	16,480	15,813	16,610	17,790
Capital and reserves	6,134	6,652	7,197	7,740	10,006
Average number of employees	11,455	11,055	11,413	12,638	12,937
Index	100	97	100	110	113
Return on capital and reserves	11.4%	13.0%	14.7%	16.3%	15.7%
Fully diluted	11.4%	12.7%	13.0%	14.5%	14.8%
Solvency ratio	41.8%	40.4%	45.5%	46.6%	56.2%
Fully diluted	41.8%	47.4%	52.9%	53.6%	56.3%
Operating margin	8.8%	10.5%	11.5%	11.1%	11.5%

DKK

	1992/93	1993/94	1994/95	1995/96	1996/97
Earnings per share	12.72	15.04	18.40	22.00	24.52
Fully diluted	12.72	14.94	17.63	20.96	23.43
Cash flow per share	31.64	30.37	32.12	30.63	35.51
Fully diluted	31.64	30.02	30.31	28.93	33.84
Net asset value per share	111	121	130	140	166
Fully diluted	111	131	140	149	167
Market price per share	159	198	217	290	386
Market price/Net asset value	1.43	1.65	1.67	2.07	2.32
Fully diluted	1.43	1.52	1.55	1.95	2.32
Price/earnings	12.52	13.19	11.79	13.18	15.74
Fully diluted	12.52	13.28	12.31	13.84	16.48
Dividend per share	2.40	2.80	3.20	4.20	5.00
Market capitalisation in DKK million	8,781	10,943	12,013	16,058	23,203

Return on capital and reserves	=	$\dfrac{\text{profit on ord. activities after tax} \times 100}{\text{average capital and reserves}}$
Solvency ratio	=	$\dfrac{\text{capital and reserves} \times 100}{\text{assets total}}$
Operating margin	=	$\dfrac{\text{operating profit} \times 100}{\text{net sales}}$
Cash flow per share	=	$\dfrac{\text{cash flow from operating activities}}{\text{average number of shares}}$
Net asset value per share	=	$\dfrac{\text{capital and reserves at 30.4.}}{\text{number of shares at 30.4}}$
Market price/ Net asset value	=	$\dfrac{\text{market price}}{\text{net asset value}}$

✓ Questions and answers

1 **Why have we been focusing so strongly on comparison when discussing financial analysis?**

Answer:
Because the absolute figures do not give the necessary background for reaching conclusions on accounting data.

2 **How can you make a common-size balance sheet?**

Answer:
By setting total assets as 100 (per cent) and the group/items as a percentage of this total (vertical analysis).

3 **Define the two most commonly used ratios for measuring profitability.**

Answer:

$$\text{Return on investment} = \frac{\text{Profit before interest expenses and taxes} \times 100}{\text{Average total assets}}$$

and

$$\text{Return on equity} = \frac{\text{Profit (before or after taxes)} \times 100}{\text{Average equity}}$$

4 **If you have calculated the return on investment in a specific case to be 6 per cent and the return on equity to be 9 per cent, how can you explain the difference?**

Answer:
First, the difference between the return on investment and the average rate of interest and, second, the ratio of debt to equity.

5 **Which ratios can be used for measuring funds management?**

Answer:
Asset turnover, stock turnover, average collection period of trade debtors.

6 **Why is the opening quotation of this chapter good advice?**

Answer:
A more efficient use of assets gives the firm a better economy and results in less money bound up in assets. This advice should be followed.

7 **What are the two most commonly used ratios for measuring liquidity?**

Answer:
Current ratio and quick ratio.

8 How do you define the equity percentage?

Answer:
Equity as a percentage of total capital.

? Problem

Calculate relevant ratios for profitability, liquidity and solvency for one of the six companies given as examples in Chapter 12.

14 An example of an annual report – Helly Hansen

LEARNING OBJECTIVES

The objective of this chapter is to revise what you have learnt in the previous chapters.

In this chapter we give an example of a full-length annual report.

This example will act as a summary of many of the issues we have discussed during the previous 13 chapters.

Helly Hansen is a Norwegian limited company, now 50 per cent owned by one of the largest listed companies in Norway, Orkla. Helly Hansen products, marketed internationally, include waterproof clothing, profile fibre clothing, sportswear and underwater wear, life jackets and survival suits.

Helly Hansen's largest segment is the outdoor sector. The group supplied outerwear to all officials and a number of the participants at the 1994 Lillehammer Olympic Games.

As you will see from the presentation of the accounts, the order of the balance sheet is not in accordance with the EU Directive. Norway, although it voted 'no' to the EU, has joined the European Economic Area and will have to apply EU directives within a few years.

ANNUAL REPORT 1996

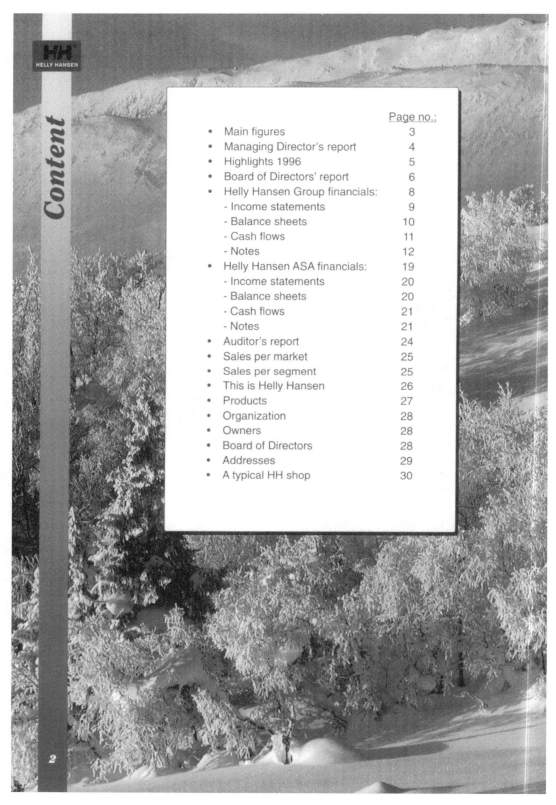

Content

2

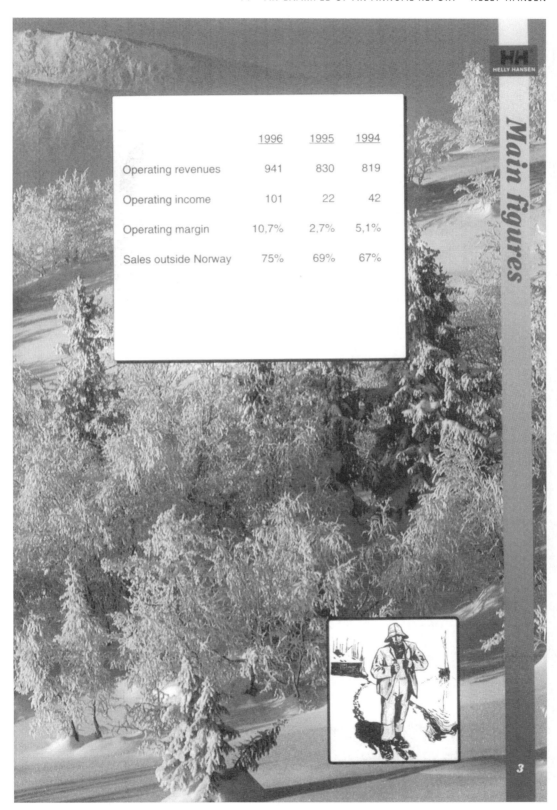

	1996	1995	1994
Operating revenues	941	830	819
Operating income	101	22	42
Operating margin	10,7%	2,7%	5,1%
Sales outside Norway	75%	69%	67%

Main figures

Managing Director's report

FOCUS ON THE BRAND

1996 was a prosperous year for Helly Hansen both on sales and results. It was also a year where we achieved more operational competence and ability to systematically further development of the HH brand.

When entering 1997 all important positions in the company are filled with persons who not only understand where we are heading, but also are fully aware of which way to choose to get there. We all join in the ambition to be the number 1 brand within outdoor/lifestyle world wide when we reach year 2000. To achieve this, our goals, and competence and will to reach them, must be deeply rooted in our own organization and with our associates. I feel that we have this!

While we in 1996 focused on the market, we are in 1997 going to focus more on the brand. Helly Hansen does not sell clothing! - We are building up a brand image! This means that every one of us must find a balanced way to visualize our identity. In other words, we must find a balance between our technical reputation and our new outdoor/lifestyle image.

In our work with marketing and product development it is of utmost importance that we make use of, and never forget to focus on the many years of technical experience Helly Hansen has. Likewise, our sales companies' ability to thoroughly investigate and question new fashion related distribution channels, will be of great importance in the future. In the end, what it is all about, is to create a well balanced brand, that again support our future image and loyalty to the brand.

If we focus on activities that only short term lead to increased sales, this surely will get us into trouble. I therefore look forward to see that our product-, marketing- and distribution processes not only emphasize but also strengthen our position of the brand long term.

Based on our technical know-how in combination with the launching of an exciting sea related range of outdoor/lifestyle products, we will protect, develop and strengthen Helly Hansen's position as the number 1 brand. Our plans to aggressively increase the number of shop-in-shops will help us inform far more customers about our new SeaGear concept. The considerable number of new shop-in-shops planned for 1997 should certainly strengthen our competitiveness in this segment.

Our mutual strong efforts within outdoor- and ski-related products will give results in 1997. We plan a considerable increase in the number of customers within this category this year, which again will make way for "the big blow" in 1998. That means that we, compared with previous years, have to double our efforts and attention to outdoor in 1997. We must reconsider our complete outdoor/ski program. Persons who pursue their activities to extreme limits must be invited to be our advisors, and we must present a creative market image, giving the impression of a company willing to do its utmost to satisfy the consumers.

Our new workwear range in Europe will "bear fruit " in 1997. We know that this new collection is very well received. Sales results are now remaining to be seen. Workwear really contributes to improved results and will therefore always be prioritized.

As I said before, 1997 is the year of brandbuilding. We all have a mutual responsibility to present an image of a united and well balanced company, in order to strengthen our identity.

If we all keep on doing our utmost to work "just in time", we can expect that 1997 will show an increased strengthening of our brand image, - and great results.

Good luck !

Johnny Austad

Highlights 1996

- 1996 was a good year for Helly-Hansen. After adjusted for 1995 production impact, gross margin improved 5% .

- A considerable improvement of results in North America and Europe.

- Most Central-European markets have managed to turn the losses into profit in 1996.

- The European markets are reorganized to function as one unit.

- The position as sales manager in several important markets is now filled with new people.

- Focus are now on development of worldwide concepts, rather than on products.

- Improved cooperation in marketing and product development throughout the world.

- Updated HH logo has been launched, and the brand image uniformed worldwide.

- License agreements have been signed for Australia, New Zealand, Finland and South-Korea.

5

Improvement in profit from operations.

Operating revenues increased by 13% over 1995 to 941 mill NOK (830 mill NOK). Income before extraordinary items and taxes amounted to 88 mill NOK (-3 mill NOK). Improvements were made in the North American market as well as the Central-European markets.

After divestment of the majority of company owned manufacturing facilities in 1995 the new Helly Hansen now has a more efficient operational structure. This structural improvement is reflected in the operating income of 101 mill NOK for 1996.

The company now focuses on product development, marketing, distribution, and sales through its own divisions in Europe and North America.

In connection with previously owned production facilities in Norway and Portugal, the company has made an extraordinary provision for losses on outstanding notes and receivables for a total of 83 mill NOK. Net income is therefore only 5 mill NOK (-3 mill NOK) before tax and -18 mill NOK (-11 mill NOK) after tax.

Market conditions

European Division

After several years of heavy investments the Central European markets turned out profitable in 1996. The growth in sales was particularly strong in UK and France with a 74% increase over 1995, followed by a 34% growth in Holland. Sales in Denmark went back to a "normal" level after a couple of years of exceptional performance on the Danish market. In 1995/1996 the company opened factory outlets in England, Switzerland and Iceland to dispose of discontinued inventory, applying the same model that has been successfully used in the US for several years. This vehicle has proved to be an effective way to phase out discontinued inventory and secure margins.

North American Division

Sales in the North American market showed a 50% increase over 1995, resulting in a substantial increase in profits. On the US market we experienced a 70% overall sales increase. This sales growth occurred mainly in traditional outdoor and specialty stores, but new markets also developed in the urban and youth sector. This growth was spurred by the development of a new product collection of Helly Hansen logoed apparel.

In Canada business lagged 10% below the 1995 sales level primarily due to restricting sales to our largest customer for credit reasons.

Members of the Board 1996:
Front from left: Kjell Inge Røkke, Olaf Eie, Bjørn Rune Gjelsten.
Back from left: Egil Bjurstøm*, Tom Vidar Rygh, Leif Lien*.
*employees representatives.

The significant strengthening of the Helly Hansen brand name, puts us in a strong position for future growth.

Licensing

Our Canadian licensee for workwear continued to see a steady 10% sales growth last year. Sales for our Japanese licensee were stable, with a 4% growth in the sportswear market in Japan. The Japanese market is very much influenced by US outdoor fashion. Our collection strategy in Japan will be modified to capitalize on these trends. Helly Hansen is a leading fashion brand in the inner-city market.

During 1996 we signed new license agreements for South-Korea, Australia, New Zealand and Finland. License agreements have also been made for Home Products in Europe and Helly Tech® as a fabric brand on an international basis.

The licensing activities will, in the long term, provide for expanded brand penetration and awareness in new markets and categories, and will generate profitable future business.

Helly Hansen Spesialprodukter AS

Also specialty products had a good year in 1996 with a turnover growth of 28%. Among the interesting projects undertaken during the year, were a cover for a football stadium in Bergen, offshore fishfarming tanks and specially designed silos. We have also experienced strong sales in boat canopies.

Improved inventory turnover.

During 1996 the company took strong measures to reduce inventories, and average turnover increased to 3,0 (2,2). The inventories at the end of 1996 totalled 164 mill NOK (179 mill NOK). The aging is good and the bulk of inventories consists of current styles. Sufficient provisions have been made for potential inventory obsolescence.

6

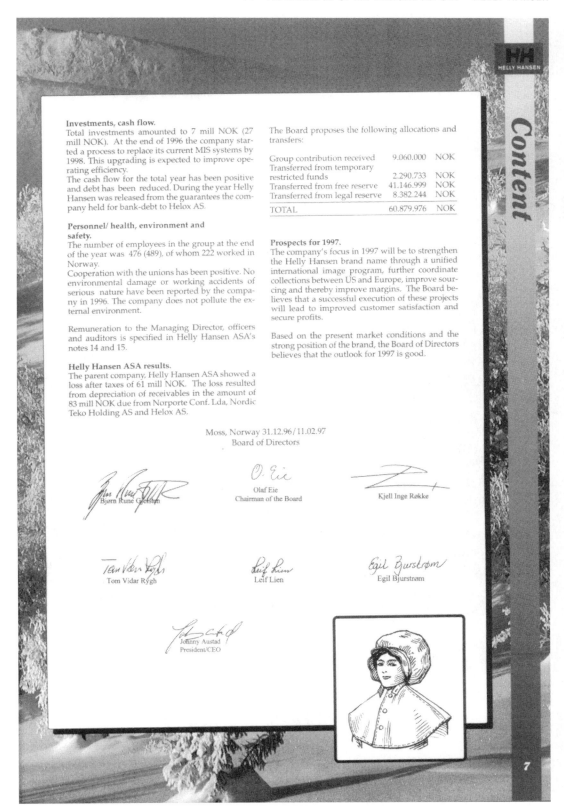

Investments, cash flow.

Total investments amounted to 7 mill NOK (27 mill NOK). At the end of 1996 the company started a process to replace its current MIS systems by 1998. This upgrading is expected to improve operating efficiency.

The cash flow for the total year has been positive and debt has been reduced. During the year Helly Hansen was released from the guarantees the company held for bank-debt to Helox AS.

Personnel/ health, environment and safety.

The number of employees in the group at the end of the year was 476 (489), of whom 222 worked in Norway.

Cooperation with the unions has been positive. No environmental damage or working accidents of serious nature have been reported by the company in 1996. The company does not pollute the external environment.

Remuneration to the Managing Director, officers and auditors is specified in Helly Hansen ASA's notes 14 and 15.

Helly Hansen ASA results.

The parent company, Helly Hansen ASA showed a loss after taxes of 61 mill NOK. The loss resulted from depreciation of receivables in the amount of 83 mill NOK due from Norporte Conf. Lda, Nordic Teko Holding AS and Helox AS.

The Board proposes the following allocations and transfers:

Group contribution received	9.060.000	NOK
Transferred from temporary restricted funds	2.290.733	NOK
Transferred from free reserve	41.146.999	NOK
Transferred from legal reserve	8.382.244	NOK
TOTAL	60.879.976	NOK

Prospects for 1997.

The company's focus in 1997 will be to strengthen the Helly Hansen brand name through a unified international image program, further coordinate collections between US and Europe, improve sourcing and thereby improve margins. The Board believes that a successful execution of these projects will lead to improved customer satisfaction and secure profits.

Based on the present market conditions and the strong position of the brand, the Board of Directors believes that the outlook for 1997 is good.

Moss, Norway 31.12.96/11.02.97
Board of Directors

Bjørn Rune Gjelsten

Olaf Eie
Chairman of the Board

Kjell Inge Røkke

Tom Vidar Rygh

Leif Lien

Egil Bjurstrøm

Johnny Austad
President/CEO

Helly Hansen Group Financials

Helly Hansen ASA and subsidiaries - N GAAP

CONSOLIDATED INCOME STATEMENTS

(mill NOK)	Notes	1996 US Dollars (Unaudited)	Year ended December 31, 1996 NOK	1995 NOK	1994 NOK
Operating revenues	2	146	941	830	819
Raw materials and goods		78	507	378	345
Wages, salaries and social benefits		23	148	216	218
Other operating expenses	3	26	170	187	179
Depreciation	13	2	11	25	31
Loss on receivables	10	1	4	2	4
Operating expenses		130	840	808	777
Operating income		16	101	22	42
Financial income		3	17	8	4
Financial expenses		5	30	33	32
Net financial income (expense)	5	(2)	(13)	(25)	(28)
Net income (loss) before extraordinary items		14	88	(3)	14
Extraordinary items	7	(13)	(83)	-	-
Net income (loss) before taxes		1	5	(3)	14
Taxes	8	4	23	8	16
Net income (loss)		(3)	(18)	(11)	(2)

The accompanying notes are an integral part of the consolidated financial statements.

Translation of amounts from kroner (NOK) into U.S. dollars ($) has been made for the convenience of the reader using the exchange rate in effect of December 31, 1996 of $ 1.00 = NOK 6,45

Helly Hansen ASA and subsidiaries - N GAAP

CONSOLIDATED BALANCE SHEETS

(mill NOK)	Notes	1996 US Dollars (Unaudited)	December 31, 1996 NOK	1995 NOK
ASSETS				
Cash and cash equivalents	9	6	39	18
Accounts receivable, net	10	24	154	140
Other short term receivables	11	2	12	100
Inventories	12	25	163	179
Current assets		57	368	437
Long-term receivables		-	2	58
Fixed assets, net	13	6	40	44
Goodwill, net	13	1	4	5
Long-term assets		7	46	107
TOTAL ASSETS		64	414	544
LIABILITIES AND SHAREHOLDER'S EQUITY				
Short-term interest-bearing debt	15	13	85	155
Other current liabilities	14	18	144	94
Current liabilities		31	199	249
Long-term interest-bearing debt	16	19	126	184
Other long-term liabilities		1	5	10
Deferred tax liabilities	8	-	1	-
Long-term liabilities		20	132	194
Share capital		7	42	42
Restricted reserves		3	18	28
Other equity		3	23	31
Shareholder's equity	17	13	83	101
TOTAL LIABILITIES AND SHAREHOLDER'S EQUITY		64	414	544
Secured debt	18			
Guarantees	18			

The accompanying notes are an integral part of the consolidated financial statements.

Translation of amounts from kroner (NOK) into U.S. dollars ($) has been made for the convenience of the reader using the exchange rate in effect of December 31, 1996 of $ 1.00 = NOK 6,45

Helly Hansen ASA and subsidiaries - N GAAP

CONSOLIDATED STATEMENTS OF CASH FLOWS

(mill NOK)	1996 US Dollars (Unaudited)	1996 NOK	1995 NOK	1994 NOK
Cash flows from operating activities:				
Net income	(3)	(18)	(11)	(2)
Adjustments to reconcile net income to net cash provided by operating activities :				
Depreciation	2	11	25	31
Allowance for doubtful accounts	13	83	(2)	2
Deferred taxes	-	1	(1)	(1)
Working capital changes that provided (used) cash :				
Receivables	-	2	(75)	5
Inventories	2	15	65	(26)
Accounts payable	3	16	(23)	13
Interest and income taxes payable	-	1	(7)	(12)
Other current liabilities	1	3	(9)	11
Net cash from operating activities	18	114	(38)	21
Cash flows from investing activities:				
Investments in fixed assets	(1)	(7)	(27)	(27)
Net proceeds from sales of fixed assets	-	2	33	5
(Increase) decrease in long-term receivables	7	45	(4)	18
Net cash from investing activities	(6)	40	2	(4)
Cash flows from financing activities:				
Loan proceeds	-	-	221	36
Principal repayments	(10)	(66)	(248)	(26)
Net change use of credit lines	(11)	(67)	60	(24)
Group contribution	-	-	-	(4)
Effect of new accounting principle, pension	-	-	-	(10)
Net cash from financing activities	(21)	(133)	33	(28)
Effect of exchange rate changes	-	-	(2)	(3)
Net increase (decrease) in cash and cash equivalents	3	21	(5)	(14)
Cash and cash equivalents at beginning of year	3	18	23	37
Cash and cash equivalents at end of year	6	39	18	23
Supplemental credit line information:				
Unused credit line	18	115	58	25

The amounts in the consolidated statements of cash flows for 1995 is affected by the sale of the manufacturing companies Helox AS and Norporte Conf. Lda. The cash effect of the sale for 1995 was limited.

The accompanying notes are an integral part of the consolidated financial statements.

Translation of amounts from kroner (NOK) into U.S. dollars ($) has been made for the convenience of the reader using the exchange rate in effect of December 31, 1996 of $ 1.00 = NOK 6,45

Helly Hansen ASA and subsidiaries - N GAAP

NOTES TO CONSOLIDATED FINANCIAL STATEMENTS

1. ACCOUNTING POLICIES

The consolidated financial statements of Helly Hansen ASA and its subsidiaries have been prepared according to generally accepted accounting principles in Norway (Norwegian GAAP). References in the consolidated financial statements to Helly Hansen (the Company) are to Helly Hansen and its subsidiaries.

Changes in 1996
As described in note 23 Helly Hansen sold its manufacturing subsidiaries in December 1995. The income statements and balance sheets for the years ended December 31, 1996, 1995 and 1994 are therefore not comparable.

Consolidation principles
The consolidated financial statements include the accounts of Helly Hansen ASA, all wholly-owned and majority-owned subsidiaries. All significant intercompany transactions and accounts have been eliminated.

Excess of the investments in subsidiaries over the book value of the net assets acquired is accounted for by increasing the carrying value of the identifiable asset to market value, with any remaining amounts shown as goodwill. Goodwill is amortized on a straight line basis over the periods estimated to be benefited, which may not exceed 20 years according to Norwegian Law.

Subsidiaries acquired or sold during the year are included in the consolidated income statements from date of acquisition or up to the date of sale, respectively.

Foreign subsidiaries are classified as either integral to the operations of Helly Hansen ASA or as relatively self-contained operations. The balance sheets of foreign integral operations are translated using historical exchange rates for inventories and capital assets, and the rate of exchange in effect at the balance sheet date for the remaining assets and liabilities. The income statements of foreign integral operations are translated using the average exchange rate for the year, except for income statement items from inventory or capital asset balances, which are translated at historical exchange rates. Translation differences are reported as financial income or expense. The balance sheets of foreign self-contained operations are translated at the exchange rate in effect at the balance sheet date. The income statements of foreign self-contained operations are translated using the average exchange rate for the year. Translation differences are charged or credited to shareholders' equity.

All foreign subsidiaries are classified as integral to the operations of Helly Hansen ASA from 01.01.1996.

Operating revenues
Operating revenues comprise the goods and services delivered during the accounting period. The recorded amounts are net of VAT, discounts, bonuses and sales freights. Royalties are recognized in income as earned.

Extraordinary income and expenses
Events or transactions which are material to Helly Hansen's activities are classified as extraordinary income or expense when they are considered not to occur in the normal course of business, to be of unusual nature and expected to occur infrequently.

Cash and cash equivalents
Cash and cash equivalents are stated at cost plus accrued interest, and include cash, bank deposits and short-term investments.

Inventories
Inventories of raw materials and purchased finished goods are valued at the lower of cost (first in, first out) or net realizable value. Inventories manufactured are valued at the lower of manufacturing cost, including an appropriate portion of manufacturing overhead, or net realizable value.

Fixed and intangible assets, depreciation and amortization
Fixed and intangible assets are recorded at cost less accumulated depreciation and amortization, except for some assets which have been revalued.

Depreciation and amortization are computed over the estimated useful lives of the various classes of·assets using the straight-line method. The following rates are being used:

Machinery, equipment, vehicles	10 - 20%
Buildings	2 - 4%
Goodwill	5 - 20%

Research and development
Research and development costs are expensed as incurred.

Foreign currency assets and liabilities
Cash and cash equivalents denominated in a foreign currency are remeasured using the exchange rate as of balance sheet date.

Other assets and liabilities denominated in foreign currencies are valued at the lower/higher of the exchange rate at the date of the transaction or the date of the balance sheet. The company's foreign currency forward contracts do not meet the criteria set for hedge accounting for firm commitments and specifically identified anticipated cash flows, and are valued at the lower/higher of the contract exchange rate or exchange rate at the balance sheet date. Total net unrealized losses are included in financial expense.

Pensions
The projected benefit obligation (funded and unfunded) is the actuarial present value of benefits based upon the pension benefit formula considering years of service rendered and assumptions about future compensation levels. Pension plan assets are measured at market value, and differences between actual return on assets and the expected return on assets are deferred. The company uses the corridor approach deferring all actuarial gains and losses resulting from variances between actual results and economic estimates or actuarial assumptions. These gains and losses are amortized over the remaining average service life of active plan participants when the net gains and losses exceed 10% of the greater of plan assets and projected benefit obligation.

The period's pension cost includes benefits earned in the period, interest cost of projected benefit obligations, estimated returns on pension plan assets and amortization as described above. Net pension costs for the year are included in wages, salaries and social benefits.

Some of the subsidiaries abroad have defined contribution plans, where annual contributions are included in the wages, salaries and social benefits.

Income taxes
Income tax expense includes both current taxes and deferred tax expense. Deferred taxes are, in accordance with N Gaap, recognized only if their realizability is assessed as more likely than not, and they do not exceed deferred tax liabilities. Deferred taxes are not provided for retained earnings in subsidiaries that are intended to be permanently reinvested. Deferred tax liabilities and assets are presented net in the balance sheets.

Helly Hansen ASA and subsidiaries - N GAAP

NOTES TO CONSOLIDATED FINANCIAL STATEMENTS

2. OPERATING REVENUES

(mill NOK)	1996	1995	1994
Sales	924	804	809
Royalty	8	9	6
Gain on sales of shares in subsidiaries	-	14	-
Gain on sales of building	7	-	-
Other operating revenue	2	3	4
Total operating revenues	**941**	**830**	**819**

3. OTHER OPERATING EXPENSES

(mill NOK)	1996	1995	1994
Sales expenses and commissions	39	31	28
Marketing expenses	45	46	40
Office space expenses	21	30	26
Other	65	80	85
Total operating expenses	**170**	**187**	**179**

4. RESEARCH AND DEVELOPMENT COSTS

Research and development costs are included in operating expenses. The amounts expensed for the years ended December 31, 1996, 1995 and 1994 are 20 mill NOK, 20 mill NOK and 18 mill NOK, respectively.

5. FINANCIAL INCOME AND EXPENSES

(mill NOK)	1996	1995	1994
Interest income	17	3	4
Interest expenses	(26)	(33)	(30)
Net foreign exchange gain (loss)	(4)	5	(2)
Net financial income (expense)	**(13)**	**(25)**	**(28)**

6. GEOGRAPHIC SEGMENT INFORMATION

When preparing geographic segment information, operating revenues and net income have been allocated based upon the location of the company's subsidiaries generating the operating revenues and net income. Identifiable assets have been allocated based upon the location of the assets. The company's policies and practices with respect to interarea transfers are described in note 23, related party transactions.

(mill NOK)	Norway	Sweden & Denmark	Other Europe	North-America & Other	Elimi-nations	Total
1996 Operating revenues:						
Unaffiliated customers	238	161	210	337	(5)	941
Interarea transfers	26	2	6	206	(240)	-
Total	264	163	216	543	(245)	941
Net income	(52)	11	12	11	-	(18)
Identifiable assets	88	58	115	153	-	414
1995 Operating revenues:						
Unaffiliated customers	258	194	159	210	9	830
Interarea transfers	127	1	198	159	(485)	-
Total	385	195	357	369	(476)	830
Net income	-	11	(20)	(2)	-	(11)
Identifiable assets	214	81	116	133	-	544
1994 Operating revenues:						
Unaffiliated customers	273	198	163	194	(9)	819
Interarea transfers	336	1	206	149	(692)	-
Total	609	199	369	343	(701)	819
Net income	27	15	(49)	2	-	(5)
Identifiable assets	94	91	235	144	-	564

(milll NOK)	1996	1995	1994
Export sales from Norway to unaffiliated customers	13	16	44
Royalty revenue from outside Norway	8	9	6

7. EXTRAORDINARY INCOME AND EXPENSES

In December 1995, as described in note 23 transactions with related parties, the company sold the shares of its manufacturing companies to NTH. The companies were sold at market price. The operation of these companies, especially Norporte Conf. Lda., has not performed as well as expected in 1996, and the financial position of the NTH Group has declined in a way that could not be foreseen at the time the 1995 annual accounts were issued. Therefore receivables totalling 83 mill NOK, from the companies in the NTH group, have been written down to 0 in 1996 as they have been assessed to be not collectible. The write down has been classified as extraordinary expences, and should be seen together with the gain on the sale of shares of 14 mill NOK recorded as operating revenues in 1995.

8. INCOME TAXES

(mill NOK)	1996	1995	1994
The income tax expense (income) consists of the following:			
Current taxes:			
Norway	1	1	6
Outside Norway	21	8	11
Total current taxes	22	9	17
Deferred taxes:			
Norway	-	-	-
Outside Norway	1	(1)	(1)
Total deferred taxes	1	(1)	(1)
Total income taxes	23	8	16

Helly Hansen ASA and subsidiaries - N GAAP

NOTES TO CONSOLIDATED FINANCIAL STATEMENTS

Temporary differences between the financial reporting basis and the tax basis of the company's assets and liabilities give rise to deferred tax assets and liabilities at December 31 as follows:

(mill NOK)	1996 Basis deferred tax assets	1996 Basis deferred tax liabilities	1995 Basis deferred tax assets	1995 Basis deferred tax liabilities
Receivables	89	-	6	-
Inventories	14	1	26	2
Other short-term differences	10	-	31	-
Fixed assets	-	11	-	13
Accrued pension liability	5	-	6	-
Other long-term differences	11	10	6	5
Loss carry forwards	99	-	145	-
Basis for deferred tax assets/liabilities	228	22	220	20
Calculated deferred tax assets/liabilities	72	7	71	6
Valuation allowance	66	-	65	-
Deferred tax asset/liability	6	7	6	6

Net operating loss carry forwards were available in Norway and various foreign tax jurisdictions at December 31, 1996. The amounts and expiration dates of these carry forwards are as follows:

(mill NOK)	Norway	Outside Norway	Total
1997	-	2	2
1998	-	5	5
1999	-	12	12
2000	-	14	14
2001	-	20	20
2002 and thereafter	8	38	46
Total	8	91	99

Provisions have not been made for taxes on undistributed earnings of subsidiaries abroad.

9. CASH AND CASH EQUIVALENTS

(mill NOK)	1996	1995
Cash and bank deposits	35	15
Cash and bank deposits restricted for payment of employee taxes	4	3
Cash and cash equivalents	39	18

10. ACCOUNTS RECEIVABLE

(mill NOK)	1996	1995
Accounts receivable	163	149
Allowance for doubtful accounts	(9)	(9)
Accounts receivable, net	154	140
Allowance for doubtful accounts per January 1	9	11
Realized losses for the year	(4)	(4)
Provision for doubtful accounts for the year	4	2
Allowance for doubtful accounts per December 31	9	9

11. OTHER SHORT-TERM RECEIVABLES

(mill NOK)	1996	1995
Related party receivables:		
Trade receivables Nordic Teko Holding Group	34	40
Note receivable for sale of manufacturing companies to NTH	49	49
Allowance for doubtful accounts	(83)	-
Loan to employees	1	-
Other current receivables	11	11
Other short-term receivables	12	100

12. INVENTORIES

(mill NOK)	1996	1995
Finished goods	146	164
Work in progress	2	4
Raw materials	15	11
Inventories	163	179

Helly Hansen ASA and subsidiaries - N GAAP

NOTES TO CONSOLIDATED FINANCIAL STATEMENTS

13. FIXED AND INTANGIBLE ASSETS

(mill NOK)	Good-will	Machinery, equipment, vehicles	Buildings, inclusive sites	Total
Cost:				
Cost at January 1, 1995 (incl. previous revaluation)	3	148	107	258
Additions at cost	6	19	2	27
Disposals at cost	3	97	72	172
Cost at December 31, 1995	**6**	**70**	**37**	**113**
Foreign currency translation	-	(3)	2	(1)
Additions at cost	-	7	-	7
Disposals at cost	-	4	6	10
Cost at December 31, 1996	**6**	**70**	**33**	**109**
Accumulated depreciation/amortization:				
Accumulated depreciation/amortization January 1, 1995	-	92	35	127
Depreciation/amortization	1	20	4	25
Disposals	-	61	27	88
Accumulated depreciation/amortization Dec 31, 1995	**1**	**51**	**12**	**64**
Foreign currency translation	-	(4)	2	(2)
Depreciation/amortization	1	9	1	11
Disposals	-	3	5	8
Accumulated depreciation/amortization Dec 31, 1996	**2**	**53**	**10**	**65**
Book value December 31, 1995	**5**	**19**	**25**	**49**
Book value December 31, 1996	**4**	**17**	**23**	**44**

INVESTMENTS IN AND SALES PROCEEDS FROM FIXED AND INTANGIBLE ASSETS

(mill NOK)	1996	1995	1994	1993	1992
Investments :					
Goodwill	-	6	3	-	-
Machinery, equipment, vehicles	7	19	20	19	23
Buildings incl. sites	-	2	4	10	-
Translation difference (currency)	-	-	-	1	5
Total	**7**	**27**	**27**	**30**	**28**
Sales :					
Goodwill	-	2	-	-	-
Machinery, equipment, vehicles	1	13	2	3	1
Buildings incl. sites	8	18	3	-	-
Total	**9**	**33**	**5**	**3**	**1**

14. OTHER CURRENT LIABILITIES

(mill NOK)	1996	1995
Accounts payable	37	24
Accrued employees taxes, social security taxes and value added taxes	24	23
Accrued income taxes	-	(1)
Other liabilities	53	48
Other current liabilities	**114**	**94**

15. SHORT-TERM INTERESTBEARING DEBT

(mill NOK)	Weighted average interest rates (effective)	Balance NOK 1996	Balance NOK 1995
NOK	5.67%	48	110
NLG	3.96%	35	40
Current portion of long-term debt		2	5
Short-term interestbearing debt	**4.94%**	**85**	**155**

Helly Hansen has a group bank account for its Norwegian entities with the Union Bank of Norway. Bank overdraft limit as of December 31, 1996 amounted to 127 mill NOK, whereof 115 mill NOK was unused at year-end.

In addition Helly Hansen has unused long term committed lines of credit amounting to 36 mill NOK and 9 mill NLG.

Helly Hansen ASA and subsidiaries - N GAAP

NOTES TO CONSOLIDATED FINANCIAL STATEMENTS

16. LONG-TERM DEBT

(mill NOK)	1996 Interest rate spread	Weighted average interest rates (effective)	1996 Duration	Balance NOK 1996	Balance NOK 1995
Bank loans :					
NOK	5.00%-11.00%	6.05%	3	85	145
USD	6.06%- 9.00%	6.97%	3	43	44
Average/Total	5.00%-11.00%	6.35%	3	128	189
Less current portion of long-term debt				(2)	(5)
Long-term debt				126	184

Payment on long-term debt (including current portion) fall due as follows :	(mill NOK)
1997	2
1998	37
1999	36
2000	53
Total	128

Certain of the financing agreements of the company contain certain restrictive covenants relating to cashflow, equity, debt and liquidity and limit the incurrence of additional indebtedness. Some of these covenants were not met at 31 December 1996. The company has obtained waivers from the banks in this respect.

17. SHARE CAPITAL AND SHAREHOLDER'S EQUITY

(mill NOK)	Helly Hansen ASA Ordinary shares Number	Amount	Legal reserves	Other equity	Total shareholder's equity
Balance December 31, 1993	423,500	42	34	58	134
Net income 1994			4	(10)	(6)
Foreign currency translation			-	(4)	(4)
Change in accounting principles			-	(10)	(10)
Balance December 31, 1994	423,500	42	38	34	114
Net income 1995			(10)	(1)	(11)
Foreign currency translation			-	(2)	(2)
Balance December 31, 1995	423,500	42	28	31	101
Net income 1996			(10)	(8)	(18)
Balance December 31, 1996	423,500	42	18	23	83

As per December 31 1996 the shares in Helly Hansen are held by RGI Norway (50%) and Orkla ASA (50%).

18. SECURED DEBT AND GUARANTEES

(mill NOK)	1996	1995
Secured debt :		
Bank overdraft	83	150
Mortgage loans	128	143
Total	211	293
Book value of assets pledged as security :		
Receivables and inventories	329	419
Machinery, equipment and vehicles	17	19
Buildings incl. sites	16	18
Total	362	456
Guarantees (off-balance sheet) :		
Guarantees for other companies	1	8
Surety on behalf of employees	1	1
Total	2	9

19. COMMITMENTS AND CONTINGENCIES

Lease commitments related to operating leases on vehicles as of December 31, 1996	(mill NOK)
1996	1
1997	1
1998	1
Total	3

Non-cancelable rental agreements as of December 31, 1996	(mill NOK)
1996	15
1997	14
1998	12
1999	9
2000	9
2001	9
2002 and thereafter	11
Total	79

Helly Hansen is not involved in or threatened with legal, tax or environmental matters which could have a material adverse effect on its consolidated results of operation, liquidity or financial position.

Helly Hansen ASA and subsidiaries - N GAAP

NOTES TO CONSOLIDATED FINANCIAL STATEMENTS

20. DERIVATIVE FINANCIAL INSTRUMENTS AND RISK MANAGEMENT

The company, having NOK as its base currency, operates internationally with distribution facilities in various locations in Europe and North America. The company may reduce its exposure to fluctuations in interest rates and foreign exchange rates by the use of derivative financial instruments. The company does not use derivative financial instruments for trading or speculative purposes.

Foreign currency:
Forward contracts are used to hedge the future value of income and expenses denominated in foreign currencies. The company generally hedges a defined portion of anticipated one year cash flows in all material currencies. These foreign currency forward contracts do not meet the criteria set for hedge accounting for firm commitments and specifically identified anticipated cash flows, and are valued at the lower/higher of the contract exchange rate or exchange rate at the balance sheet date. The net gain/loss from this valuation is included with the net gain/loss from other assets and liabilities denominated in foreign currency as described in note 1.

Interest rates:
The company does not use interest rate swaps or related derivative interest rate financial instruments. The interest rates on the company's debt is normally floating rates or adjusted at 3 or 6 month intervals.

Credit risk:
Financial instruments which potentially subject the company to concentrations of credit risk consist principally of temporary cash investments and accounts receivable. The company places temporary cash investments with its bank connection or high credit quality institutions. Concentrations of credit risk with respect to accounts receivable are mainly related to the economic trends in the apparel retail industry, but reduced by the large number of customers comprising the company's customer base.

The counterparties to the agreements relating to the company's foreign exchange instruments consist of high credit quality Norwegian or foreign financial institutions. The company does not believe that there is significant risk of nonperformance by these counterparties.

Forward contracts:
The table below summarize by currency the amounts of the company's forward exchange contracts. Bought and sold in the table represents the amounts bought and sold in each currency, translated to NOK at the exchange rate in effect at the balance sheet data:

	Bought (mill NOK)	Average remaining days	Sold (mill NOK)	Average remaining days
USD	58	64	-	-
PTE	21	64	-	-
NLG	-	-	19	106

The fair value of the forward currency contracts, based upon estimates from brokers and dealers in such financial instruments, is 1 mill NOK. The carrying amount of the contracts is NOK 0.

21. FAIR VALUE OF FINANCIAL INSTRUMENTS

The fair value of Helly Hansen cash and cash equivalents, receivables and debt approximate the amount carried on the balance sheet.

22. PENSION PLANS

The company's non-contributory pension plans cover substantially all employees of Helly Hansen and its Norwegian subsidiaries. Plan benefits are generally based on years of service and final salary levels. The plans are administered by Storebrand, an independent Norwegian life insurance company. In addition, unfunded non-contributory plans supplement the benefits provided by the funded plans. For purposes of financial statement presentation these plans are treated as defined benefit plans.

Employees of subsidiaries abroad participate in pension plans in accordance with local practice, laws and tax regulations. These pension plans are defined benefit plans or defined contribution plans and vary as to legal form and funding status, and covers 117 persons.

Contributions to plans are made in accordance with local laws and tax regulations.

Plan assets and liabilities are based on estimated actuarial value as of December 31. Asset values are adjusted annually in accordance with information from the insurance company.

Net pension cost for the years indicated includes the following components:

(mill NOK)	1996	1995	1994
Defined benefit plans:			
Service cost	3	4	5
Interest cost	2	3	2
Assumed return on plan assets	(2)	(2)	(2)
Net periodic pension cost, defined benefit plans	3	5	5
Defined contribution plans:			
Company's contributions	2	1	1
Net pension cost, defined contribution plans	2	1	1

The following table shows the plans' funded status and amounts recognized in the balance sheet:

	1996		1995	
	Assets exceed accumulated benefits	Accumulated benefits exceed assets	Assets exceed accumulated benefits	Accumulated benefits exceed assets
Vested benefits	17	16	16	12
Accumulated benefit obligation	18	17	17	13
Projected benefit obligation	20	18	19	14
Fair value of plan assets	34	2	27	-
Assets in excess of (less than) projected benefit obligation	14	(16)	8	(14)
Unrecognized net (gain)loss	(4)	1	-	-
Prepaid (accrued) pension cost	10	(15)	8	(14)

Helly Hansen ASA and subsidiaries - N GAAP

NOTES TO CONSOLIDATED FINANCIAL STATEMENTS

Pensions are presented net in the balance sheet.

Assumptions:				
Discount rate	6%	6%	6%	6%
Salary increase/assumed pension increases	3%	3%	3%	3%
Increase in social security contribution ceiling	2%	2%	2%	2%
Assumed rate of return	7%	7%	7%	7%
Average remaining years of service	15	15	15	15

Actuarial assumptions applied are based upon demographic factors generally used by insurance companies.

The projected benefit obligations as of December 31, 1996 for the Norwegian plans amounted to 35 mill NOK (representing 337 persons), and for the non-Norwegian plans to 3 mill NOK (representing 19 persons).

Pension plan assets is invested as follows:	1996	1995
Money market investments	1	1
Bonds	16	12
Loans	7	5
Shares	9	6
Real estate	3	3
Total pension assets	**36**	**27**

23. TRANSACTIONS WITH RELATED PARTIES

Transactions with RGI ASA and Orkla ASA:
In 1995 the company sold the shares of its manufacturing companies Helox AS (Norway) and Norporte Confeccoes Lda (Portugal) to Nordic Teko Holding AS, a company owned by the company's shareholders RGI and Orkla. The company realized a gain of 14 mill NOK on the transactions. The sales price, 49 mill NOK, were not settled in cash, but a note payable was issued by NTH. The note receivable was written down in 1996.

Balances with related parties that are included in the consolidated financial statements are not material in current or prior years except as follows:

(mill NOK)	1996	1995
Short term receivables Helox AS and Norporte Confeccoes Lda	34	40
Long term receivables Helox AS and Norporte Confeccoes Lda	-	55
Short term loan NTH AS - sale of shares in Helox and Norporte Conf. Lda	49	49
Allowance for doubtful accounts	(83)	-
Total	**-**	**144**

Interarea transfers:
All internal transactions between companies in the group are based on the "Arm-length-principle". All sales companies pay a royalty- and trademark fee to Helly Hansen ASA, based on total external net sales for each company, payable every quarter.

24. STOCK BASED COMPENSATION

The managing director in the US subsidiary has an agreement which gives him the right to buy shares in the US subsidiary at a certain price, and the right to sell the issued shares back to the subsidiary at a price dependent on the company's operating income. Provision has been made for the full estimated value of this agreement, and the related expenses have been included as operating expenses with 13 mill NOK in 1996 and 3 mill NOK in 1995. An agreement to buy back the shares and options has been signed.

25. COMPANIES INCLUDED IN THE CONSOLIDATED FINANCIAL STATEMENTS

Company name	Country	Currency	capital (1.000)	Share Ownership %
Helly Hansen ASA	Norway	NOK	42.350	100%
A/S Helly Hansen	Denmark	DKK	6.000	100%
Helly Hansen (US) Inc.	USA	USD	3.250	100%
Helly Hansen Distributie B.V.	Netherlands	NLG	5.000	100%
Helly Hansen AB	Sweden	SEK	4.000	100%
Helly Hansen Spesialprodukter AS	Norway	NOK	3.000	100%
Helly Hansen Verkaufs G.m.b.H.	Germany	DEM	250	100%
Helly Hansen (UK) Ltd.	England	GBP	400	100%
Helly Hansen G.m.b.H.	Austria	ATS	1.000	100%
Helly Hansen Benelux B.V.	Netherlands	NLG	40	100%
Helly Hansen (Suisse) SA	Switzerland	CHF	600	100%
Helly Hansen France S.A.R.L.	France	FRF	3.450	100%
Helly Hansen N.V.	Belgium	BEF	1.250	100%
FCO Maritim AS	Norway	NOK	50	100%
Oban Wetsuit Ltd.	Scotland	GBP	50	100%
Helly Hansen Leisure Inc.	Canada	CAD	132	100%
Helly Hansen Far East Ltd.	Hong Kong	HKD	1.500	100%
Retis Ltd.	Iceland	ISK	1.000	100%
Eurcen Retail (UK) Ltd.	England	GBP	100	100%

ARTHUR ANDERSEN

TRANSLATION FROM NORWEGIAN

AUDITORS' REPORT FOR 1996

To the Annual General Meeting of
 Helly-Hansen ASA

Arthur Andersen & Co.
Statsautoriserte Revisorer

Drammensveien 165
Postboks 228 Skøyen
0212 Oslo
22 92 80 00 Telefon
22 92 89 00 Telefax

Medlemmer av Norges Statsautoriserte
Revisorers Forening

We have audited the annual accounts of Helly-Hansen ASA for 1996, showing net profit before extraordinary items and and taxes of NOK 23,000,000 and net loss of NOK 60,879,976 for the company and net profit before extraordinary items and taxes of NOK 88,000,000 and net loss of NOK 18,000,000 for the group. The annual accounts, which consist of the Board of Directors' report, income statements, balance sheets, statements of cash flows, notes and the corresponding consolidated financial statements, are the responsibility of the Board of Directors and the Chief Executive Officer.

Our responsibility is to examine the company's annual accounts, its accounting records and the conduct of its affairs.

We have conducted our audit in accordance with applicable laws, regulations and generally accepted auditing standards. We have performed the auditing procedures we considered necessary to determine that the annual accounts are free of material errors or omissions. We have examined, on a test basis, the accounting material supporting the financial statements, the appropriateness of the accounting principles applied, the accounting estimates made by management and the overall presentation of the annual accounts. To the extent required by generally accepted auditing standards we have also evaluated the company's asset management and internal controls.

The appropriation of net loss, as proposed by the Board of Directors, complies with the requirements of the Joint Stock Companies Act.

In our opinion, the annual accounts have been prepared in conformity with the Joint Stock Companies Act and present fairly the company's and the group's financial position as of 31 December 1996 and the result of its operations for the fiscal year in accordance with generally accepted accounting principles.

ARTHUR ANDERSEN & CO.

Olve Gravråk (sig.)
State Authorised Public Accountant (Norway)

Oslo,
 11 February 1997

This is Helly Hansen

Helly Hansen was founded in Norway in 1877 and has built one of the most recognized and respected brands of high-performance, technically sophisticated seagear in the world. Over its 119-year history, the company has developed a reputation for superior quality and performance, and Helly Hansen's products have been the apparel of choice for use in the world's most "extreme" maritime activities. As a result of its unique heritage, Helly Hansen has come to be known as the authentic brand among users of its products. In the past two decades, the company has successfully introduced new products and complementary product categories that incorporate the same standard of excellence offered in its seagear products. Today, the company's expanded product offerings include high-performance, technically oriented outdoor apparel, skiwear, workwear and special products designed for rigorous use in a variety of adverse weather conditions. In 1997, nearly five million people will purchase Helly Hansen products through over 10,000 points of distribution around the world.

In August 1995, a new management team began implementing a variety of strategic and operational improvements to enhance sales and improve profitability. The company cut overhead by reducing the headcount at its corporate headquarters and country sales offices, divesting the majority of its company-owned manufacturing facilities, and implementing new sourcing initiatives to manufacture products in Asia. During 1997, the company intends to continue to implement operational, management and marketing initiatives.

To pursue its growth objectives, Helly Hansen's management team has implemented a strategy to (i) increase brand visibility in all of its markets, (ii) expand its target customer base beyond "enthusiasts" to the larger group of less frequent outdoor "participants", (iii) broaden distribution in all of its markets, (iv) continue to engage in innovative product design and development, and (v) upgrade its management information systems and concentrate on one distribution centre in Holland for Europe.

The company intends to enhance brand visibility by increasing the resources directed to marketing and promotion from five percent of revenues in 1996 to seven percent of projected revenues in 1998. The company intends to use such additional resources to improve products brochures, increase point-of-sale promotion and establish a stronger retail presence. Finally, the company intends to target the large and growing "participants" market. In order to appeal to this market segment, the company will seek to introduce innovative, attractively designed products that offer a high degree of functionality and performance.

Helly Hansen historically has focused on selling its products to retail accounts in all of its geographic markets. The company intends to grow the number of retail distribution points from 1.800 to 2.800 in North America and from 8.200 to 9.700 in Europe by the end of 1999. In addition, Helly Hansen intends to selectively expand its retail presence in its markets through a combination of company-owned flagship stores and authorized Helly Hansen dealer stores. By the end of 1998, the company plans to have 10 dealer stores and three flagship stores in North America (one will be opened in 1997) and five dealer stores and three flagship stores in Europe. The company believes that, in addition to increasing revenues, these new retail formats will enhance Helly Hansen's brand awareness in its key markets. In existing retail accounts that sell large volumes of Helly Hansen products, the company will continue to open shop-in-shops to more effectively promote the brand. The company currently has 30 such shops in North America and 50 in Europe and expects to open an additional 30 in North America and 40 in Europe by the end of 1998.

The company has two sales and marketing divisions, one in North America and one in Europe, and markets its products in Japan and certain other countries through licensees. The company forecasts that its sales in North America will increase at a faster rate than the company's overall sales due to untapped distribution opportunities in the United States. The company also anticipates attractive sales growth in selected European markets such as Germany and UK. To date, sales in Japan have been limited primarily to seagear. However, the company believes there is potential to broaden its product offerings in Japan to include outdoor apparel and skiwear.

Helly Hansen maintains its own sourcing office in Hong Kong which coordinates the sourcing of up to 80% of the company's products through approximately 20 contractors located throughout the Far East. The company's remaining product is primarily sourced through North American and European contractors and certain special products are manufactured by the company in Norway. Through direct oversight of its sourcing relationships, the company believes it is better able to oversee quality control and production at a lower cost than through traditional agency relationships.

26

Products

Today, Helly Hansen is one of the dominant brands in the high-performance seagear category. Over the last two decades, the company has expanded its product offerings, and in addition to seagear the range now includes many different products for protection against the elements.

The core of Helly Hansen's product line is based on Helly Tech®, Helly Hansen's brand of waterproof, breathable fabric.

Outdoor apparel.
This line is designed to comfortably protect the wearer from a range of cold, wet and windy weather conditions. It includes outdoor apparel that addresses the specific needs of hikers, mountaineers and fishermen, as well as rainwear for less active pursuits.

SeaGear.
Helly Hansen offers a full range of technical SeaGear designed for use in a variety of "extreme" maritime activities. This product group includes the Razorfish line which caters to all the specific needs of the dinghy sailor.

Thanks for support and cooperation towards Atlanta Olympics 1996
NORGES SEILERFORBUND

Skiwear.
The skiwear range is designed for extreme skiing in remote areas but has become increasingly popular among a wider group of recreational skiers. In addition Helly Hansen can offer a line of apparel specifically designed for snowboarders.

Workwear.
The workwear products of Helly Hansen are designed to meet the needs of workers and work crews that spend large amounts of time outdoors and require protection in a variety of weather conditions.

Special Products.
This group designes and distributes cold water survival suits, boat canopies, textile based agricultural products - including silos and fish farm tanks - etc.

27

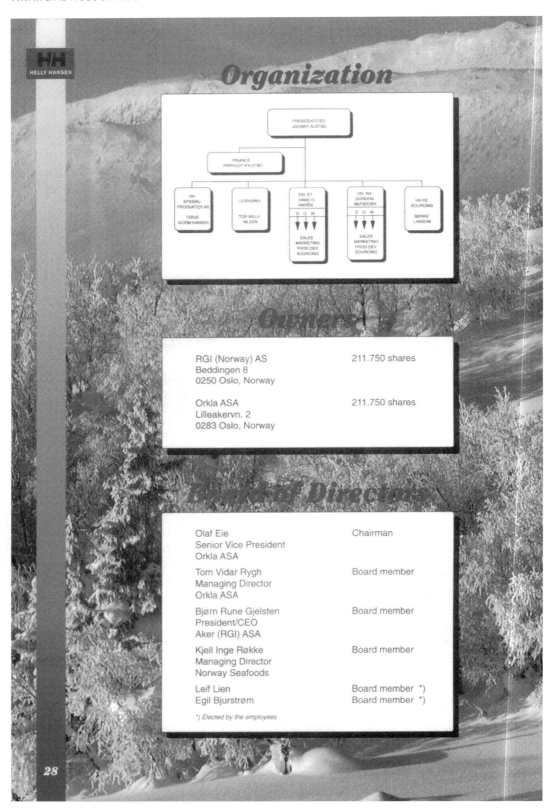

Organization

PRESIDENT/CEO
JOHNNY AUSTAD

FINANCE
FRITHJOF KYLSTAD

HH SPESIAL-PRODUKTER AS	LICENSING	DIV. ET. HANS O. HARÉN	DIV. NA GORDON McFADDEN	HH FE SOURCING
TERJE GORM HANSEN	TOR WILLY NILSEN	S O W	S O W	BØRRE LANGUM
		SALES MARKETING PROD.DEV. SOURCING	SALES MARKETING PROD.DEV. SOURCING	

Owners

RGI (Norway) AS Beddingen 8 0250 Oslo, Norway	211.750 shares
Orkla ASA Lilleakervn. 2 0283 Oslo, Norway	211.750 shares

Board of Directors

Olaf Eie Senior Vice President Orkla ASA	Chairman
Tom Vidar Rygh Managing Director Orkla ASA	Board member
Bjørn Rune Gjelsten President/CEO Aker (RGI) ASA	Board member
Kjell Inge Røkke Managing Director Norway Seafoods	Board member
Leif Lien	Board member *)
Egil Bjurstrøm	Board member *)

*) Elected by the employees

28

15 Price change accounting ('Inflation accounting')

'Historically the cycle of inflation always returns, though the timing cannot be foreseen.'

ASC (Accounting Standards Committee), Great Britain

LEARNING OBJECTIVES

The literature on price change accounting is in many ways confusing. It is, therefore, very important to clarify the main questions within the field. These clarifications are for the most part of a theoretical kind, but practical illustrations will both demonstrate the theory and show the international clarifications and agreements reached during the last few decades.

After studying this chapter you will:

- understand, even better than before, the limitations of historical cost accounting when prices are increasing;
- have been given a short history of developments in this field of accounting;
- understand why price change accounting is a better term to use than inflation accounting;
- see the alternatives to historical cost accounting (HCA): current value accounting (CVA) and current purchasing power accounting (CPPA);
- understand why current cost accounting (CCA) is the leading alternative to HCA;
- know the difference between nominal and real price increases;
- have learnt about the 'value to the business' philosophy;
- have reflected on whether an increase in value can be part of the profit for the year;
- know of three different views on the capital maintenance concept;
- have learnt that the effect of financing must be taken into consideration;
- understand gearing and the gearing adjustment reasoning;
- have a full understanding of price change reporting by studying in depth a concrete example.

Since this chapter is even more concentrated than the other chapters in this book, it could be wise to refer to Albert Einstein before starting to read: 'Make everything as simple as possible, but not simpler.'

15.1 Background and a brief history

In Chapter 1 we underlined the basic principles of traditional accounting. One of the central principles was historical cost. This principle is so fundamental that traditional accounting is often referred to as historical cost accounting (HCA).

So far in this book we have discussed the basic measurement problems and built the analysis on this basic assumption. We have also seen that internationally financial statements and reporting are based on historical cost. The principal limitations of HCA in times of price increases are well understood and may be summarized as follows:

- *Reported results* HC accounts match current revenues with out-of-date costs, leading to an overstatement of reported results.
- *Capital employed* The HC of asset is not an up-to-date measure of the resources employed in a business.
- *Return on capital* The use of HC profit and HC asset values overstates the return on capital because it both overstates profit and understates the asset amounts.
- *Maintenance of capital* HC accounts do not show the extent to which a company earns sufficient funds to maintain its operating capability or the purchasing power of shareholders' equity.
- *Trends* HC accounts can give misleading impressions of the trends of growth and profitability because they do not take account of changes in the value of the unit of money.

These deficiencies are most apparent in periods of relatively high inflation. Therefore, criticism of HCA and discussion of the alternatives are always at their highest in such periods, and in countries with high inflation.

The discussion of alternatives to traditional HCA has a long history both in literature and in teaching. The origins of the development within the field of business economics were in continental Europe in the 1920s, particularly Germany (Fritz Schmidt) and the Netherlands (Limpberg). However, the ideas had little impact on practice at that stage, although the writings were absorbed into the body of accounting thought. Later, some Dutch companies adopted a system of value accounting which has remained a minority practice in the Netherlands up to the present day.

A milestone in accounting literature was passed in the early 1960s with the publication of the book *The Theory and Measurement of Business Income* from two leading US accounting researchers, Edgar Edwards and Philip Bell.

This book was a bridge builder to economic thinking and economic theory. It developed a meaningful theory of the concept of business income and the authors showed how the ideas can be applied in accounting. The philosophy and thinking of Edwards and Bell had an important impact on both theory and teaching and also practice in the US and other countries.

During the early 1970s, when inflation accelerated, there was a series of academic and professional proposals for alternatives to HCA. Both the US and the UK developed accounting standards as a supplement to HCA. There was, however, a lack of interest in both countries and the standards were withdrawn in the mid-1980s. This illustrates that practical interest in price change accounting is directly related to the rate of inflation: the greater the inflation, the greater the interest.

At present, price change accounting is limited to certain economies in Latin America which have experienced high levels of inflation. Elsewhere, traditional historical cost accounting dominates. We must also add that price change accounting has always been a supplement to HCA. Most certainly, this will remain the case in the future.

Price change accounting is, however, an important field of study for at least three main reasons:

- as mentioned in this chapter, inflation is likely to return;
- there will always be some countries in the world with high inflation;
- companies operating in many countries may operate in countries with high inflation, and there is a need to take this fact into the accounting information.

The short study here will aim to discuss the main measurement problems in the field of price change accounting, to give theoretical clarifications and to show what practical discussion and experience in the 1970s and 1980s gave in clarification. The purpose of this is twofold: to be able to use price change accounting if necessary and to be prepared to use it whenever inflation occurs.

15.2 Terminology

The first clarification regards terminology. Strictly speaking, the word 'inflation' means a general increase in the prices of goods and services in a country. It is measured by broad-based indices. Changes in the prices of particular goods may not move exactly in line with those of others. This you can see from published indices of particular categories of assets, such as an index of property prices. Thus there is a choice between taking specific price changes into consideration or just changes in the general price level. It is therefore better to use the broader term *price change accounting*, rather than the narrower term inflation accounting, since the latter implies that only the change in the general price level is taken into consideration.

15.3 The alternatives

Traditional financial accounting, historical cost accounting, does not take price changes into consideration at all. Assets are therefore measured in the balance sheet at cost prices (less depreciation on depreciable assets). In addition, all assets are summarized without taking into consideration the different points in time at which they were acquired. We summarize a building bought ten years ago and machinery bought five years ago at prices at that time (less depreciation) and cash and bank accounts at tod ay's monetary value. In fact, this is a parallel to summarizing German marks, British pounds and Norwegian kroner without currency translation!

Since we want to get the full overview in relation to the term price change accounting, we start with the flow chart in Fig. 15.1.

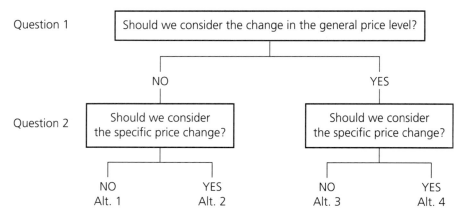

Alternative 1 In this alternative both questions have negative answers, and we are back to the basis of historical cost accounting (HCA).

Alternative 2 In this case the answer is 'yes' to considering specific price change, but 'no' to considering the general price change. This alternative will give the value of assets at any time. Therefore, a good name for this alternative is current value accounting (CVA).

Alternative 3 In this alternative the effect of the change in the general price level will be considered, but not the price change of the specific asset. This accounting alternative is current purchasing power accounting (CPPA).

Alternative 4 In this case the answer is 'yes' to both considerations. We will have an alternative where the final valuation of the asset is current value (see Alternative 2), but we will also see this value compared with the general change in price level. We have current value accounting in real terms (CVA – Real Terms).

Figure 15.1 Historical cost (traditional financial accounting)

We see that in Alternatives 2 and 4 we end up with the current value of the building. In Alternative 2 we just add the nominal price increase to the value of the building at the beginning of the year. In Alternative 4 the focus will be on the real price increase, i.e. the increase after having taken the increase in the general price level into consideration. If, for example, the building has increased in value by 10 per cent and the general price level increase has been 4 per cent, then the real increase in the value of the building is 6 per cent.

15.4 Current values

As we have seen, Alternative 2 and Alternative 4 both represent current value accounting. Figure 15.2 illustrates the difference between the two.

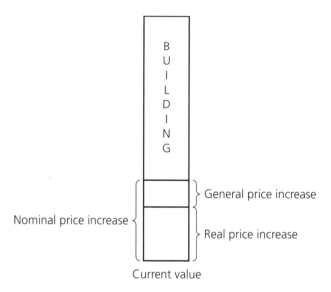

Figure 15.2 Current value accounting

In Alternative 2 we move directly to the current value of the asset (building). In Alternative 4 we will make a distinction between the change explained by the change in general price level and the change above that level.

We have used the term current value accounting for Alternatives 2 and 4. Current means that this accounting system is updated at any time and thus these alternatives give today's values of all assets. The question is whether we should look at the input market or the output market as far as current value is concerned. In the first case the question to be asked is: what is the *cost* of the specific asset?, and in the latter: what is the *sales value* of the asset?

In some cases the value of the asset could be almost identical under the two alternatives, but in other cases there could be big differences. This depends on the prevailing market conditions and also the fact that you operate in different markets when you compare input values with output values.

In choosing between the two alternatives the going concern view is quite important. You will remember that one of the fundamental concepts in traditional financial accounting is the going concern concept. That means that the accounts are prepared and presented under the condition that the company will continue. In line with this view, there are strong arguments in favour of the input view.

The international development confirms this view, leading to current cost accounting (CCA) being the preferable alternative to current value accounting (CVA).

15.5 The 'value to the business' philosophy

We have to underline a further aspect of CCA: it is equal to replacement cost or recoverable amount, whichever is the lower. Recoverable amount is the maximum value which could be derived from the asset either from sale or from use in the business. This view is based on the 'value to the business' (VTB) philosophy, known in the literature from the 1920s (J.C. Bonbright). This philosophy has a clear parallel to the 'lower of cost or market' view (and test) in traditional accounting. It takes care of the general principle: prudence or conservatism. Thus in the CCA, the VTB test sees to it that the asset is not overvalued.

In symbolic terms, we can think of the following relations between the three value alternatives: NPV = net present value, CCV = current cost value and CSV = current sales value

1   NPV > CCV > CSV
2   NPV > CSV > CCV
3   NSV > NPV > CCV
4   NSV > CCV > NPV
5   CCV > NPV > CSV
6   CCV > CSV > NPV

The question we ask in the VTB test is: what loss do we suffer if we lose the asset in question?

In situations 1 and 2 the decision is to use the asset, not sell it. The maximum loss, however, will be CCV. Then you will be able to replace the asset. The VTB in 1 and 2 is therefore CCV. In situations 3 and 4 the optimal decision will be to sell the asset. The loss, however, will be limited to CCV, since you then will be just as well off as before the asset was lost. In situations 5 and 6 the optimal decision is not to replace the asset. In 5 you will sell it, but in 6 you will use it. The maximum recoverable amount, VTB, however, will be NPV in 5 and NSV in 6.

We have seen that in four of the six situations the answer to the VTB test is CCV, but in those cases where CCV is the highest, the VTB test is effective and will result in an answer other than CCV. Thus the test must be done in order not to over-value the asset according to the VTB philosophy. This test is quite parallel to the test 'lower of cost or market' that we make in traditional financial accounting.

15.6 Can an increase in value be part of the profit for the year?

A key question within value accounting is whether or not an increase in value could be part of the profit for the year. In order to answer this question, we have to find the economic explanation of such an increase. That part of the increase of a specific asset representing the general price level change is uncomplicated: there can be no profit since it just compensates for the change in general purchasing power of money. The other part, the real price (or value) increase, must be due to a change in demand for this specific asset. Since the real value has increased, the expectation of the income (or cash flow) from that asset must have changed in a positive way. Using the 'well off' philosophy, there are good arguments for accepting this part as profit for the year. It is obviously better for a company to have assets that increase in value rather than those that do not.

Although this economic argument is very strong, many accounting authors, and especially practitioners, will not agree to reporting this part as profit. The main argument against it is that, physically, it is the same asset we have at the end of the year as in the beginning. The asset will have to be replaced with another that would be equally expensive, so no gain should therefore be registered.

This discussion leads us to the main question, namely: when is capital maintained?

15.7 Capital maintenance

There are three alternative capital maintenance concepts:

- unadjusted money amount;
- adjusted for the general increase in purchasing power; and
- adjusted for the increase in the prices of the specific assets of the company.

The first alternative follows automatically in HCA. In the CVA system this alternative is not relevant. We will therefore concentrate on the other two alternatives.

In the second alternative a general price level index adjustment is used in order to ensure that the (equity) capital is maintained. In this case, there can be no increase in equity before this effect has been taken into consideration. The specific change in prices (the real price increase) is, however, an effect beyond the capital maintenance concept.

The third alternative makes an adjustment according to the specific changes in prices. The view here is that capital (equity) is maintained by including the investment of the capital, i.e. the change in the prices of specific assets.

There is a conflicting view of the concepts both in accounting literature and in practice. In practice, this difference can be seen from the accounting standards in this field. The US view will be in accordance with the second alternative, and thus include part of the real specific price (value) change as something to be reported as part of income. The UK view will not accept any part of a price (value) change as part of the year's result. Thus this view will be in accordance with the third alternative.

15.8 The effect of financing

A common feature of inflation is that debtors gain in purchasing power in times of price increases, while creditors lose. The reason for this is that if a person borrows money in a period of inflation, the repayment will take place with money of lower purchasing power than when the loan was granted. In most economies, however, where a free lunch is not a common feature, this seems strange. Creditors will protect themselves by increasing the interest rate when inflation is expected. Therefore, the nominal rate of interest can be broken down into two parts: one representing the real interest rate, the other the inflation part. If, for example, the real interest (the rate which would have been charged in the absence of inflation) is 3 per cent and inflation is 5 per cent, then the nominal interest rate is 8 per cent.

If we return to the field of business, this question requires us to consider the impact of debt financing on non-monetary assets. Once more we illustrate the issue using a figure, again a building, but partly financed by debt (Fig. 15.3).

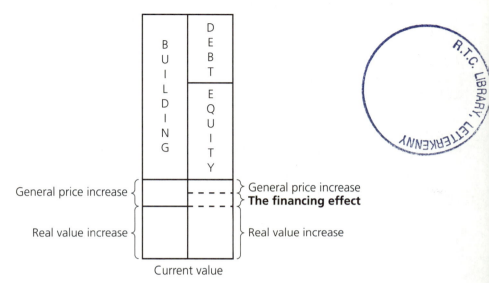

Figure 15.3 The effect of financing

In the figure there is nothing new as far as the assets side (the building) is concerned. But on the debt/equity side, we see a new phenomenon, referred to as 'the financing effect'. The explanation is as follows.

We see that the part taking care of the general price level change is different on the assets side – the building – than that part taking care of the maintenance of the equity. This is due to the debt financing of the building. The total increase in the value of the building will have full effect on the equity. Thus a gain exists because of the financing.

We underline this phenomenon by the following example based on different percentages of debt financing:

The current value of the building at the beginning of the year was 100. The price increase of the building this year was 15 per cent, and the general price level increased by 5 per cent.

Alternatives:	A	B	C	D
Debt/equity ratio	0/100	20/80	50/50	80/20
Nominal increase in equity, absolute figures (= total increase in the value of the building)	15	15	15	15
Equity, absolute figures	100	80	50	20
Increase in equity	15%	18.75%	30%	75%

We see an enormous variation in the increase in equity when we compare the alternatives: from 15 to 75 per cent in the extreme cases (A and D).

Both in theory and in the international accounting standards on value accounting it is agreed that the effect of financing must be taken into consideration when profit is being reported under a CVA system. In practice, however, not all countries and/or companies agree.

There are two different ways to take the financing effect into consideration: either to calculate the gain on net monetary liabilities or to make a correction to the relevant costs or expenses.

Alternative 1: The net monetary effect

Liabilities (long-term and short-term):	X
less	
Monetary assets (debtors, bank accounts, cash):	X
Net monetary liabilities	X

Gain on net monetary liabilities: Net monetary liabilities • (multiplied by) the increase in the general price level index.

Alternative 2: The gearing effect

Gearing is expressed as the debt financing of the non-monetary assets. Thus we find the same basic view as we have discussed under Alternative 1, but the measurement of the effect is different. The gearing ratio (the debt financing of the non-monetary assets) is used as a correction of the additional costs in a CCA system. The logic behind such a view can be illustrated in the following way:

Operating profit, HC	X
Effect of CC system:	X
Additional cost of stocks	X
Additional cost of depreciation	X
Operating profit, CC	X
Interest expenses	X
Gearing*	–X
Profit after financial items	X

* Additional costs (stocks and depreciation) multiplied by the gearing ratio/percentage (net monetary liabilities/non-monetary assets × 100)

When calculating the additional costs of stocks and depreciation due to price change, we look at the non-monetary assets (NMA) on the assets side. This gives a current operating result based on the available resources regardless of the financing of the assets. The effect of the financing is then taken care of in the financing section of the reporting of results. This is logical, since in fact it is a correction of the interest (the interest is measured in nominal terms); thus the inflation rate is part of the nominal interest rate. Therefore, this correction (of the additional cost corrections) must be taken into consideration in order to give the full effect of price changes.

This clarification and practical ways to carry out the correction underline the importance of taking the financing effect into consideration when we decide on a CCA system. It also raises the following important and controversial question: when is capital maintained?

15.9 Capital maintenance and the financing effect

If we go back to Fig. 15.3, we can see directly how the capital maintenance concept and the financing effect can be explained. When the capital maintenance view is to keep the equity updated according to the increase in the general price level, we have the following two explanations,

either:

● the nominal increase in the value of the asset (building)
  less
● equity adjusted for the general price level increase

or:

● the gain on net monetary liabilities
  plus
● the real value increase in non-monetary assets.

In both alternatives we will have the same result, as you will see from the figure.

If we keep to the second capital maintenance view, the whole increase in the value of the non-monetary assets will be part of the capital adjustment. The financing effect is taken care of by the gearing technique. In this way we will have the following explanation:

Equity at January 1		X
Net profit for the year		X
Value increase on NMA	X	
less		
Gearing	X	X
Equity at December 31		X

If we compare the two capital maintenance concepts, we see two differences. In the first alternative, the effect of monetary items is calculated by using the general price level index. This is not the case in the second alternative, since the correction is linked to the specific price changes of the non-monetary assets. Second, the gain on net monetary liabilities is measured from the balance sheet situation, but in the latter alternative the effect is linked to the realization (i.e. the disposal of the non-monetary assets). This difference in technique will give different figures for a specific year, but the phenomenon is the same. Over time the difference will balance.

15.10 An example

Ajour Ltd was founded five years ago, starting with a total capital of 100 (million), financed 50/50 by loan and equity. The capital was immediately invested in a building at a cost of 40 (million) and machinery at a cost of 60 (million).

Since the year of formation there has been an increase in prices, especially during the last two years, so the company also presented value data for last year, but only balance sheet figures. The presentation was as follows (all figures in millions):

Balance sheet, December 31	Year 4	
	Historical cost	Current cost
Building	36.0	43.2
Machinery	36.0	39.6
Stocks	15.0	15.0
Debtors	12.0	12.0
Cash	1.0	1.0
Assets	100.0	110.8
Equity	60.0	70.8
Long-term liabilities	30.0	30.0
Short-term liabilities	10.0	10.0
Equity and liabilities	100.0	110.8

In the section 'Accounting policies' Ajour Ltd gave the following information:

Depreciation

'The building is depreciated over 40 years, the machinery over 10 years (no residual value), both according to the straight-line method.'

Stocks

'Stocks are valued according to the lower of cost or market price principle and the assumption of FIFO for the cost flow.'

Comments

As we see from the CC balance sheet figures, the assets side of the balance sheet is 10.8 per cent higher than the HC figures. We also see that the equity figure in the CC balance sheet is 18 per cent higher than the HC figure. The difference in these percentages can be explained by the effect of debt financing.

Although the additional information about current cost values is positive, it must be said that the price increase also affects the profit and loss figures. Such figures are not presented. Further, there are no current cost figures for Year 3, and thus no total explanation of the change in equity for the year.

For Year 5 we want to present full CC figures for Ajour Ltd with an illustration of the different views presented in the last section.

The following figures are given:

Profit and loss account, HC	Year 5
Sales	100.0
Cost of goods sold	75.0
Depreciation	7.0
Other operating expenses	12.0
Operating profit	6.0
Interest expenses	3.0
Profit before taxes	3.0
Taxes	1.0
Net profit	2.0

The following indices are given as a representation of the price changes:

	19 × 0	19 × 4	19 × 5
Building	100.0	120.0	138.0
Machinery	100.0	110.0	121.0
Stocks	100.0	115.0	124.2
General price level index	100.0	108.0	114.5

We see that the nominal price increases in Year 5 on the non-monetary assets were 15, 10 and 8 per cent, respectively. The general price level increase was 6 per cent. This means real price increases of the three non-monetary assets of 9, 4 and 2 per cent, respectively.

Given this information, and the HC data for Year 5, we get the following CC figures:

Balance sheet, December 31, current cost

	Year 5		Year 4	
	CC	(HC)	CC	(HC)
Building	48.3	(35.0)	43.2	(36.0)
Machinery	36.3	(30.0)	39.6	(36.0)
Stocks	16.0	(16.0)	15.0	(15.0)
Debtors	14.0	(14.0)	12.0	(12.0)
Cash	3.0	(3.0)	1.0	(1.0)
Assets	117.6	(98.0)	110.8	(100.0)
Equity	81.6	(62.0)	70.8	(60.0)
Long-term liabilities	28.0	(28.0)	30.0	(30.0)
Short-term liabilities	8.0	(8.0)	10.0	(10.0)
Equity and liabilities	117.6	(98.0)	110.8	(100.0)

Comments

Building and machinery can be adjusted from HC to CC by using the indices at the end of this year directly (138/100 and 121/100, respectively). The figure can also be found by using the CC figures for Year 4, adding on the price increase for Year 5 and reducing the figures to allow for the CC depreciation.

Stocks are valued according to the FIFO principle, and are approximately updated.

The monetary items are the same in the CC system as in the HC. That is also the case as far as liabilities are concerned.

The equity at the end of the year can be found as a difference. However, the total change of 10.8 needs an explanation. The first is the profit for the year, and the next is the increase in the value of non-monetary assets.

Thus we have to work out the profit and loss account in the CC model. This calculation and presentation is done in different steps: (1) the operating profit; (2) the effect of financing; and (3) the change in the values of non-monetary assets connected with the capital maintenance concepts. This should give a good illustration of the alternative views discussed earlier.

	Year 5	
(1) Operating profit	Current cost	Historical cost
Sales	100.0	(100.0)
Cost of goods sold	76.2	(75.0)
Depreciation	8.7	(7.0)
Other operating expenses	12.0	(12.0)
Operating profit	3.1	(6.0)

The CC figure of cost of goods sold is 1.2 higher than the HC figure, due to the adjustment of the stocks at the beginning of the year. The depreciation is 1.7 higher, due to 0.4 additional depreciation on the building and 1.3 additional depreciation on the machinery.

(2) Capital maintenance

The CC equity figures are given in the beginning of this example:

	Year 5	Year 4
Equity	81.6	70.8

As we have discussed earlier, there are three different views on capital maintenance:

• unadjusted money amount;
• adjusted for the general increase in purchasing power; and
• adjusted for the increase in the prices of specific assets of the company.

We have mentioned before that in a CCA system the first alternative is of little relevance. Consequently, the real alternatives are either to adjust the equity capital by a general purchasing power index or specific indices for the non-monetary assets of the company.

In our example the capital maintenance figure will be:

Equity at the end of last year	70.8
General price level increase this year (6%)	4.3
Equity at the end of this year	75.1

In this capital maintenance concept, the equity capital is maintained according to the increase in the general purchasing power of money.

If we calculate according to the specific capital maintenance concept, we will get the following figures:

Equity at the end of last year	70.8
Specific price increase of non-monetary assets*	11.7
Equity at the end of this year	82.5

* Nominal increase on the building (15% this year)	6.5
Nominal increase on machinery (10% this year)	4.0
Nominal increase on stocks (8% this year)	1.2
Total nominal increase on non-monetary assets	11.7

(3) The financing effect

Alternative: the net monetary effect

Liabilities (at the end of last year)	40.0
Monetary assets (debtors, cash)	13.0
Net monetary liabilities	27.0

Gain on net monetary liabilities: 1.6 (27.0 x 6% (increase in the general price level index)).

Alternative: Gearing

	Year 5
Additional cost of stocks	1.2
Additional cost of depreciation	1.7
	2.9

Gearing ratio percentage (based on the balance sheet data last year): 27.6%

(Net monetary liabilities: 27.0, non-monetary assets (building, machinery and stocks): 97.8)

Gearing: 0.8 (27.6% x 2.9)

The final presentation

The final presentation is shown in two ways, the first representing the UK view, the other the US view. Both are based on the accounting developments experienced by the two countries according to the accounting standards during the 1980s.

UK-inspired	Year 5
HCA, *operating profit*	6.0
Additional cost of goods sold	1.2
Additional cost of depreciation	1.7
CCA, *operating profit*	3.1
Interest expenses	3.0
Gearing	0.8
Profit before taxes	0.9
Taxes	1.0
Net profit	–0.1

Balance sheet, December 31, CCA	Year 5	Year 4
Building	48.3	43.2
Machinery	36.3	39.6
Stocks	16.0	15.0
Debtors	14.0	12.0
Cash	3.0	1.0
Assets	117.6	110.8
Equity	81.6*	70.8*
Long-term liabilities	28.0	30.0
Short-term liabilities	8.0	10.0
Equity and liabilities	117.6	110.8

*Equity, December 31, Year 4	70.8
Net profit, Year 5	–0.1

The effect of price increase:

Nominal increase on building	6.5
Nominal increase on machinery	4.0
Nominal increase on stocks	1.2
	11.7
Less gearing	0.8
	10.9
Equity, December 31, Year 5	81.6

US-inspired

Income statement	Year 5 Historical cost	Current cost
Sales	100.0	100.0
Cost of goods sold	75.0	76.2
Depreciation	7.0	8.7
Other operating costs	12.0	12.0
Operating profit	6.0	3.1
Interest expenses	3.0	3.0
Gain on net monetary liabilities	–	1.6
Taxes	1.0	1.0
Net profit	2.0	–
Profit after gain on net monetary liabilities	–	0.7
Real increase on stocks (2%)		0.3
Real increase on building and machinery (9% and 4%)		5.5
Profit including real increase on non-monetary assets		6.5

Balance sheet, December 31, current cost

	Year 5 CC	Year 5 (HC)	Year 4 CC	Year 4 (HC)
Building	48.3	(35.0)	43.2	(36.0)
Machinery	36.3	(30.0)	39.6	(36.0)
Stocks	16.0	(16.0)	15.0	(15.0)
Debtors	14.0	(14.0)	12.0	(12.0)
Cash	3.0	(3.0)	1.0	(1.0)
Assets	117.6	(98.0)	110.8	(100.0)
Equity	81.6*	(62.0)	70.8*	(60.0)
Long-term liabilities	28.0	(28.0)	30.0	(30.0)
Short-term liabilities	8.0	(8.0)	10.0	(10.0)
Equity and liabilities	117.6	(98.0)	110.8	(100.0)

* Equity December 31, Year 4	70.8
Maintenance of the general purchasing power of money	4.3
Profit including real increase on non-monetary assets	6.5
Equity December 31, Year 5	81.6

✓ **Questions and answers**

1 What are the principal limitations of HCA?

Answer:
The reported results overstate the profit for the year while the capital employed is undervalued. These two factors lead to an overstatement of the rates of return. Furthermore, the HC figures do not show whether the capital employed is maintained. Finally, the trend of, for example, sales is misleading because the change in the value of money is not taken into consideration.

2 Why do you think the term 'price change accounting' is better than 'inflation accounting'?

Answer:
Because, strictly speaking, inflation means the general change in prices of goods and services. Thus specific price changes in the value of goods and services are not included. This restriction is not relevant for business.

3 What are the alternatives to HCA?

Answer:
Current purchasing power accounting (CPPA), taking just the general price level change into consideration, and current value accounting (CVA), taking the specific changes in prices of assets into consideration.

4 Illustrate the difference between nominal and real price change with an example.

Answer:
If the increase in the price of a building is 10 per cent in a specific year, and the increase in the general price level that year is 6 per cent, then the real increase in the price of the building is 4 per cent.

5 Why do you think current cost accounting (CCA) is preferred to current sales value accounting?

Answer:
Because the input view is more realistic for a company and also in accordance with the traditional 'going concern' view.

6 What is 'value to the business' or 'recovery value'?

Answer:
It is the value you will come up with by asking the following question: what is my loss in money terms if this specific asset is taken away from me? The answer to this question will usually be the current cost figure, but it can also be the net present value or the sales value if the current cost figure is lower.

7 How will you argue in favour of the view that a real increase in the value of a non-monetary asset could be part of profit for the year?

Answer:
The reason for the real price change of the asset must be a change in expectation about the future income (cash flow) of the asset. Therefore, one can argue that since this took place this year, it should be reported as income this year.

8 Why is it necessary to take the effect of financing of the non-monetary assets into consideration?

Answer:
Because that effect follows from the fact that the interest includes compensation for inflation. If we do not take the financing effect into consideration in accounting, we overestimate the financial cost and thus underestimate the result for the year.

9 Which two forms of calculations can be used for measuring the effect of financing?

Answer:
The gain or net monetary view and the gearing view.

10 Explain how the gearing ratio is calculated.

Answer:
First, the gearing percentage is found by measuring how much (what percentage) of the non-monetary assets is financed by debt. Second, this percentage is used on the additional costs for calculating current costs instead of historical cost for the relevant items (stocks, depreciation).

11 How would you like to see CC figures and the effect of price changes presented in the annual report?

Answer:
First of all, such figures should be presented as a supplement to HCA. All effects should be taken into consideration and presented, and both the profit and loss accounts and balance sheets for two years should be included. In many ways the UK model seems easy to understand, but on the other hand the US model has more relevant components. The main point, however, is that the change in equity during the year is fully explained. Finally, trend figures should be adjusted for the effect of the fall in the purchasing power of money.

? Problems

1 Calculate the 'gain on net monetary items' in this example, assuming that the development in the general price level has been 10 per cent this year.

Balance sheet, December 31

Building	1200
Machinery	1000
Stocks	800
Trade debtors	600
Other debtors	400
Bank account	200
Cash	100
Assets	4300
Nominal share capital	1000
Additional paid-up capital	500
Retained earnings	600
Total equity	2100
Mortgage loan	500
Bank loan	500
Overdraft	200
Trade creditors	400
Other creditors	600
Equity and liabilities	4300

2 Machinery is bought at the beginning of the Year 1 at a purchase price of 100. The economic life is expected to be five years. No residual value of the machinery is expected.

(a) Calculate the yearly depreciations and the values at the end of each year using the straight-line method in the HCA system.

(b) Calculate the yearly depreciations and the values at the end of each year using the straight-line method in the CCA system. The current cost calculation should be based on an expectation of 10 per cent yearly increase in the price of the machinery.

3 Company X Ltd presents the following accounting figures:

Profit and loss account	This year
Sales	1000
Cost of goods sold	750
Depreciation	60
Other operating costs	90
Operating profit	100
Interest expenses	50
Net profit	50

Balance sheet, December 31	This year	Last year
Building	490	500
Machinery	250	300
Stocks	200	200
Debtors	150	200
Bank	110	50
Assets	1200	1250
Equity	500	450
Long-term liabilities	600	600
Creditors	100	200
Equity and liabilities	1200	1250

The building is depreciated by the straight-line method over 40 years, machinery over 10 years. Stock is valued according to the FIFO principle for the flow of cost. Information about the development of specific prices and of general price level is all expressed by indices.

Building	at time of purchase	100
	December 31 last year	200
	December 31 this year	250
Machinery	at time of purchase	100
	December 31 last year	139
	December 31 this year	150
Stocks	December 31 last year	150
	December 31 this year	165
General price index	at time of foundation	100
	December 31 last year	150
	December 31 this year	156

Based on the HCA data and the information about the development in prices, you should calculate the CCA data. The presentation should be made in two ways (1) and (2), as follows:

(1) (UK-inspired)

Results	This year
Results	**This year**
HCA operating profit	100
Additional cost of goods sold	
Additional cost of depreciation	____
CCA operating profit	____
Interest expenses	50
Gearing	____
CCA profit	____

Balance sheet, December 31

	This year	Last year
Building		
Machinery		
Stocks		
Debtors		
Bank	____	____
Assets	____	____
Equity		
Long-term liabilities		
Short-term liabilities	____	____
Equity and liabilities	____	____

(2) (US-inspired)

	This year	
Income statement	Historical cost	Current cost
Sales	1000	1000
Cost of goods sold	750	
Depreciation	60	
Other operating costs	90	90
Operating profit	100	
Interest expenses	50	50
Net profit	50	
Gain on net monetary items	–	____
Result after gain on net monetary assets	–	
Real increase in stocks	–	
Real increase in building and machinery	–	
Result after real increase in non-monetary assets	–	____

273

Answers to problems

Chapter 1

1 (a), (b), (e), (g), (i), (j), (l).

2 (a) The prudence principle (lower of cost or market value).
    (b) The historical cost principle.
    (c) The transaction principle, registering the purchase of the new machinery and the sale of the old one. The matching principle, so that the cost of using the machinery is matched against the revenue.
    (d) The principle of consistency, or in fact the change of it.

Chapter 2

1 **Assets**	(000s)	(000s)
Fixed assets		
Land	200	
Quay	300	
Ship	200	
Building	900	
Machinery	1400	
Office equipment	300	
Shares in Alfa	200	
		3500
Current assets		
Finished goods	200	
Work in progress	80	
Raw material	70	
Debtors	200	
Postal account	40	
		590
Total assets		4090
Equity and liabilities		
Equity		1450

Long-term liabilities

Debenture	1400	
Bank loan	600	
		2000

Short-term liabilities

Bank overdraft	400	
Creditors	40	
Bill payable	20	
Advance payments from customers	30	
Social Security amounts due	120	
Tax from employees	30	
		640
Total equity and liabilities		4090

2 Balance sheet, December 31, 19XX   (000s)

Assets

Building	600
Machinery	200
Shares in Beta	100
Stocks	270
Debtors	180
Bank account	100
Total assets	1450

Equity and liabilities

Equity	350	(difference)
Debenture	800	
Local authorities	200	
Other short-term liabilities	100	
Total equity and liabilities	1450	

Chapter 3

1 Profit and loss account for 19XX   (000s)

Operating revenues and expenses

Sales	3800
Rental income	50
Operating revenues	3850
Cost of goods sold	2150
Wages and social security expenses	600
Administrative expenses	200
Rent	300
Loss on trade debtors	50

Operating expenses	3300
Operating profit	550
Financial income and financial expenses	
Dividends on shares	50*
Interest on mortgage loan	200
Interest on overdraft	100
Net financial expenses	250
Net profit	300

(* This is deducted (50 – (200 + 100) = 250))

2 As operating income:

Profit on sale of old factory	3.5[1]

As operating expense:

Depreciation on factory	3[2]

[1] Sale amount less book value at December 31, last year, less half a year's depreciation.

[2] Half a year's depreciation on the old factory plus half a year's depreciation on the new building.

3 Profit and loss account for 19XX (000s)

Operating revenues and expenses

Sales	9090
Cost of goods sold	4050
Wages and social security expenses	3600
Rent expenses	300
Administration expenses	800
Loss on trade debtors	50
Depreciation on machinery and equipment	100
Total operating expenses	8900
Operating profit	190
Financial income and expenses	
Dividends on shares	(10)
Interest on mortgage loan	200
Interest on bank overdraft	50
Net financial expenses	240
Net loss	(50)

Balance sheet, December 31, 19XX (000s)

Fixed assets

Quay	200
Machinery and equipment	900
Total fixed assets	1100

Current assets

Stock	850
Trade debtors	600
Shares	100
Bank account	50
Total current assets	1600
Total assets	2700
Equity	1200
Long term liabilitites	
Mortgage	800
Short-term liabilities	
Trade creditors	200
Tax liability	100
Other short-term liabilities	100
Bank overdraft	300
Total short-term liabilities	700
Total equity and liabilities	2700

Chapter 5

1 (a) Debit purchased goods, credit cash.
  (b) Debit bank account, credit cash.
  (c) Debit creditors, credit cash.
  (d) Debit debtors, credit sales of goods.
  (e) Debit machinery, credit creditors (for machinery).
  (f) Debit bank account, credit mortgage loan.
  (g) Debit value added tax, credit cash.
  (h) Debit mortgage loan, credit bank account.
  (i) Debit cash, credit debtors.
  (j) Debit equity, credit cash.

2

	Account for goods purchased		Account for goods sold	
	Debit	Credit	Debit	Credit
Stock, January 1	500			
Purchase goods in January	8500			
Sales in January				12 000
Profit and loss account, Jan. 31		8000	12 000	
Balance, January 31		1000		
	9000	9000	12 000	12 000
Stock, February 1	1000			

3

Account for machinery

	Debit	Credit
Balance, January 1	800	
Bank, January 1–December 31	2000	
Profit and loss account, December 31		600
Balance, December 31		2200
	2800	2800
Balance, January 1	2200	

4 **Balance sheet, January 31**

Building	395
Stock	350
Trade debtors	100
Postal account	250
Total assets	1095
Equity (difference)	425*
Debentures	300
Trade creditors	200
Bank overdraft	150
Unpaid operating expenses	20
Total equity and liabilities	1095

Profit and loss account, January

Sales	4000
Cost of goods sold	2950
Wages	600
Other operating expenses	420
Depreciation of building	5
	3975
Profit	25

*Balance, December 31: 400, plus profit for January: 25.

Chapter 6

1 4 (realized loss plus the increase in the calculated loss).

2 Cost of goods sold 24 600 (100 units at 100 plus 20 units at 110 plus 80 units at 110 plus 30 units at 120).
Stock: 8400 (70 units at 120).

3

Raw material cost (1000 units at 20, 4500 units at 21)	114 500
Other operating costs	2 400 000
Decrease in work in progress and finished goods	50 000
Operating costs	2 564 500

4

	Straight line 20%	Reducing balance 30%
Year 1	16	30
Year 2	16	21
Year 3	16	14.70
Year 4	16	10.30
Year 5	16	7.20

5 Book value according to the straight-line principle: 20.
Book value according to the reducing-balance principle: 16.80.
Gain on sale of asset: 10 (straight line) and 13.20 (reducing balance).

6

Year:	19X1	19X2	19X3	19X4	19X5
Firm A					
R&D expense	20	10	15	10	5
Firm B					
R&D expense	4	6	9	11	12
Difference	−16	−4	−6	+1	+7

(At the end of year 19X5 Firm B will have an R&D balance of 18. We see from the figures that this amount is exactly the difference between the R&D expenses charged in the profit and loss account of the two firms.)

Chapter 7

1 7.20 and 5.50.

2 Fixed asset: plus 100; deferred taxes: plus 30; equity (restricted): plus 70.

Chapter 15

1 Total liabilities:

Mortgage loan	500
Bank loan	500
Overdraft	200
Trade creditors	400
Other creditors	600
	2200

Monetary assets:

Trade debtors	600
Other debtors	400
Bank account	200
Cash	100
	1300

Net monetary liabilities 900

Gain on net monetary items: 90

2 a)

HCA	Year:	1	2	3	4	5
Depreciation		20	20	20	20	20
Accounting value		80	60	40	20	0

b)

CCA	Year:	1	2	3	4	5
Depreciation		22	24.2	26.6	29.3	32.2
Current cost value		88	72.6	53.3	29.3	0

Comments

We see that depreciation increases by 10 per cent per year.

The current cost values are always updated and represent the current values of the used machinery; for example at the end of Year 3 the machinery has been in use for three years out of the total of five years, so the value at that time will be 40 per cent of the cost of new machinery (40 per cent of 133.1 = 53.3).

We also see the connection between the current cost values from one year to another. At the end of Year 3, for example, the CCV is 53.3, and at the end of Year 4, 29.3. This last CCV can be explained as follows:

Value at December 31 in Year 3 (53.3) plus the increase in the value (10 per cent of 53.3 = 5.3) less current cost depreciation for Year 4 (29.3). This gives a value of 29.3 at December 31 in Year 4.

3 *(1) (UK-inspired)*

Results	This year	
HCA operating profit	100	
Additional cost of goods sold	20	(1)
Additional cost of depreciation	40	(2)
CCA operating profit	40	
Interest expenses	50	
Gearing	20	(3)
CCA profit	10	

Balance sheet, December 31	This year		Last year	
Building	1225		1000	(3)
Machinery	375		420	(3)
Stocks	200		200	
Debtors	150		200	
Bank	110		50	
Assets	2060		1870	
Equity	1360	(4)	1070	(4)
Long-term liabilities	600		600	
Short-term liabilities	100		200	
Equity and liabilities	2060		1870	

1 The index for stock shows 10 per cent increase during the year. Based on the opening stocks (200), this gives a higher CC of goods sold of 20.

2 The index for the building has increased by 150 per cent since the date of acquisition. The depreciation cost therefore has to be up by 15. For the machinery the price index shows an increase of 50 per cent, so the CC depreciation should be up by 25.

3 In order to calculate the gearing ratio, we will have to adjust the balance sheet for December 31 last year to CC data. The building and the machinery are adjusted according to the development of the relevant indices since the time of acquisition, and the equity is found by subtraction.

The gearing ratio is approximately 34%.

(Additional costs (stock and depreciation): 60, non-monetary assets (building, machinery, stocks): 620, financed by debt (liabilities less monetary assets): 550.

Gearing ratio: 550/1.620 ≈ 34%).
Gearing: 34% of 60 ≈ 20.

4 Increase in equity   290
   Net profit   10
   Increase in non-monetary assets   300
   Gearing   −20
   Net   280

(2) (US-inspired)

Income statement	This year Historical cost	Current cost
Sales	1000	1000
Cost of goods sold	750	770
Depreciation	50	90
Other operating costs	90	90
Operating profit	100	40
Interest expenses	50	50
Net profit	50	–
Gain on net monetary items		22 (1)
Result after gain on net monetary assets		12
Real increase in stocks		12 (2)
Real increase in building and machinery		227 (2)
Result after real increase in non-monetary assets		251

1 (Last year's figures)

Liabilities (800), less monetary assets (debtors, bank; 250) = 550. Increase in the general price level index: 4 per cent gives 22.

2 The nominal increase in the index of stock is 10 per cent, the increase in the general price level 4 per cent; leaving the real increase on stock at 6 per cent. For the building and the machinery the real increases are 21 and 4 per cent, respectively.

Balance sheet at December 31 last year and this year are as presented in (1) UK.

Glossary:
Financial accounting
from A to Z

'Accounting is the language of business and, in the twentieth century,
English is the language of accounting.'

This glossary defines, explains and illustrates more than 400 words and expressions of most relevance for understanding financial accounting information. Where English and American English differ greatly, both are given, with English first, as in stocks/inventories.

AAA American Accounting Association.

Above the line A rather vague term referring to that part of the profit and loss account/income statement above the measure of earnings on which earnings per share are based. Extraordinary items are normally not above the line. Contrasts with *below the line*.

Absorption costing That method of costing whereby all costs of production are attributed to the identified units of production. Contrasts with *direct* or *marginal* costing.

Accelerated depreciation Methods of depreciation that allocate larger amounts of depreciation in the earlier years than in the later years. See *depreciation*.

Account A record in which the changes for a balance sheet or profit and loss/income statement item are recorded.

Accountancy The official journal of the Institute of Chartered Accountants in England and Wales, published monthly.

Accounting An information system for measuring economic activity and communicating the result (of these measurements) to users.

Accounting concepts (assumptions, axioms, conventions, postulates) Attempts by accountants to determine the assumptions (etc.) on which the practice of accounting either is based or ought to be based. Numerous lists have been prepared in the literature.

Accounting income Income measured according to accounting principles.

Accounting policies Accounting bases selected and consistently followed, usually published in the annual report.

Accounting principles See *generally accepted accounting principles*.

Accounting Review The journal of the American Accounting Association (AAA), published quarterly.

Accounting standards Accounting rules and procedures relating to measurement, valuation and disclosure, prepared by accounting bodies.

Accounting Standards Board The standard-setting body in the UK, formed in 1990. Successor to the Accounting Standards Committee, established in 1976.

Accounts payable A US term for short-term liabilities arising from purchases on credit from suppliers. See *creditors*.

Accounts receivable A US term for short-term assets that arise from sales on credit to customers. See *debtors*.

Accrual accounting Accounting for revenues in the period in which they are earned and for expenses in the period in which they are incurred. A basic assumption in accounting. Contrasts with *cash accounting*.

Accumulated depreciation The total amount of depreciation of an asset accumulated to date.

Acid test (ratio) See *liquidity ratio*.

Acquisition (accounting) The purchase of a previously independent business. Acquisition accounting (or acquisition method) is the preparation of consolidated financial statements on the assumption that one company has acquired another. Contrasts with *merger accounting/pooling of interests* that may be used only in precisely defined circumstances.

Affiliated company See *associated company*.

All-inclusive concept of profit The perspective which regards the profit as including all gains, whether likely to be repeated or not.

Allocation problem How to allocate cost when only part of the goods or services is used up in one accounting period. The problem arises particularly in the case of stock/inventory valuation and of the depreciation of fixed assets.

Amalgamation The absorption by one company of another.

American Accounting Association (AAA) A US academic association of accountants, established in 1916. Publisher of the *Accounting Review* since 1926 and of numerous books and research studies.

American Institute of Certified Public Accountants (AICPA) The professional association of Certified Public Accountants (CPA) in the US.

Amortization The same as depreciation, but generally used in relation to intangible assets.

Anglo-Saxon accounting Accounting and financial reporting as practised in English-speaking countries, based mainly on a common philosophy of presenting a true and fair view to users of accounting information, especially investors. Compared with European accounting, Anglo-Saxon accounting is much less influenced by creditors and tax authorities.

Annual general meeting A meeting of members of an organization held every year, most often as required by law. The usual business transacted includes reception and consideration of the directors' report, accounts and the auditors' report, declaration of a dividend, election of directors, and the appointment and the fixing of the remuneration of the auditors.

Annual report A document published by a company as part of the management's responsibility to report to shareholders and other interested parties.

Appreciation An increase in the value of an asset, normally not recognized in financial accounting. If recognized, normally not regarded as part of income.

Asset A valuable item owned or controlled by the firm as a result of past transactions or events.

Asset stripping A process whereby a company acquires a controlling interest in another company for the purpose of disposing of its assets.

Asset turnover ratio A ratio that measures how efficiently assets are used to produce sales (sales divided by average total assets).

Associated company A company in which an investment fulfilling certain conditions is held. Normally an investment for the long term, a substantial involvement (not less than 20 per cent of the voting rights) and in a position to exercise a significant influence.

Auditing The process of examining and testing the financial statements of a firm in order to render an independent professional opinion as to the fairness of their presentation.

Auditor Independent chartered/certified public accountants who check and test the accounting records. Necessary to determine the quality of the financial statements.

Auditor's report A report by an independent auditor that accompanies the financial statements, communicating the nature of the audit and the conclusion as to the fair presentations of the financial statements.

Authorized shares/stocks The maximum number of shares/stocks a company is permitted to issue.

Average collection period The speed of collection of debts, calculated as an average: debtors × 365 days divided by credit sales.

Average cost method A stock/inventory costing method assuming that the cost of stock/inventory is set to the average cost of all goods available for sale.

Bad debt An amount owing which is not expected to be recovered and is therefore written off either to a bad debt account or to a previously established provision for doubtful debt.

Balance sheet A statement of the assets, liabilities and capital/owner's equity at a particular date. The format has been developed on different lines in the UK and the US. In the UK the balance sheet normally starts with fixed assets, then current assets; in US the order is opposite.

Bank overdraft An overdrawn balance of cash in a bank account. A very common form of borrowing. The maximum size of the overdraft is agreed upon, but interest is only charged according to use.

Bankruptcy Legal status made by the court because of inability to meet financial liabilities.

Below the line A rather vague term referring to that part of the profit and loss account/income statement below the measurement of earnings (on which earnings per share is based). Thus extraordinary items are below the line.

Beta (ß) A measure of the systematic risk of a company's shares/stocks. A share/stock with a beta of 1.0 will on average move in line with the market, a share/stock with a beta greater than 1.0 will on average go up faster and down faster than the market and a share/stock of less than 1.0 will on average fluctuate less than the market as a whole.

Big Six The six largest international public accounting firms, Arthur Andersen & Co; Coopers & Lybrand; Deloitte Touche; Ernst & Young; KPMG; Price Waterhouse.

Board The directors of a company, collectively known as the board of directors.

Bond A fixed interest security, usually long term, representing money borrowed by a firm from the investing public.

Bonus shares/stock dividend An issue of shares/stocks to existing shareholders/stockholders without payment on their part.

Bookkeeping The systematic recording of financial transactions and other events. A process of accounting. Double-entry bookkeeping, a system of recording financial events which recognizes that each event has a dual aspect (debit/credit entry), was first used in about the year 1300 in Northern Italy and first described by Pacioli in 1494. It remains one of the principal techniques used by accountants.

Book value The amount of an asset or a liability as stated in the balance sheet.

Bottom line The last line in the profit and loss account; net profit.

Business profit The sum of current cost operating profit and realizable gains in a current cost (Edwards & Bell) model.

Called-up share capital In the UK, the amount of the issued share capital which has been called up, i.e. the amounts the shareholders have been asked to pay to date.

Capital A word used in many different senses. The primary meaning in accounting is ownership interest given in the balance sheet as the contributed and accumulated capital (assets less liabilities). The primary meaning in economics is capital goods (fixed assets and stocks/inventories). Both accountants and economists, however, use the word on occasion for the asset side or the equity-liability side of the balance sheet.

Capital allowances Allowances made to tax payers in relation to depreciation of fixed assets. Since the amounts and timing of capital allowances change continually, these amounts often have little relation to profit measurement in financial accounting and thus create (problems of) deferred taxes.

Capital asset pricing model (CAPM) A model of the securities market based on portfolio analysis. The model rests on the assumption that securities are traded in a perfect market. The CAPM has proved a fruitful framework for financial research, with important implications for the measurement of cost of capital and for capital structure.

Capital employed The total of equity plus long-term debt; and sometimes also fixed assets plus net current assets.

Capital expenditure An expenditure on assets not written off completely against revenue in the accounting period when the expenditure is made.

Capital gain A gain resulting from the holding of an asset. In practice usually applied to fixed tangible assets and investments.

Capital gearing See *gearing (leverage)*.

Capitalization A word with several meanings. It can refer to a firm's capital structure (long-term sources of funds), the total market value of shares, the net present value of future earnings or cash flows, and that amount of expenses shown as an asset in the balance sheet.

Capital lease US term for finance lease. See *leasing*.

Capital maintenance A concept where profit is measured only after capital has been maintained. The problem is the definition of capital (financial or physical) and the measurement either in nominal or real terms.

Capital reserve A reserve in the balance sheet which is not available for distribution to the owners. There are several ways such a reserve may arise: an earmarked part of retained earnings, a revaluation of a fixed asset (Revaluation reserve), new shares at a price in excess of nominal value (Share premium account), a buy or redemption of own shares (Capital redemption reserve) or it may arise from the process of consolidation in a consolidated balance sheet.

Capital stock The US equivalent of share capital.

Cash accounting Recording and measuring the financial activities and performance in cash terms. Contrasts with *accrual accounting*.

Cash flow The flow of cash into and out of a firm. Often used loosely as net profit plus depreciation.

Cash flow accounting See *cash accounting* and *cash flow statement*.

Cash flow statement A statement explaining how cash and cash equivalents have changed during a period. Usually cash flows are divided into flows from operating activities, investing activities and financing activities.

Certified public accountant (CPA) The US title of a public accountant who has met stringent licensing requirements.

Chairman's statement A statement in the annual report, not audited or regulated by accounting standards. Usually reviews recent performance, outlines current plans and even budget figures.

Chartered accountant Member of recognized professional accountancy bodies. They have acquired theoretical and practical knowledge in accounting. Chartered or certified accountants may act as auditors.

Common size analysis Financial analysis where figures for different years or items within the same year are related to a base (= 100) in order to compare them over years or between companies.

Common stock US term for ordinary shares.

Company A corporate enterprise with a legal identity separate from that of its members. May be used also in a more general sense for any business organization.

Comprehensive income Income including all changes in equity during a period except changes from investment or withdrawals by owners.

Concept An idea forming part of a framework.

Conceptual framework A set of concepts, explicit or implicit, underlying the procedures of financial accounting.

Conservatism (prudence) An accounting convention which, where there is a choice of accounting treatments, chooses the one with the least favourable immediate effect on reported profit and financial position.

Consistency An accounting principle requiring that a particular accounting procedure will not be changed from period to period. It does not mean that accounting treatment may never change, but such changes must be disclosed and quantified (where material).

Consolidated financial statements/group accounts Financial statements incorporating a parent company and its subsidiaries into one set of statements.

Contingent liability (contingency) A potential liability that can develop into a real liability if a possible subsequent event occurs.

Continuing and discontinued activities (operations) A classification of income items making it possible to see what income might reasonably be expected from on-going activities.

Contribution profit and loss account/income statement Disclosure of contribution margin with the distinction between variable and fixed costs.

Controlling interest An investment in a company sufficiently large to enable control, normally more than 50 per cent of the shares' voting rights.

Corporation Persons or bodies of persons authorized by law to act as one person and having rights and liabilities distinct from the individuals forming the corporation.

Cost A term with many uses but always connected to the sacrifice of resources, generally expenditure required to produce output or a benefit.

Cost accounting That area of accounting concerned with the determination and analysis of costs.

Cost flow assumptions Assumptions made about the flow of individual items of stocks/inventories which cannot be physically identified. The most common assumptions: FIFO, weighted average and LIFO.

Cost of goods sold (cost of sales) The cost of goods sold during a period, calculated by adjusting cost of goods purchased with the change in stocks/inventories during the period.

Creative accounting Accounting which follows the rules and standards, but still presents a too favourable picture of a firm's position or progress.

Credit 1. A period of time allowed before payment. 2. The right-hand side of a double-entry account.

Creditor One to whom money is owed, normally classified under current liabilities in the balance sheet.

Cumulative preference shares/stocks See *preference shares/stocks*.

Current asset An asset held temporarily as a stage in the earning cycle, usually: stocks/inventories, debtors and cash.

Current cost A basis of valuation where an asset is valued at the amount it would currently cost to obtain.

Current cost accounting That method of accounting which bases valuation on the current replacement cost of assets.

Current liability A liability to be paid in the relatively near future, usually within one year.

Current operating profit The profit of operating activities when expenses are measured at current cost.

Current purchasing power accounting A system of inflation accounting where all amounts are indexed by means of a general index reflecting changes in the purchasing power of money.

Current ratio The ratio between current assets and current liabilities.

Current value accounting The general accounting term for accounting systems where assets are valued at current replacement cost, net realizable value, net present value or a combination thereof.

Debenture The most common form of long-term loan; interest bearing, usually, but not necessarily, secured on the assets.

Debit The left-hand side of a double-entry account. Contrasts with *credit*.

Debt An amount owed by one person or business to another. A near synonym for liability.

Debtor One who owes money to another. The balance sheet includes the following debtors: trade debtors, amounts owed by group and related companies, prepayments and accrued income, and called-up share capital not paid. The US term *accounts receivable* does not include prepaid expenses and other current assets not arising from trading transactions.

Debt-to-equity ratio Total liabilities divided by owner's equity.

Declining balance method US term for the reducing balance method. An accelerated method of depreciation, computed by applying a fixed rate to the book value (the declining balance).

Deferred expenditure Cash paid for goods or services to be supplied later.

Deferred income (deferred revenue) Cash received in advance for goods or services to be delivered.

Deferred taxation Taxation, which, owing to tax legislation, results in timing differences, i.e. differences between income computed for taxation purposes and for financial accounting purposes. Unlike permanent differences, timing differences are capable of being reversed in future periods. In the deferred tax model, deferred tax is a long-term liability. Depending on the direction of the difference, deferred taxation could also be deferred charges. Discounting of deferred tax liabilities to present value is not generally practised and has not been adopted in any accounting standard.

Depletion (accounting) The proportional allocation of the cost of a natural resource to the unit removed. See *unit of production method*.

Depreciable cost The cost of an asset less its residual value.

Depreciation A measure of the wearing out, consumption or other loss of value of a fixed asset arising from use, time or obsolescence. The term is sometimes restricted to fixed tangible assets, but in some countries, for example the UK, it is regarded as a general term that also includes intangible assets. The most important depreciation methods are: straight-line method, the reducing-balance method/the declining-balance method, and the production-unit method.

Deprival value The value of an asset measured as the loss suffered from being deprived of it. See *value to the business*.

Different cost for different purposes The philosophy that a measure of cost is dependent upon the purpose for which it is required (measured).

Direct costing US term for marginal costing, or more precisely variable costing, contrasts with *absorption costing*.

Direct costs Costs that can be, conventionally and economically, traced to a specific cost objective.

Directives See *EU directives*.

Directors' report An annual report by the directors of a company to its shareholders, required by law (Companies Act). The 'directors' could, in some countries, be the board of directors or, in other countries, the board. Usually, the directors' report must disclose: a fair review during and at the end of the financial year, important events which have occurred since the year end, likely future developments, research and development activities, proposed dividend and proposed transfers to reserves.

Disclosure Presentation of information. *Full disclosure* means that all relevant material information is given.

Discounted cash flow The discounting of expected future cash flows to take care of the time value of money.

Disposal value (residual value, salvage value) The estimated value of a tangible asset at the estimated date of disposal.

Dividend That part of the profits distributed to shareholders. May be either interim (and paid during the year) or final (recommended by the directors for approval by the shareholders at the annual general meeting).

Dividend cover The ratio between earnings (per share) and ordinary dividend (per share).

Dividend yield The ratio between dividend paid (per share) and the market price (per share).

Double-declining-balance method An accelerated (declining-balance) method of depreciation where the fixed rate used is double the straight-line rate.

Double-entry bookkeeping A recording system making use of double entry. Forms of it have been in use since about the year 1300. First text published in 1494 (Pacioli).

Doubtful debt A debt where there is doubt as to its receipt. Usually such a debt is not written off as a bad debt, but a provision for doubtful debts is established.

Dow Jones index An index of share prices calculated for the US stock exchange.

Dual (duality) The characteristic double effect of accounting transactions embodied in the double-entry system.

Du Pont system A method (certain ratios and their combination) of analysing financial accounts in order to assess the underlying health of the firm.

Early warning Signs or signals indicating negative economic development of the firm.

Earnings The after-tax profit; net income.

Earnings per share (EPS) Net income, usually before extraordinary items, divided by the weighted average number of shares of common stock.

Economic value The value of an asset computed by discounting its future cash flows.

ECU European Currency Unit.

ED Exposure Draft.

Efficient market (efficient market theory) A market where stock prices respond immediately to available information.

Eighth Directive A directive on company law approved by the EC in 1984, dealing with various aspects of the qualifications of auditors and authorizations.

Employment report A report included in a company's annual report, giving details of the employees, for example the number, age and sex, geographical location, the costs of employing, training schemes, health etc.

Entity concept A concept of accounting where a business is seen as an entity of its own, separate from its owners or managers.

Entry values Values based on purchase prices either at date of acquisition (historical cost) or at the date of the balance sheet (current replacement cost).

Equity Normally a synonym for owners' equity.

Equity accounting The method of accounting for investments in associated companies, where the share of profits (or losses) is taken as income rather than dividends, and the investment is carried at cost plus the share of undistributed profits. In some countries (for example the UK) equity accounting can only be implemented in consolidated financial statements. In other countries (for example, the US), it can also be used in the accounts of the investor company.

EU directives European Union directives.

Exceptional items Items which are exceptional because of size and/or incidence, but derive from ordinary activities. Should be distinguished from extraordinary items.

Exit values Values based on sale prices in the market at the date of the balance sheet, i.e. net realizable values.

Expenditure Cash spent on goods or services, that may or may not become an expense in the profit and loss account/income statement depending on whether any residual value remains at the end of the period.

Expense Cash spent on goods and services which no longer represent an asset and therefore are shown as a charge against profit in the profit and loss account/income statement.

Exposure Draft (ED) A draft of a proposed accounting standard, published for comment by interested parties.

Extraordinary items Items that derive from events or transactions outside the ordinary activities and are expected not to recur frequently or regularly (the UK definition) or by their unusual nature and by the infrequency of their occurrence (the US definition). Extraordinary items are shown below the line in the profit and loss account/income statement and thus do not affect the calculation of earnings per share.

Fair value The value of an asset through a transaction in an open market.

FASB Financial Accounting Standards Board. The board responsible for developing accounting standards in the US, established in 1973.

FIFO (First-in, first-out) A cost measurement method based on the presumption that goods are used in the order they were acquired.

Financial accounting income Income as measured according to accounting principles.

Financial capital maintenance See *capital maintenance*.

Financial leverage See *gearing*.

Financial statements Statements giving financial information about an accounting entity. The traditional financial statements are the balance sheet and the profit and loss account/income statement. Many firms also publish a cash flow statement or funds statement, fewer a value-added statement.

Financial statement analysis The collective term for the techniques showing relationships in financial statements and which facilitate comparisons from period to period and among companies.

Fixed assets Assets intended for use on a continuing basis.

Fixed costs Costs that remain constant within a relevant range.

Forecast reporting The reporting of projected data to external users of financial statements; prohibited in some countries, becoming more popular in others. Detailed quantitative forecasts are provided in prospectuses and during takeover (battles).

Foreign currency translation The restatement of transactions or accounts in one currency into another. The two main translating methods are the temporal method, where translations are at the rate of exchange at the time of the transaction, and the closing rate method, where the rate of exchange at the balance sheet date is applied.

Fourth Directive A directive on company law approved by the EC in 1978, covering both public and private companies. Deals with valuation rules, format of financial statements and disclosure requirements.

Free reserve A reserve, withheld from profit, not allocated to any defined purpose.

Full cost A cost including an element of fixed overhead.

Full disclosure An accounting convention requiring that financial statements contain all information relevant to the user's understanding of the situation.

Functional currency The currency which a foreign subsidiary handles on a day-to-day basis and in which it generates net cash flows. In the context of foreign currency translation.

Fund Money, normally cash or highly marketable securities, held for a specified purpose.

Fund accounting In the public sector, stewardship accounting where a fund forms the accounting entity.

Fundamental accounting assumptions (concepts) Broad basic assumptions underlying the financial accounts of business firms and having general acceptability. In the EC Fourth Directive they are: going concern, accruals, consistency and prudence; in the IAS, the first three.

Fundamental analysis The study of financial reports and other relevant information to gain insight into the 'real worth' of a company's shares.

Funds flow statement See *cash flow statement*.

Futures Commodities or currencies priced on the basis that they are to be delivered in the future. Enable protection against some of the risks of price fluctuations.

Gains Profits of an irregular or non-recurrent nature.

Gearing (leverage) The ratio between debt finance and equity finance.

Gearing adjustment An adjustment for borrowed funds in accounts prepared on a current cost basis.

Generally accepted accounting principles (GAAP) Principles so widely used and accepted that they are presumed to underlie all accounting statements. The term was coined in the US by the FASB. Often referred to as US-GAAP.

General reserve A reserve withheld from profits; created for unspecified purposes.

Going concern A fundamental accounting concept, stating that a firm is presumed to be carrying on business for the foreseeable future.

Golden parachutes (handshakes) Benefits to directors/managers in case of being given notice to quit.

Goods A general term for physical items of trade.

Goodwill The value of a firm above the realizable value of its separate assets. Internally generated goodwill is not valued in the balance sheet, but when a firm is acquired as a going concern, the purchaser will normally pay explicitly for goodwill as an element of the total purchase price. Such goodwill may appear in the balance sheet.

Goodwill on consolidation Arises on a business combination when acquisition accounting is used.

Group Two or more companies where one controls the other(s). Gives rise to the need for consolidated accounts.

Group accounts Accounts of a group constituted by the parent company and its subsidiaries.

Group companies Companies that are subsidiaries or holding companies.

Harmonization The process of increasing the comparability of accounting practices by reducing the degree of variation. An important task for the International Accounting Standards Committee.

Hidden reserves (secret reserves) Undisclosed understatement of net worth.

Highlights Brief summaries of financial and operating data, especially those included in the annual report.

Historical cost The basic principle for measurements in traditional financial accounting.

Holding company A company which controls one or more other companies (subsidiaries). More narrowly, in some countries defined as one which has no operating activities.

Holding gain A gain made when the market value of an asset rises after acquisition.

Horizontal integration An amalgamation of two businesses or divisions engaged in the same stage of manufacture or distribution. Contrasts with *vertical integration*.

Human assets The value of human beings in an organization. Not conventionally recorded in financial statements.

Human resource accounting A financial representation of the value of employees in an organization. Disregarded in conventional accounting, except insofar as included under goodwill.

IAS, IASC International Accounting Standards, International Accounting Standards Committee.

Income (net income) The net result, revenues less expenses, for a period, or the increase in equity as a result of operations during a period.

Income smoothing To smooth income between periods.

Income statement US term for the profit and loss account.

Independence (of the auditor) The ability of an auditor to act with integrity and objectivity.

Indexation The adjustment by a price index in order to allow for price changes. Used in contracts, and also for adjusting financial statements (other than those based on historical cost).

Indirect costs Costs not directly attributable to a unit of production.

Inefficient market A market where new information is absorbed slowly. Contrasts with *efficient markets*.

Inflation accounting An imprecise term for any system of accounting that attempts to take account of changes in the general price level, specific prices or both. Strictly used: a system where just the decline in the value of money is adjusted for.

Initial allowance A form of capital allowance given for tax purposes in the year the asset is acquired.

Insider dealing The use of information not publicly available in order to trade shares at amounts different from their 'real worth'.

Insolvency The inability to pay debts as they fall due.

Institute of Chartered Accountants in England and Wales (ICAEW) The largest body of professional qualified accountants in the UK, founded in 1880.

Institutional investor Shareholders other than persons: industrial and commercial companies, the public sector and financial institutions such as banks, insurance companies and pension funds.

Intangible asset An asset with no tangible form, such as goodwill, patents and trade marks, copyrights.

Intercompany profits Profit made by one member of a group as a result of trading with another company in the same group. Eliminated in the consolidated profit and loss account/income statement.

Intercompany transactions Transactions between the member companies of a group. Eliminated in the consolidated financial statements.

Interest in shares Significant shareholdings in a public company; in the UK a 5 per cent interest must be notified to the company.

Interim dividend A dividend paid or proposed to be paid in the course of a financial year.

Interim financial statements (reports) Financial statements for a period shorter than a year, e.g. half-yearly, quarterly. In some countries a legal obligation. Normally a requirement for listed companies.

International accounting The international aspects of accounting, including accounting principles, disclosures, reporting practices in different countries, harmonization, international standards.

International Accounting Standards Accounting standards agreed upon internation-ally, in particular the standards (IAS) issued by the International Accounting Standards Committee (IASC), founded in 1973. IASC works for the improvement and harmonization of financial reporting, primarily through the development and publications of IAS. IASC has so far approved 33 International Accounting Standards.

International harmonization The process of increasing the consistency and comparability of accounts.

Inventories The US term for stock, comprising goods held for sale by a retailer or wholesaler (merchandise inventory) or a manufacturer (finished goods), work in progress, and raw materials and supplies.

Inventory turnover See *stock/inventory turnover*.

Investment grants A cash grant by a government to an enterprise in order to encourage investments of a particular kind or in a particular location.

Investments Assets held for the investment income rather than for use, such as shares, loans, bonds and debentures. They can be either fixed assets, i.e. providing a continuing source of income, or current assets, i.e. a temporary means of earning income on funds intended for other uses.

Issued (share) capital That part of the nominal amount of the authorized share capital which has been issued.

Joint venture A transaction carried out by more than one person or an association of persons jointly undertaking a non-permanent business. (Contrasts with *partnership*.) Accounting for joint ventures requires that revenues, expenses etc. are divided among the participants.

Journal A chronological record of all transactions in which a firm is engaged. Applies also to the book (general journal) that records the transactions.

Journal of Accountancy The journal of the American Institute of Certified Public Accountants (AICPA), published monthly.

Knowhow Skill or knowledge acquired from research and/or experience. Normally not to be found in the balance sheet.

Leaseback Taking a lease on property which was previously sold by the lessee to the lessor. Motive: to release funds previously tied up in fixed assets.

Leasing Hiring rather than buying fixed assets. An *operating* lease is one where the user hires the asset for part of its life, while a *finance* lease is one where the lessee uses the asset for most of its useful life, and assumes the benefits and risks associated with ownership. Assets held under a finance lease are treated as if the asset is purchased and financed by a loan.

Ledger Accounts making up a double-entry system, often subdivided into cash book, sales ledger, purchase ledger.

Lessee One who leases property from another.

Lessor One who leases property to another.

Leverage US term for gearing: the use of debt financing. Debt-to-equity ratio measures the relation between debt and equity financing.

Liability A legal obligation expressed in money. Payable in the short run, current liability, or in the long run, long-term liability.

LIFO (Last-in, first-out) A cost measurement method based on the presumption that the last items purchased should be assigned to the first items used or issued to the production process.

Limited company A company where the members have limited liability.

Liquid assets Assets either in cash or which can readily be converted into cash.

Liquidation The process of turning assets into cash; usually the process of ending a business.

Liquidity Convertibility into cash. The position of having enough funds on hand to pay bills when due.

Liquidity ratios 1. The ratio between current assets and current liabilities. 2. The ratio between the most liquid current assets and current liabilities (acid test).

Long-term assets Assets that are acquired for use in the operation of the business, not intended for resale to customers. Often considered as having a useful life of more than one year.

Long-term contract A contract for the supply of a single substantial asset or service where the time taken to complete the contract falls into more than one accounting period. If certain criteria are met, profit earned on such contracts may be taken into the profit and loss account/income statement as the project advances.

Long-term debt (liability) Debt to be paid in the future, usually more than one year ahead.

Lower of cost or market A generally accepted prudent basis for valuing stock/inventory at an amount below cost if the market value is less than cost. In the UK, market is normally the net realizable value; in the US, the replacement value.

Macro-accounting Those aspects of accounting concerned with nations rather than individuals or organizations. A field developed by economists and statisticians rather than accountants.

Management The group of people having overall responsibility for operating the business and for achieving its goals.

Management accounting That part of accounting concerned mainly with internal reporting to the managers, emphasizing control and decision making rather than the stewardship aspects of accounting.

Marginal costing UK term for direct costing. Contrasts with *absorption costing*.

Mark down To reduce prices below a previously stated level.

Marketable Readily saleable. Marketable securities, for example, are those quoted on a stock exchange.

Market capitalization The total value of a company (or all companies) determined by multiplying the stock market price of the shares by the total number of shares.

Market value The value of an asset if sold.

Matching A fundamental accounting principle in computing profit, whereby all costs are matched against the related revenues.

Materiality The threshold for recognition of an accounting item in a financial statement.

Maturity The date when a long-term financial obligation falls due.

Merger The amalgamation of two or more separate enterprises.

Merger accounting/pooling of interests The preparation of consolidated financial statements on the assumption that one company has merged with another rather than acquired another. Contrasts with *acquisition accounting*.

Miller and Modigliani theory A theorem that capital structure is not a factor in determining the cost of capital.

Minority interests That part of the profit or equity of a subsidiary attributable to shares owned by interests other than the parent company or other group companies. Usually shown as a separate item in the profit and loss account/income statement (as a part of net income) and in the balance sheet (between equity and liabilities).

Minute A record of a decision taken at a meeting, e.g. a meeting of a board (of directors).

Monetary assets (and liabilities) Assets (and liabilities) with a value fixed in monetary terms; important distinction in inflation accounting.

Money-measurement concept Accounting records which report only facts that can be expressed in monetary amounts.

Mortgage A type of long-term debt secured by real property.

Multi-column reporting The side-by-side presentation of financial data drawn up on several different measurement bases.

Mutual fund US term for unit trust: an institution set up to enable the small investor to invest in a wide spread of securities.

Negative goodwill (badwill) Where the sum of the values of the separate assets is higher than the value as a whole. In consolidated accounts it is credited to reserve and in certain circumstances released later to profit and loss account/income statement.

Net assets Total assets less all liabilities, i.e. equal to the equity.

Net current assets Current assets less current liabilities.

Net present value The discounted value of the anticipated cash flows.

Net profit Revenues over expenses, usually after all expenses, although it may be calculated before or after extraordinary items and before or after tax depending on the context.

Net realizable value The amount received if an asset were sold after deduction of outstanding charges and sales expenses.

Nominal (share) capital The share capital of a company at its nominal amount.

Nominal value The face value of a security, e.g. a share.

Non-monetary assets Assets other than monetary assets; a distinction useful for inflation accounting.

No par value shares/stock Shares without a par value. Fairly usual in the US but illegal, for example, in the UK.

Notes to the accounts/financial statements Information relating to the financial statements not given on the face of the statements.

Objectivity An accounting concept stressing independency for recording transactions and for measurements of financial events.

Obsolescence The process of becoming obsolete, one of the factors leading to depreciation of fixed assets.

Off-balance-sheet financing Indirect finance not appearing on the balance sheet, for example leasing (but note that in some countries finance leases are required to be capitalized and hence will appear on the balance sheet).

Operating activities Activities by a firm as part of its normal trade.

Operating lease See *leasing*.

Operating profit The profit from carrying out the firm's basic business operations. The excess of operating revenues over operating expenses.

Operating ratios Ratios which throw light on profit-making activities, for example profit and costs as a percentage of sales.

Opportunity cost The cost of an action in terms of the value of the best opportunity thereby foregone. A term borrowed from economics, but with basic relevance for financial decision making.

Option The right to decide whether or not to enter into a transaction on agreed terms within an agreed period of time, on stock market securities used as a hedge against price fluctuations.

Ordinary activities Activities forming part of normal trading, expected to recur regularly.

Ordinary shares The basic risk capital of a limited company.

Overdraft See *bank overdraft*.

Overhead Costs which do not directly become part of the product or service.

Own shares/treasury stocks A company's own shares acquired by purchase redemption, gift, surrender or forfeiture. Illegal in some countries, legal under stringent conditions in other countries, for example the UK, or fully legal in some countries, for example the US (treasury stock).

Parent company A company controlling one or more other companies (subsidiaries).

Partial tax allocation Taxes deferred only when tax benefits or tax obligations are likely to be reversed within a reasonable time in the future.

Partnership Two or more persons carrying on a business in common.

Par value Equal to *nominal value*.

Patent The legal right to exclusive use of the idea for an invention for a period of time, in accounting classified as an intangible asset.

P/E (ratio) Price/earnings (ratio).

Permanent differences Differences between financial accounting profit and taxable profit that do not reverse, i.e. they exist forever. Contrasts with *timing differences*.

Plant and machinery Equipment used in an industrial production process, shown in the balance sheet as a fixed asset.

Ploughed-back profit Profit retained in a business rather than being distributed to owners.

Pooling of interests US term for merger.

Portfolio In a financial context, a collection of different securities, or other assets which can be evaluated in terms of their combined risks and returns.

Post-balance-sheet events Events occurring after the date of the balance sheet but before the accounts are approved by the board.

Preference shares/stocks A class of share capital with special rights or restrictions compared with other classes of stock in the same company; usually giving prior rights to dividends.

Present value See *net present value*.

Price/earnings ratio (P/E) The relationship between the market price of a share and the earnings per share.

Price-level adjustments Adjustments compensating for the effect of inflation, made by applying a price index to the original figures.

Prior-year adjustments Material adjustments relating wholly to matters occurring in a previous period, arising from changes in accounting policies or fundamental errors.

Private company A company which restricts the transfer of its shares to those approved by the directors, designated by the term 'limited' (Ltd) and not quoted on the Stock Exchange. Contrasts with *public company*.

Profit A surplus of revenues over expenses. In the profit and loss account/income statement usually both profit before tax and profit after tax are shown.

Profit and loss account/income statement The most important of the financial statements, showing revenues, expenses and profit for a defined period of time. The EC Fourth Directive gives a choice of four formats: two (vertical or horizontal) based on the type of expenditure; two based on function.

Profit sharing A scheme whereby the employees are entitled to some share in profits.

Pro forma (In the form of) A pro-forma balance sheet is a statement showing what the position would be if certain proposed steps were taken, rather than one showing the actual position.

Proper accounting records Records of financial transactions in a form sufficient to explain them fully.

Proposed dividend A dividend proposal for payment by the board. Subject to the approval of the shareholders in general meeting. Conventional UK accounting practice is to show the proposed dividend as a current liability.

Prospectus A document inviting an application for shares or other securities.

Prudence (conservatism) A principle of accounting to the effect that accounting statements should be prepared on a cautious basis, avoiding undue optimism.

Public accounting The field of accounting offering services in auditing, taxes and management advices to the public for a fee.

Public company A company having no restrictions on ownership or transfer of its shares.

Purchasing power loss or gain A loss or gain from holding net monetary assets during a period of change in the general price level.

Qualified audit report An auditor's report expressing reservations. See *auditor's report*.

Quality of earnings A common phrase used by financial analysts to describe a company's earnings. High-quality earnings are, for example, earnings coming from operations, not financial manoeuvres.

Quick assets Highly liquid assets (current assets less stocks/inventories). Quick ratio is the relationship between quick assets and current liabilities.

Quoted company A company whose shares are quoted on a Stock Exchange.

R&D Abbreviation for research and development.

Rate of exchange The rate at which the currency of one country can be exchanged for the currency of another. See *foreign currency translation*.

Realizable value Amount received if an asset were sold.

Realization concept A fundamental accounting concept stating that profits should be recognized only when they have been realized.

Real value Value expressed independent of the value of money.

Recoverable value The greater of the net realizable value and net present value of an asset; an important test in determining the value to the business.

Recurring (and non-recurring) income A net income concept based on recurring events (non-recurring events).

Red figures Negative figures.

Reducing-balance method See *depreciation*.

Registrar of Companies A public official with the responsibility of receiving and holding prescribed information about companies.

Relevance A quality characteristic of accounting information, capable of making a difference to a decision by a user.

Reliability A quality characteristic of accounting information with three components: verifiability, representational faithfulness and neutrality.

Rent Amount paid for the use of land or buildings.

Replacement cost The cost of replacing an asset by the same or similar type of asset.

Research and development expenditure (costs) Expenditure on pure research and applied research and development.

Reserves Items of owners' equity arising for example from share premium, the retention of profits and the revaluation of assets.

Residual value The value of a fixed asset after it has reached the end of its useful life.

Results The financial outcome of the activities of a company (for a specified accounting period).

Retained earnings (profits) That part of the profit not distributed to shareholders.

Return on investment (capital employed) The relation between profit and investment, used as a measure of performance.

Revaluation The writing up of a fixed asset.

Revenues Original meaning: amounts received. The income items in the profit and loss account/income statement. The most typical revenue: sales.

Sale and leaseback Sale of a fixed asset to a finance company and then making a leasing arrangement on the sold asset.

Sales The value, at selling prices, of goods sold in a period.

Scrap value The realizable value of a fixed asset at the end of its useful life.

Secret reserves See *hidden reserves*.

Securities and Exchange Commission (SEC) The official US body responsible for overseeing the operation of listed companies.

Segmental reporting Reporting on segments of the business activity.

Simplified financial statements Statements with a reduced information content for better understanding for those unskilled in accounting.

Share Unit of capital in a limited company.

Share capital The total nominal value of the shares issued by a company.

Shareholder/stockholder One who owns shares in a company.

Shareholders' equity The balance sheet value of the total value of share capital and reserves.

Share premium (account) A capital reserve created when shares are issued in excess of nominal value.

Share split Dividing shares into a larger number of a lower nominal value.

Single-entry bookkeeping A system of bookkeeping recording just one aspect of a transaction. Contrasts with *double-entry bookkeeping*.

Sinking fund A fund established to accumulate the amount required to pay a debt at a set date in the future. Sinking fund method is a depreciation method where the time value of money is taken into account.

Sleeping partner A member of a partnership who takes no active part in the operation of the business.

Social (responsibility) accounting A form of accounting where the benefits and costs to society of a business's activities are reported. Related to recent concern with environmental issues.

Sole proprietorship (trader) An unincorporated business enterprise owned by a single person.

Source and application of funds (statement) See *cash flow statement*.

SSAP Statement of Standard Accounting Practice.

Standard & Poor's A US company providing detailed information related to investment in the Stock Exchange.

Standard setting Setting the rules to be followed in the preparation of financial statements. The standard-setting body in the UK is the Accounting Standards Board (ASB), Foreningen Statsautoriserede Revisorer (FSR) in Denmark, Redovisningsrådet (RR) in Sweden, Norsk RegnskapsStiftelse (NRS) in Norway and Financial Accounting Standards Board (FASB) in the US.

Statutory reserve A reserve in the balance sheet required by the Companies Act.

Step-by-step acquisition Shareholding giving control of a company when shares are acquired gradually.

Stewardship Responsibility for the property of others. With stewardship goes accountability, enabling judgement on the effectiveness of the stewardship function.

Stocks/inventories Physical goods or other assets purchased or produced for sale: in the balance sheet divided into raw material and consumable work in progress/process, and finished goods and goods for resale. US term: inventories.

Stock exchange An organized market in securities.

Stock/inventory turnover A ratio showing how many times stock was replaced (sold) during the year, calculated by dividing the average stock into cost of sales.

Straight-line method See *depreciation*.

Subsidiary A company controlled by another.

Substance The economic reality of a transaction or situation.

Substance over form An accounting concept whereby accounting information is presented in accordance with economic reality rather than legal form.

Sum of the years' digits A method for calculating the depreciation of an asset. See *depreciation*.

Sunk costs Costs incurred in the past and not affected by any future action and thus irrelevant to decision making.

Super profit Profit in excess of a normal rate of return.

Takeover One company acquiring control of another.

Takeover bid An offer by one company to acquire all of, or a controlling holding in, another company.

Tangible asset An asset having physical existence. Contrasts with *intangible asset*.

Taxes The expense for taxes shown in the profit and loss account/income statement. In the deferred tax model the amount represents the total tax to be paid on the accounting profit for that year, in other models just the amount to be paid according to the taxable income for that year.

Tax liability Amount to be paid in taxation; current liability in the balance sheet.

Tax integrated model The financial accounts and the tax accounts are the same.

Tax link model A financial accounting reporting model, originally developed in Sweden, where accounting income and taxable income are linked by a special section in the profit and loss account/income statement. In the balance sheet the accumulated figures are shown also in a separate section (untaxed equity).

Temporal method See *foreign currency translation*.

Temporary differences See *timing differences*.

Timing differences Differences between accounting profit and taxable profit arising from the inclusion of items of income and expenditure in tax computations in periods different from those in which they appear in financial statements. See *deferred taxation*.

Trade creditors/accounts payable Creditors arising out of trading transactions.

Trade debtors/accounts receivable Debtors arising out of trading transactions.

Trade mark A symbol used to represent a business or its products in a quickly recognizable way. If appearing in the balance sheet classified as an intangible asset.

Transaction A financial event recorded in the accounting system. The transaction principle is basic in accounting.

Treasury stock US term for the approximate UK equivalent of own shares.

True and fair view The overriding financial reporting requirement in the UK and also in the EU through the Fourth Directive; a view which accurately conveys the situation it seeks to portray. It overrides the form and content of financial statements, the notes and the accounting principles.

Turnover The total value of goods or services sold in a period.

Uniform accounting A system where a number of firms in a similar activity prepare accounts on a uniform basis to aid comparison.

Unit of production method A method of calculating depreciation in which the depreciation charge is proportionate to the amount of product turned out by the asset. Normally used in oil and gas accounting.

Unrealized profit An increase in the value of an asset not sold or used up. It is generally not regarded as good accounting practice to take any account of this.

Useful economic life The length of time of use of a fixed asset. An important factor in deciding the rate of depreciation.

Users' needs The need of presumed users of financial statements. In the UK and US, equity investors are presumed to be the dominant users. In Europe, loan creditors and government are also important.

Valuation Attaching a monetary value to an asset or, less usually, a liability.

Value added The value which the firm adds to a bought-in product by its own efforts.

Value-added statement A financial statement showing for a period how much value has been added by the operations of an enterprise and how this value has been distributed among employees, providers of capital, government and for reinvestment in the business.

Value-added tax (VAT) A multi-stage indirect sales tax.

Value to the business A value concept valuing an asset at the lower of the following two values: replacement cost and the higher of net present value and realizable value (recoverable value).

Venture capital Funds invested in a venture in which the expected risks and returns are higher than normal on the basis that the investor receives a share in the outcome.

Vertical integration The merger of businesses in sequential stages of production or distribution.

Wasting asset A non-renewable resource, such as oil and gas.

Windfall gains and losses Totally unexpected gains and losses.

Window dressing To make accounts look better than they are.

Working capital Current assets less current liabilities.

Work in progress/work in process Partly completed production or services.

Written-down value Net amount after depreciation of a fixed asset.

Yield The amount, normally as a percentage, of income from an investment.

Z-score A measurement, calculated from a linear equation, incorporating more than one financial ratio, used especially as a measure of the solvency of a company.

Selected additional reading

Financial Accounting Theory

Hendriksen, E.S. and van Breda, M.F., *Accounting Theory*, 5th edn (Irwin, 1992).

Financial Statement Analyses

White, G.I., Sondhi, A.C. and Fried, D., *The Analysis and Use of Financial Statements* (Wiley, 1997).

International Accounting

Black, J. and Amat, O., *European Accounting* (Pitman Publishing, 1993).

Nobes, C. and Parker, R., *Comparative International Accounting* (Prentice-Hall, 1995).

Samuels, J.M., Brayshaw, R.E. and Craner, J.M., *Financial Statement Analysis in Europe* (Chapman & Hall, 1995).

Index